FRANK GEHRY, ARCHITECT

FRANK GEHRY, ARCHITECT

J. Fiona Ragheb, editor

*essays by Jean-Louis Cohen, Beatriz Colomina, Mildred Friedman,
William Mitchell, and J. Fiona Ragheb*

GuggenheimMUSEUM

Published on the occasion of the exhibition
Frank Gehry, Architect
Organized by Mildred Friedman and J. Fiona Ragheb

Solomon R. Guggenheim Museum, New York
May 18–August 26, 2001
Guggenheim Museum Bilbao
October 29, 2001–February 3, 2002

This exhibition is sponsored by **HUGO BOSS**

Additional support is provided by ❦ National Endowment for the Arts

ISBN 0-89207-245-6 (softcover)
ISBN 0-8109-6929-7 (hardcover)

Guggenheim Museum Publications
1071 Fifth Avenue
New York, New York 10128

Hardcover edition distributed by
Harry N. Abrams
100 Fifth Avenue
New York, New York 10011

Hardcover edition distributed in German-speaking countries by
Hatje Cantz Verlag
Senefelderstrasse 12
D-73760 Ostfildern, Germany

Design: Bruce Mau Design Inc., Toronto, Canada
Production: Elizabeth Levy, Melissa Secondino, Cynthia Williamson
Editorial: Meghan Dailey, Elizabeth Franzen, Jennifer Knox White, Carey Ann Schaefer, Edward Weisberger
Printed in Germany by GZD
Cover: Current design model for Guggenheim Museum New York, 2000. Photo by Ellen Labenski.

FRANK GEHRY, ARCHITECT

Acknowledgments

An exhibition of this magnitude and ambition could not have been accomplished without the collaboration and support of numerous individuals and institutions to whom we wish to extend our sincere gratitude. Above all, we are indebted to Frank Gehry himself, whose unparalleled vision we are celebrating. We are equally obliged to partners Jim Glymph and Randy Jefferson, who shepherded the project along with the same skill they bring to the management of Frank O. Gehry & Associates, and to Edwin Chan and Craig Webb for generously sharing their extensive knowledge of the firm's work. Gehry and his staff are also to be congratulated for the stunning exhibition design that animates the museum. Along with Keith Mendenhall, whose essential guidance ensured the smooth development of this project and its myriad components, many other talented staff members of Gehry's firm whose names appear in the Project Team contributed to the realization of this exhibition and catalogue.

A project such as this is truly the result of a team effort. We are very fortunate that Mildred Friedman, who curated the first retrospective on Gehry's work in 1986, and is also the author of an important monograph on the architect, has joined us as Guest Curator. This exhibition was also organized by J. Fiona Ragheb, Associate Curator for Collections and Exhibitions, who has firsthand experience working in the context of a Frank Gehry building, for she was instrumental in mounting the premier exhibition at the Guggenheim Museum Bilbao. I am grateful to Fiona for bringing her wide-ranging talent and considerable energy to bear on the successful realization of this exhibition and its accompanying catalogue, for which she served as editor. Kara Vander Weg, Curatorial Assistant, also demonstrated enormous dedication and enthusiasm from the project's inception. I am indebted to numerous additional staff members of the Guggenheim who made this extensive and complicated exhibition possible, and who are credited in the Project Team. The skillful work of the museum staff at all levels has made this project a pleasure; I am fortunate to work with such exceptional and engaged people. As always, Lisa Dennison, Deputy Director and Chief Curator; Jane DeBevoise, Deputy Director for Program Administration and Operations; Anthony Calnek, Managing Director and Publisher; and Karen Meyerhoff, Managing Director for Exhibitions, Collections, and Design, contributed widely and wisely along with their respective staffs to the progress of the exhibition.

Bruce Mau, Anita Matusevics, and their colleagues must be commended for their design of the catalogue, which captures the essence of Gehry's work, as well as for their role in the exhibition design. I am also indebted to authors Jean-Louis Cohen, the Institut Français d'Architecture and New York University; Beatriz Colomina, Princeton University; William J. Mitchell, Massachusetts Institute of Technology; and the exhibition curators for their insightful and engaging essays. Their work would have been much more difficult without that of the photographers who have captured Gehry's buildings with stunning results. We are indebted to those photographers whose work appears throughout this volume, and to their representatives, in particular to Erika Stoller of Esto Photographics, Inc.

In the course of designing buildings all over the world, Frank Gehry has developed a large and enthusiastic base of support among clients, the art world, and the architectural community. I greatly appreciate all those individuals and institutions who lent models or furniture to this exhibition from their collections. In a very real sense, the exhibition could not have happened without their enthusiasm for this project. We are also indebted to those who generously shared insights and materials for the project. In particular, we would like to thank Gwen Bitz, Wim DeWit, Rainald Franz, Fred Hoffman, Kirsten Kiser, Sheila Lesh, Ricky Renier, and Robert Violette. Gehry's clients, past and present, generously made themselves available and shared their knowledge; Nicole Nathan of the Experience Music Project (EMP) and Lyndel King of the Frederick R. Weisman Art Museum at the University of Minnesota were particularly helpful in this capacity. For their interest in the project, I am also appreciative of Katharine Lee Reid and Katherine Solender at the Cleveland Museum of Art; Jill Snyder at the Cleveland Center for Contemporary Art; Jeremy Strick, Paul Schimmel, and Stacia Payne at the Museum of Contemporary Art, Los Angeles; David Ross, Aaron Betsky, and Ruth Berson of the San Francisco Museum of Modern Art; and Dr. Peter-Klaus Schuster of the Staatliche Museen zu Berlin.

An exhibition of this scope could not take place without the generous support of our sponsors. We would like to extend our sincerest thanks to Enron, whose commitment to innovation in commerce is expressed through their support of this landmark exhibition. In particular, I would like to thank Kenneth Lay, Chairman, and Jeffrey Skilling, President and Chief Executive Officer, for their vision and leadership. In addition, I would like to thank Steven Kean, Executive Vice President, and his group, for their creativity and dedication to this remarkable exhibition. We are also deeply grateful to Hugo Boss for their ongoing commitment and support of exhibitions at the Guggenheim. Hugo Boss continues to set a shining example of corporate support in the arts. I am indebted to the Chairman and CEO, Werner Baldessarini, and Marty Staff, CEO, Hugo Boss, USA, for their enlightened generosity, and to Hjoerdis Janecke, Arts Sponsorship, for her support and dedication. This exhibition has also been made possible in part by a major grant from the National Endowment for the Arts, whose recognition and financial support affirms the significance of architecture and design in America's cultural life. In this context, I would also like to acknowledge the work of the museum's development staff, in particular Ben Hartley, former Director of Corporate Communications and Sponsorship, and Kendall Hubert, his successor in that role.

Significant additional support has also been provided by Dassault Systèmes, which collaborated with Frank O. Gehry & Associates, IBM, and SGI to develop CATIA sequences to enhance the understanding of the role technology plays in creating today's architectural landmarks. A. Zahner Company collaborated with the firm on the creation of the terrace architectural study, creating a dazzling exterior element so that audiences can engage with architecture on the level that it is most meaningfully experienced. We are also indebted to Fujitsu for providing essential presentation display technologies; to Knoll and to Vitra for their generous support in providing examples of Gehry's furniture; and to Target Stores for supporting the Family Activity Guide, all contributing to making this exhibition a success. I would also like to thank Sydney Pollack for the use of footage from his documentary film on Frank Gehry, to be completed early next year.

Thomas Krens
Director, The Solomon R. Gugggenheim Foundation

A Personal Reflection

Thomas Krens

Half a century ago, an architect then at the height of his fame, and whose name would become inextricably linked to the Guggenheim, was given an exhibition at this very location, the corner of Fifth Avenue and Eighty-ninth Street. Called *Sixty Years of Living Architecture*, the show was comprised of architectural models, original drawings, mural-sized photographs of finished buildings, and even furniture. The architect, or course, was Frank Lloyd Wright, and, in 1953, his last masterpiece, the Solomon R. Guggenheim Museum, was still in the design stage; the building would not open for six years. The exhibition was presented on the site that was reserved for the future museum, and the architect himself designed a temporary space using unexpected and humble materials: Masonite panels alternated with glass in the starkly tilted roof, and visible pipe columns formed the support structure.

With *Frank Gehry, Architect*, the Guggenheim once again celebrates the lifetime achievement of one of America's leading practicing architects. And, as with *Sixty Years of Living Architecture*, this exhibition occurs at a time in which the architect in question has designed a Guggenheim Museum yet to be built—the project for a new Guggenheim Museum on the shores of Lower Manhattan. Unlike Wright at the time of his exhibition, Gehry is already closely identified with this institution due to the startling success of his design for the Guggenheim Museum Bilbao, which opened in 1997. With Bilbao, Gehry came of age as an architect. Scale, design, sophistication, elegance, and the power to communicate with everyman all came together to bring his work to a new level of magisterial prominence and creative command. Bilbao also foreshadows a cornucopia of extraordinary projects on the threshold of completion at this very moment—the Walt Disney Concert Hall; the Peter B. Lewis Building at the Weatherhead School of Management at Case Western Reserve; and the Ray and Maria Stata Center at MIT most prominent among them—that will catapult his achievement onto an even higher plane of recognition and regard. But perhaps most important, certainly from the Guggenheim perspective, this exhibition provides context and an historical narrative that will frame what could come to be regarded as his greatest project of all—the new Guggenheim for New York City.

Like many architects, it took a while for Frank Gehry's work to come to the attention of a wider audience. His first museum retrospective was organized in 1986, when he was fifty-seven, by the Walker Art Center in Minneapolis, and it was when that exhibition came to the Whitney Museum in New York that my ascent began into Frank's mysteriously exuberant world of psychologically organic form rendered in steel, glass, metal, plywood, stone, and chain link. Prior to the Whitney show, my direct contact with his work was limited. I had not traveled much to the places where he had built buildings until the late 1980s, when I became a client. My friendship with Frank began with the plans for MASS MoCA (the Massachusetts Museum of Contemporary Art), a project for the conversion of twenty-eight nineteenth-century textile mill buildings into a museum. By some stroke of good fortune, the precise mechanics of which happily continue to elude me, a triumvirate of Frank, David Childs, and Robert Venturi came together as a team and was chosen to design the Master Plan for MASS MoCA. Unhappily, the project as conceived by this distinguished group never got off the preliminary drawing board; the economic crisis in Massachusetts in the early 1990s delayed the project for some five years, and by the time it regained momentum the situation had shifted and Frank, David, and Bob were no longer involved. But in the few short months that I worked with this group, always on the run, so to speak, in airports, on napkins, on site, on plans and drawings, and over the phone, it became clear to me that Frank had this wonderful propensity for collaboration. And it is here, in the climate of socio-physical problem solving, that the measure of the man as artist can really be taken.

As I came to know Frank, recognition and, more important, bigger projects were substantially moving in his direction. By 1989, as we began working on MASS MoCA, he received the Pritzker Architecture Prize. Works like the Chiat Day Building, the fish lamps, and the cardboard furniture were already the stuff of legend; and Frank was becoming the famously self-effacing architect that I now know so well. The Chiat Day Building was particularly important because it was here that he took hold of art — obviously and aggressively — by enthusiastically embracing another artist as a collaborative ally in a joint project. In retrospect it was obvious — as obvious as using common materials like plywood and chain link in his early work. In art, Frank saw a huge potential for architecture — as inspiration, as counterpoint, and as content. He placed at risk the traditional distinction and features of architecture as a practice of like-minded professionals, and thereby, of course, expanded the very definition of the field. Frank had been associated with artists in southern California for most of his career and he designed houses for painters like Ron Davis. But by making the Claes Oldenburg and Coosje van Bruggen binoculars form the dominating centerpiece of the Chiat Day Building, and fully integrating its essential form into the practical operation of the building, he opened a door to the rich world of artistic collaboration as a process and as an end in itself, from which he would never turn away.

As Bilbao was about to open, I remember doing an interview with the late Heinrich Klotz, then the former director of the Architecture Museum in Frankfurt, in which he asked me whether "Frank Gehry was as egoless as his Columbo-like persona suggested." My response, based on working intensely with Frank for more than five years was, no, rather to the contrary, I saw him as having a huge ego. He so thoroughly trusts in his own capacities to come up with the best solution that he is not afraid of criticism in the conventional sense. His self-knowledge and understanding of the creative process encourages him not to invest too heavily in the current outcome. He knows that by encouraging rather than resisting the destruction of his latest iteration or paradigm or model, he would get to design again from a higher plane of knowledge and information and do it better the second time. Frank embraced architecture as an endless, evolving process. By working with others, specific problems could be worked out, fresh directions would be suggested, and new possibilities would emerge. In other words, by so completely understanding and appropriating the creative process, Frank gets to do things and see things that occur to no one else. The special accent is that his confidence is always tempered by anxiety, and from that tension his finest work is created. Hence, his architecture and his mastery.

The primary purpose of this exhibition is to organize, synthesize, and present in a single location, the history and essence of Frank Gehry's work. This is not, of course, an easy task, and the scale and importance of this objective will not be lost on even the most casual observer. He is arguably the most important architect of our time — the Michael Jordan of bricks and mortar. *Frank Gehry, Architect* brings the world up to date with his spectacular portfolio of projects. The exhibition celebrates his pioneering designs of nearly four decades; thirty-six projects, ranging from private homes to museums, university campuses, and corporate headquarters in twenty-four cities and five countries are represented through models, drawings, and photographs. Throughout, the emphasis of the presentation is on the evolution of his visual language and working process.

One of the strengths of Frank's architectural sensibility is predicated on the relationships he forges with his clients. I am fortunate to have been a client and collaborator with him on numerous projects over the past twelve years — from MASS MoCA to Bilbao; with exhibitions like *The Art of the Motorcycle* and the installation of the current *Frank Gehry, Architect;* with new projects in New York, St. Petersburg, and Brazil; and through an almost daily exchange of views on the power and direction of architecture and art. There is nothing, however, to replicate the thrilling experience of a built building and to have been present with a courtside seat to watch the creation of a masterpiece. The Guggenheim Museum Bilbao has been lauded as "a miracle," "a life-transforming experience," and "the greatest building of our time" by architects and critics around the world, and has raised the bar for architectural innovation. Frank has accomplished this because of a preternatural openness to the concept of difference and radical juxtaposition. Place two unlikely elements together and Frank will say, "Why not?" He is a master at transforming the material environment — whether natural or artificial — into architecture. He is, in the best sense of the word, a true genius.

Sponsor Statement

Frank Gehry's art dominates skylines around the world, and yet the source of his inspiration has long been hidden in sketches and models unseen by anyone but his closest collaborators. With this exhibition, Gehry's evolving genius comes to life.

To help bring this work to the eyes of the public is truly an honor, and Enron is privileged to lend its support. Enron shares Mr. Gehry's ongoing search for "the moment of truth" — the moment when the functional approach to a problem becomes infused with the artistry that produces a truly innovative solution.

This is the search Enron embarks on every day, by questioning the conventional to change business paradigms and create new markets that will shape the New Economy. It is the shared sense of challenge that we admire most in Frank Gehry, and we hope that this exhibition will bring you as much inspiration as it has brought us.

Jeff Skilling
President and Chief Executive Officer

Sponsor Statement

Frank O. Gehry is indisputably one of the greatest architects of our time. His hallmark use of unusual materials, organic shapes, and interlocking structures has already become legendary. Breathtaking achievements like the Guggenheim Museum Bilbao and the Experience Music Project (EMP) in Seattle bear eloquent testimony to his creativity, innovation, and astounding talent.

We at HUGO BOSS are fortunate to have worked with Frank O. Gehry on many of the special events we organized when the Guggenheim Museum Bilbao first opened. Now we are delighted to continue this association, with this original retrospective. Our very special thanks are due to Thomas Krens, Director of the Solomon R. Guggenheim Foundation, Mildred Friedman and J. Fiona Ragheb, the curators of the exhibition, and everyone else who helped make this unique retrospective possible.

We wish you much pleasure in discovering the many facets of this truly outstanding architect.

Werner Baldessarini
Chairman & CEO

HUGO BOSS

Project Team

GUGGENHEIM MUSEUM

Curatorial

Mildred Friedman, *Guest Curator*
J. Fiona Ragheb, *Associate Curator for Collections and Exhibitions*
Kara Vander Weg, *Curatorial Assistant*
Sunmin Whang, *Photography Research Assistant*
Sarah Richardson, *Project Curatorial Assistant*
Michelle Anderson, *Intern*
Carolyn Begley, *Intern*
Mariana Cánepa Luna, *Intern*
Sabrina Lupero, *Intern*
Laetitia Chauvin, *Intern*
Kalliopi Minioudaki, *Intern*
Sonia Roe, *Hilla Rebay Intern*

Art Services and Preparations

Scott Wixon, *Manager of Art Services and Preparations*
Mike Asente, *Assistant Manager of Art Services*
Barry Hylton, *Senior Exhibition Technician*
David Bufano, *Senior Exhibition Technician*
Mary Ann Hoag, *Lighting Designer*
Richard Gombar, *Construction Manager*
Michael Sarff, *Assistant Construction Manager*
James Nelson, *Chief Preparator*
Elizabeth Jaff, *Associate Preparator for Paper*
Jeffrey Britton, *Associate Preparator*
Jeffrey Clemens, *Associate Preparator*
Derek DeLuco, *Technical Specialist*
Thomas Radloff, *Art Handler*
Hans Aurandt, *Art Handler*
Elizabeth Martin, *Art Handler*

Conservation

Eleonora Nagy, *Sculpture Conservator*
Mara Guglielmi, *Paper Conservator*
Nathan Otterson, *Assistant Sculpture Conservator*

Education

Kim Kanatani, *Gail Engelberg Director of Education*
Pablo Helguera, *Senior Education Program Manager*
Sharon Vatsky, *Senior Education Program Manager, School Programs*
Juliet Source, *Education Associate*

Exhibition and Collection Management and Design

Karen Meyerhoff, *Managing Director for Exhibitions, Collections, and Design*
Marion Kahan, *Exhibition Program Manager*
Sady Cohen, *Exhibition Management Assistant*
Paul Kuranko, *Media Arts Specialist*
Sean Mooney, *Exhibition Design Manager*
Alexis Katz, *Senior Exhibition Designer*
Asifa Tirmizi, *Architectural CAD Coordinator*
Marcia Fardella, *Chief Graphic Designer*
Concetta Pereira, *Production Coordinator*
Laura Bush, *Graphic Designer*

Fabrication

Peter Read, *Manager of Exhibition Fabrications and Design*
Stephen Engelman, *Technical Designer*
David Johnson, *Chief Framemaker*

Film and Video

Ultan Guilfoyle, *Director of Film & Video Production*
Alice Bertoni, *Assistant Producer, Film & Video Production*
Brainerd Taylor, *Production Research*
Cathrine Ellis, *Production Manager*

Photography

David M. Heald, *Head Photographer*
Kim Bush, *Manager of Photography and Permissions*
Ellen Labenski, *Associate Photographer*
Leslie Gravel, *Digital Imaging Specialist*

Publications

Anthony Calnek, *Managing Director and Publisher*
Meghan Dailey, *Associate Editor*
Elizabeth Franzen, *Manager of Editorial Services*
Elizabeth Levy, *Managing Editor/Manager of Foreign Editions*
Carey Ann Schaefer, *Editorial Assistant*
Melissa Secondino, *Assistant Production Manager*
Edward Weisberger, *Editor*
Jennifer Knox White, *Editor*
Cynthia Williamson, *Assistant Production Manager*

Registrar

Meryl Cohen, *Head Registrar*
Lisa Lardner, *Associate Registrar for Exhibitions*
Sarah Bradbury, *Registration Assistant*

Structural Engineering

Ramon Gilsanz Consulting Engineers
Ramon Gilsanz
Vicki Arbitrio
Raul Maestre

FRANK O. GEHRY & ASSOCIATES

Exhibition Design Team
Frank Gehry, *Principal*
Randy Jefferson, *Principal*
James Glymph, *Principal*
Edwin Chan, *Associate Principal*
Craig Webb, *Associate Principal*
Terry Bell, *Associate Principal*

Project Director
Keith Mendenhall

Project Architects
Michelle Kaufmann
Tensho Takemori
Ana Henton
Rachel Allen

Job Captains
Sean Gallivan
Leigh Jerrard

Structural Development
Karl Blette

Project Team
Reza Bagherzadeh
Anand Devarajan
Marc Digeros
Matt Gagnon
Jeff Garrett
Christoph Groth
Ali Jeevanjee
Eric Jones
Steffen Leisner
Meaghan Lloyd
David Nam
Gaston Nogues
Diego Petrate
Birgit Schneider
Christian Schulz
Paola Tassara
Aaron Turner
Gavin Wall

Photography Coordination
Whit Preston
Laura Stella

CATIA/CAD Coordination
Henry Brawner
Reg Prentice
Dennis Sheldon
Monica Valtierra-Day
Kristin Woehl
Bryant Yeh

Structural Engineering
John A. Martin & Associates
Trailer Martin
Jackie Vinkler
Marcello Sgambelluri
Diane Duvand
Nathan Tse

Fabrication
CTEK
Erik Adickes
Fred Adickes
Jim Howell
Todd Kidd

A. Zahner Company
Bill Zahner
Anthony Birchler
Tom Zahner
Paul Martin
Rodney Bassett

BRUCE MAU DESIGN
Bruce Mau
Anita Matusevics
Helen Sanematsu
Catherine Rix
Petra Chevrier

SELECTED PROJECTS

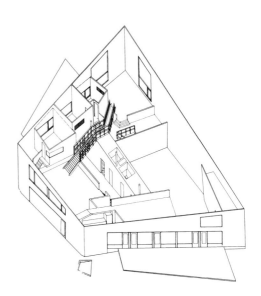

Davis Studio and Residence
Malibu, California 1968–72

The singular trapezoidal form of this studio and residence for painter Ron Davis extended the nascent concern with nonorthogonal geometry first evident in Gehry's O'Neill Hay Barn (1968) in San Juan Capistrano, California. Davis, using color and geometric form, explored perspectival space in his canvases, and for this design, Gehry probed the visual conditions of perspective in built form. The dialogue between artist and architect resulted in a boxlike building whose skewed roofline echoes the shapes of the surrounding hills. The sense of a uniform container is enhanced by the galvanized corrugated steel—unusual in a residential application, but increasingly used by Gehry—that clads exterior walls and roof alike. The simplicity outside is repeated inside, where a spinelike core containing the kitchen and bathroom articulates an otherwise highly flexible space. The loftlike interior accommodates large-scale artworks and an additional level at the highest point. The roof's interior wood framing is left largely exposed.
— JFR

Facing page, top: Completed view looking toward hills.
Left: Construction view.
Above left: View from the northeast.
Above right: Axonometric projection of interior.

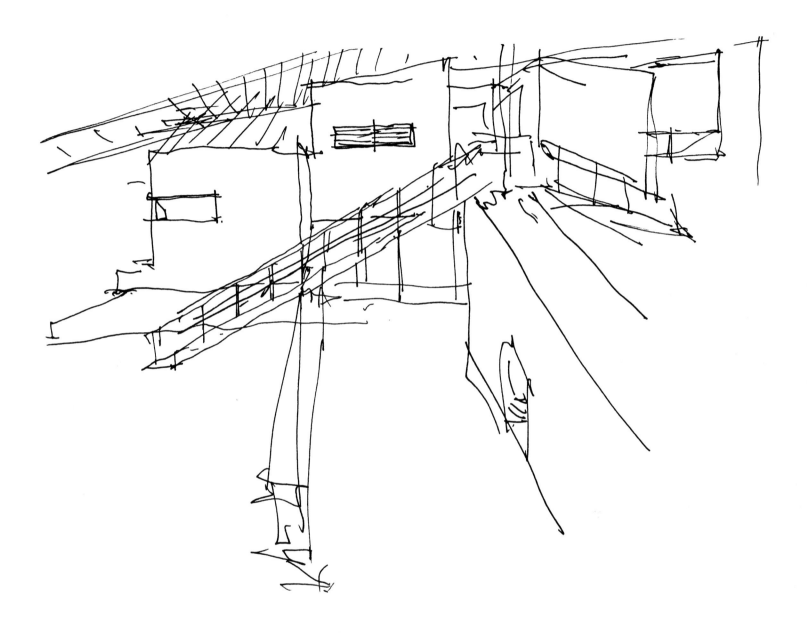

Facing page: Detail of east facade.
Above: Interior sketch.

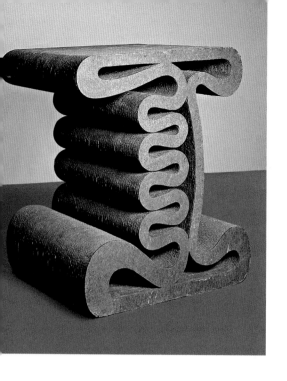

Easy Edges Cardboard Furniture
1969–73

The transformation of humble materials into elaborate and striking geometries—an intrinsic aspect of Gehry's early buildings—exists on a more intimate scale in his Easy Edges furniture. In 1968, Gehry was asked to redesign the interiors of two Joseph Magnin department stores in California. He remade the existing luxurious oak and teak display fixtures in simple plywood, and one of his furniture designers, Don Chadwick, created basic U-shaped cardboard chairs for the interiors. It was then that Gehry began to consider the further design potential of cardboard. Its rough appearance appealed to his informal aesthetic sense, and he discovered that while relatively malleable as a single sheet, it gains strength exponentially when layered. His curiosity led him to glue several sheets of stacked, corrugated cardboard together to form a desk with drawers. Gehry discovered the two-inch-thick surface of his desk could easily support his weight when he stood on it. Chairs, tables, and chaise lounges—constructed from the same material as ordinary packing boxes—have the appearance of gently draped velvet, but are at the same time immensely durable, with hardboard facing applied to the flat surfaces for increased strength.

Above: Easy Edges rocker in Gehry Residence.
Facing page: Easy Edges wiggle side chair.

Page 24: Workshop view.
Page 25, above left and below: Easy Edges bar and bar stool, Collection of Joan and Jack Quinn, Beverly Hills, California. Above right: Easy Edges slanted side chair.

The technique for making these furnishings is as simple as their name implies: A furniture profile is cut from rectilinear cardboard sheets. The individual cutouts are stacked to the desired width of the furniture. The stacks are then compressed into compact units and secured with glue. By 1972, seventeen different, modestly priced versions of Gehry's furniture were available for sale in department stores. This temporary mass distribution gave a wider public access to his uncompromising designs.—KVW

Gehry Residence

Santa Monica, California 1977–78; 1991–92

Gehry's residential designs of the late 1970s and early 1980s produced some of his most innovative work to date. The 1977–78 renovation of his own home—an unassuming two-story bungalow on a corner lot—provided an opportunity to push his experimentation with materials and spatial dynamics to greater degrees. He wrapped the existing structure in layers of corrugated metal and chain link, and pierced the outer skin with large glass apertures rotated off square. Interior spaces were opened up and plaster was stripped away to expose the wood-frame construction, imparting an unexpected sense of process and movement. The reconsideration of the architectural envelope, use of unusual materials, and rejection of the Modernist grid are concerns that have continued to preoccupy Gehry.

In 1991–92, a second renovation began modestly to accommodate the family's changing needs, and some of the earlier sense of immediacy was lost. Along with more significant changes—the addition of a lap pool, the transformation of the garage into a guest house, the reclamation of exterior spaces through extensive landscaping—some of the exposed wood framing that particularly characterized the first renovation was removed or covered over. As a result, some of the sense of process and immediacy that marked the first renovation was lost.—JFR

Right: View looking west across Twenty-second Street of the Gehry residence after the first renovation.

Right and facing page: The first renovation veiled the original structure in an envelope of corrugated metal that stood brazenly visible as seen at right. After the second renovation, the metal was partially shrouded in yet a third layer—a landscaped one—as seen at far right.

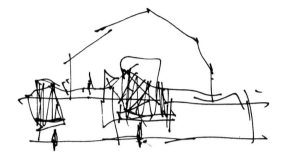

Above: Design sketch of Washington Avenue elevation that shows profile of existing bungalow wrapped by the new addition.

Right: On the second level, the interstitial spaces between the old and new structures create private outdoor spaces, such as the terrace directly above the dining area at bottom.

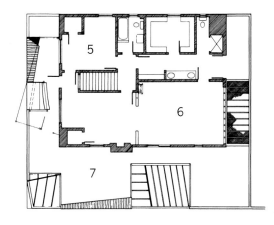

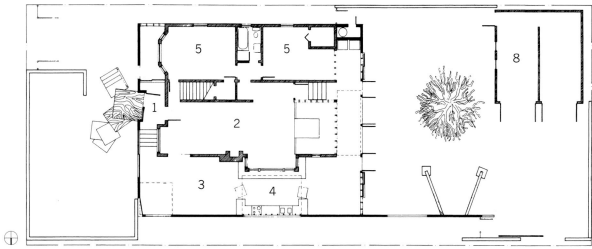

Above: Plans of first and second floors. 1. Entry, 2. Living area, 3. Dining area, 4. Kitchen, 5. Bedrooms, 6. Master bedroom suite, 7. Outdoor deck, 8. Garage.

Pages 34–35: Playing with the conventional use of a window to frame an exterior view, a trapezoidal opening along Washington Avenue frames an interior view of a monumental cactus in the backyard for passersby. The view was subsequently obscured during the second renovation.

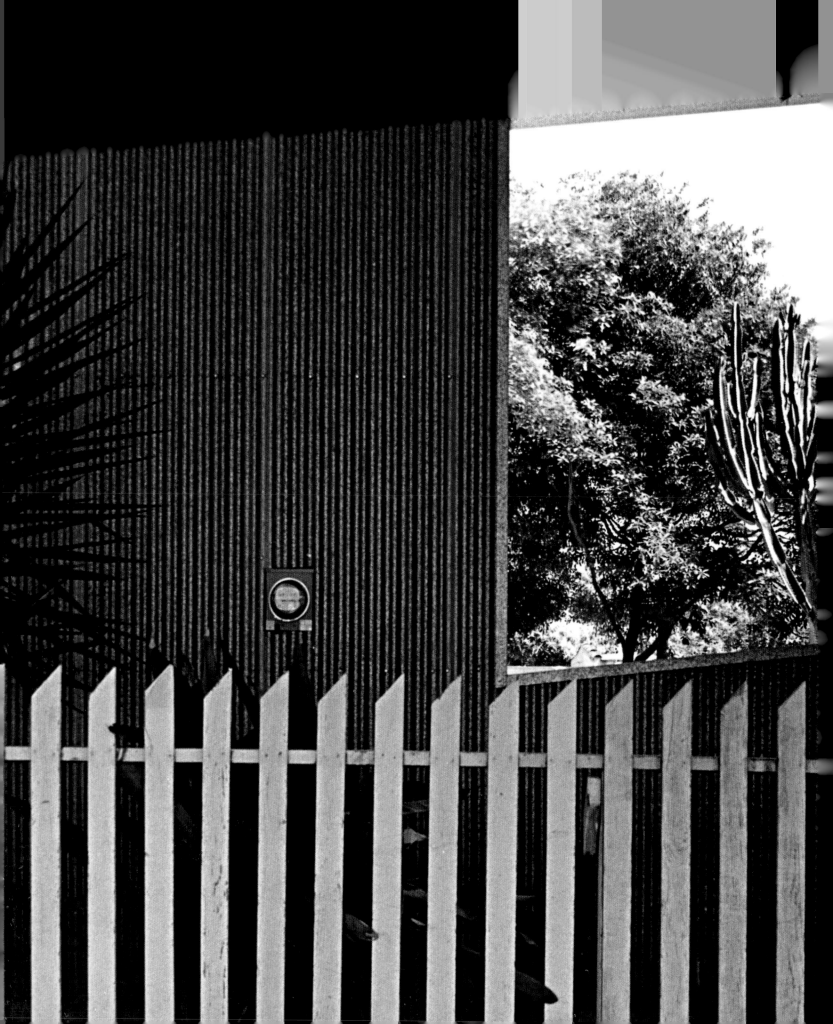

Facing page: The master bedroom on the second floor took on a much more open and airy quality after the second renovation.

Left: The first floor living area after the first renovation. Vestiges of the original house, such as the bay window at right, were retained creating a play between interior and exterior, old and new.

Pages 36–37: Along Washington Avenue, a large glass cube seems momentarily lodged between the old and new fabric of the house, its shape echoed by a chain-link form above. The cube floods the kitchen interior with light, while still maintaining privacy. The kitchen floor is covered with asphalt, suggesting a driveway just outside the original bungalow.

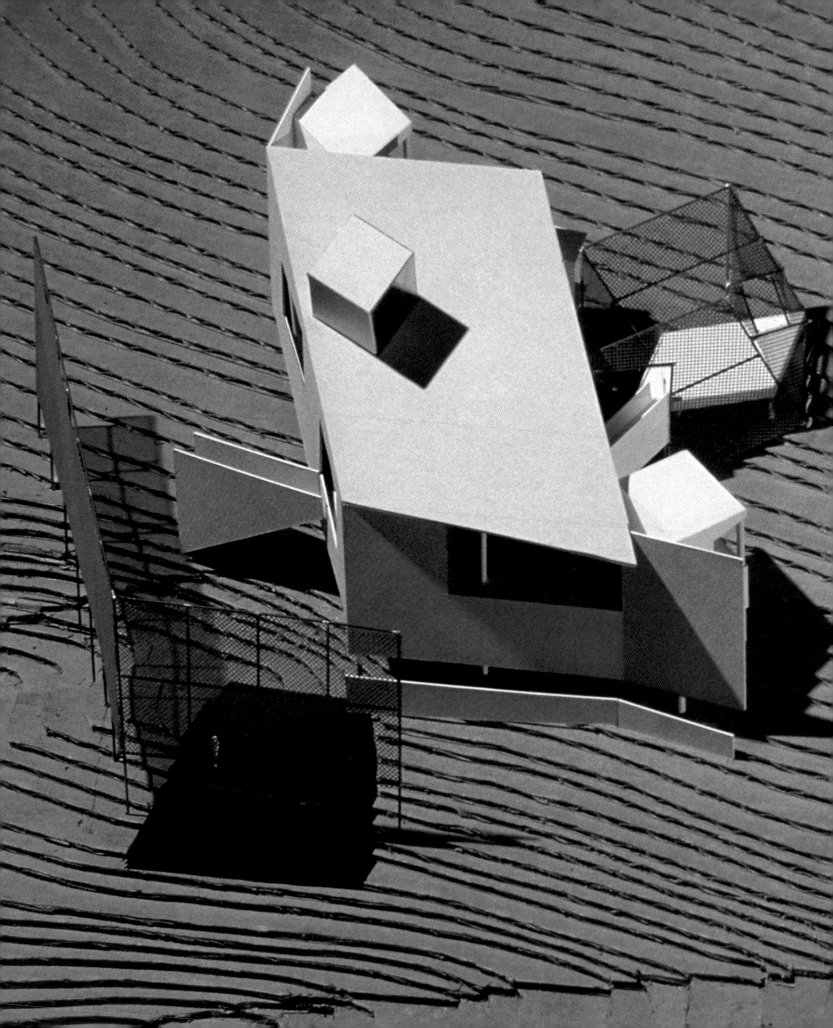

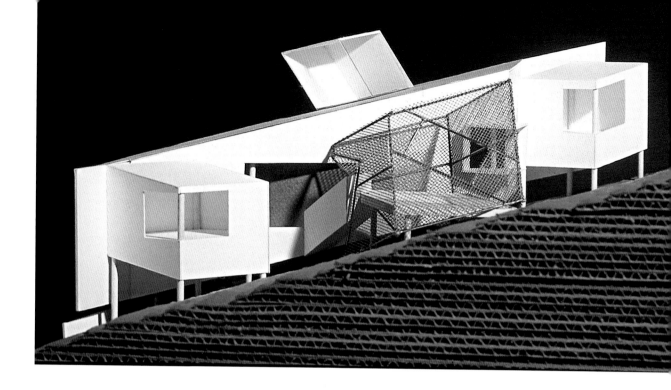

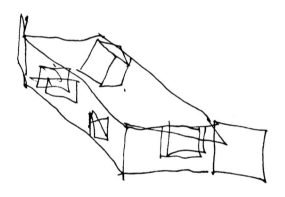

Wagner Residence (unbuilt)

Malibu, California 1978

The Wagner Residence, like Gehry's other residential projects from this period, reveals the architect's interest in rupturing the rigid, Modernist box. Gehry's design both relies on and distorts the rectilinear wood-frame substructure. It also suggests the influence of Japanese architecture upon his early work, albeit through the reconfiguration of its typically low, horizontal spaces and symmetrical lines. The split-level Wagner Residence was conceived for a sloping hillside location. Hovering above the ground on piers, the house features two upper living levels and a doctor's office and asphalt carport on the bottom story. The corrugated metal outer walls and irregular window openings are juxtaposed at oblique angles to the foundation, and the structure's nonrectilinear form creates the effect of a sculptural mass tumbling down the slope. This sense of dynamism was something that Gehry endeavored to capture in his early buildings, and it continues to inform his work.—KVW

Facing page and above: Final design model, scale unknown.
Above left: Perspective sketch.

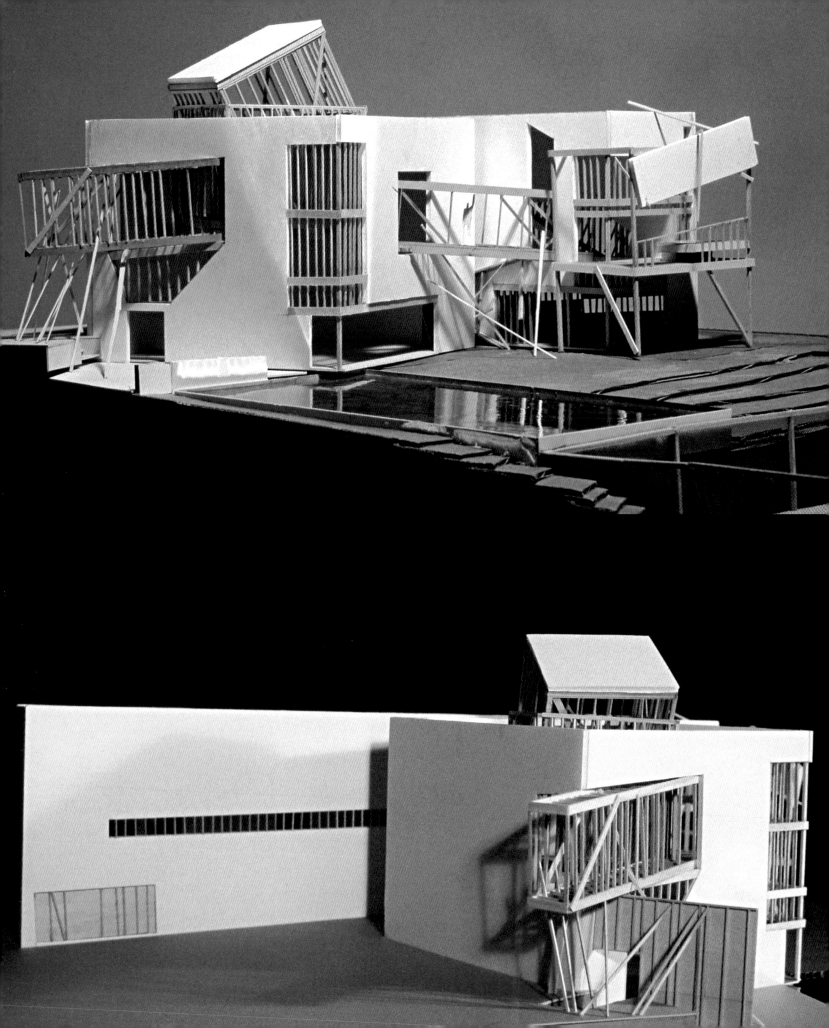

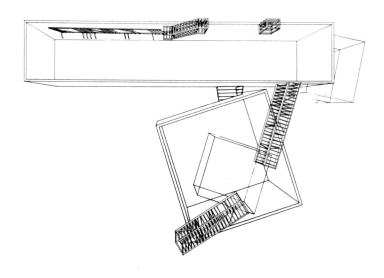

Familian Residence (unbuilt)
Santa Monica, California 1978

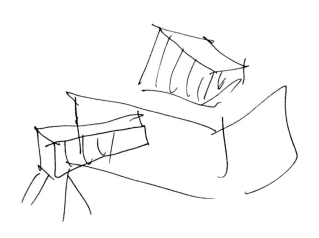

Gehry has stated that "buildings under construction look nicer than buildings finished." His design for the Familian Residence particularly captures this quality of arrested motion. In contrast to the traditional structure of single-family dwellings, Gehry's design fragmented the protective exterior shell by revealing glimpses of the wood framed exterior beneath stucco sheathing. The house is comprised of separate buildings, one rectangular and the other cube-shaped. These structures are joined by a network of wooden bridges, pavilions, and skylights intended to connect them both physically and visually, and to allow unobstructed views of the Santa Monica Mountains from the back of the house. Gehry's design also reflects his sensitivity to his clients' lifestyles; in this case, a need to accommodate both social and private use. The cube features a single open space intended for entertaining, while the rectangular building houses the living quarters.—KVW

Facing page: Design process model, scale unknown. The wood framing of the circulation space is left exposed, providing a visual link between the interrelated public and private structures. The Museum of Modern Art, New York. Gift of the architect.

Above and left: Axonometric projection with exterior circulation elements, and design sketch.

Loyola Law School

Los Angeles 1978–

In 1978, Gehry was chosen by Loyola Marymount University to develop a campus plan for their law school. The project has been executed in several stages and remains ongoing (including an additional building and a large outdoor stage area to be completed in 2002). The gradual expansion of the campus and its status as a work-in-progress is underscored by the nonaxial layout, which suggests an "unplanned" quality to the area that is heightened by the distinct, individual character of each building.

When Gehry took on the commission, the law school consisted of one building in an industrial area near downtown Los Angeles. In response to the university's request that he define a welcoming environment for the school and its commuting student population, Gehry created a parklike atmosphere. Mounds of grass and trees are scattered between the buildings, and the main entrance is elevated slightly and accessed by several steps from Olympic Boulevard. Gehry's design conveys a palpable sense of place, but one that is also seamlessly integrated into its urban environment—an important consideration for the architect. A subdued, light gray stucco was used for the street-side exterior of the renovated Fritz B. Burns Academic Center. A long rectangular structure, it reinforces the patron's desired sense of privacy, while also giving the campus a sufficiently unobtrusive presence that feels very much a part of the neighborhood.

Within the campus, the architecture is more animated. The yellow interior side of the Burns building provides a backdrop for a scattering of smaller, dissimilar structures. Here Gehry's design makes reference, however obliquely, to classical architecture, drawing on the configuration of a Roman acropolis for the arrangement of buildings and for several structural details. His historical allusions acknowledge the school's wish to visually communicate the history and solemnity of the legal profession, while his surprising reconfigurations of familiar elements suggest the lively debates that might occur within the classrooms.—KVW

Left: View of the campus looking northeast with downtown Los Angeles in the distance.

45

Facing page: The Burns building was renovated during the first phase of construction and provided a backdrop for the more animated buildings that followed. The main stairway punctures the facade as it snakes from ground to roof, asymmetrically cutting the building. The pronounced passage in and through the building emphasizes its importance as the campus's social center.

Above right: Sketch of Burns building facade.

Right: Campus site plan. Phase 1: Fritz B. Burns Academic Center; Phase 2: 2a. Chapel of the Advocate; 2b. Joseph J. Donovan Hall; 2c. Merrifield Hall; 2d. Hall of the '70s; Phase 3: Rains Library renovation; Phase 4: 4a. Rev. Charles S. Casassa building; 4b. Hall of the '80s; Phase 5: Parking garage; Phase 6: 6a. Trial Advocacy Center; 6b. Site of Girardi Moot Court [projected].

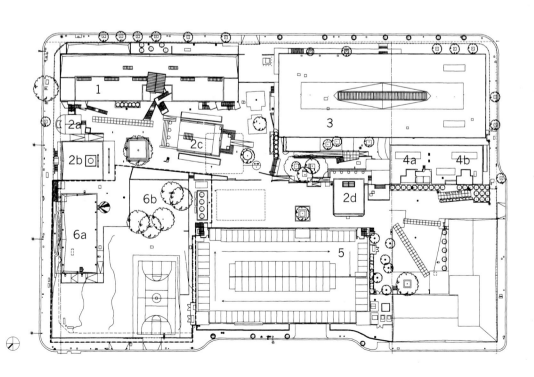

DARLING PAVILION

CHARLES S. CASASSA, S.J.
BUILDING

Facing page: The Casassa building was completed in 1991 during the fourth construction phase and houses a library annex, classrooms, and offices. Like the Burns building, it provides a strong visual anchor for the campus.

Below: Two tiers of columns adorn Donovan Hall and echo the thick columns of Merrifield Hall, opposite, which remain detached from the building as purely sculptural objects.

Facing page: Site model, scale 1/8"=1'. The Burns
building is in left foreground, the chapel is in center
foreground, and Casassa building is at rear.

Below: Chapel interior.

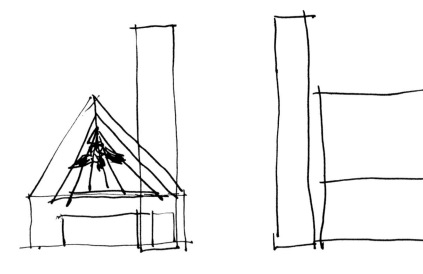

Facing page: Design sketches of chapel (above). Sheathed in copper sheet metal, the chapel was originally covered in Finnish plywood treated to withstand weathering (below).

Above: View of Donovan Hall and Chapel of the Advocate as seen from courtyard, provide a visual terminus along Olympic Boulevard. The chapel's glass-sided campanile is transformed during the evening into an elegant column of light.

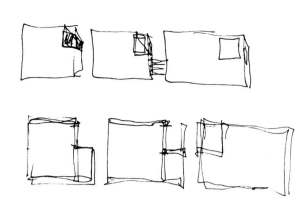

Above: View of south facades. The three studios are tightly grouped on a narrow lot, and their materials and exterior details are varied to break up the mass.

Facing page, top left: Interior view of a studio. As a means to collaborate with the residents, Gehry left Sheetrock and wood framing exposed so that they were able to finish the interiors as desired. Top right: Preliminary design sketches. Below: View looking east along Indiana Avenue.

Indiana Avenue Studios
Venice, California 1979–81

By the early 1970s, Gehry had become acquainted with a number of artists who were part of the thriving Southern California art scene. The use of Pop aesthetics, and the manipulation of light and space were crucial aspects to the work of artists such as Larry Bell, Billy Al Bengston, and Robert Irwin; Gehry too was exploring these ideas in his architecture. His involvement with the Los Angeles art community resulted in the commission to build the Indiana Avenue Studios for three local artists.

The sculptural nature of his design solution for the project speaks to Gehry's artistic predilections. In each of the three 1,500 square-foot live-in studios, the aesthetics of the surrounding community and the needs of the buildings' inhabitants are integrated. While modest in size, the two-story buildings project above the low Venice skyline. To minimize the boxlike masses, Gehry abstracted the exteriors with oversized details: a chimney, stairway, and protruding bay window. The coverings, one each in green asphalt shingles, unpainted plywood, and blue stucco, contribute to the quirky overall appearance. The spacious, loftlike interiors accommodate the dual function of the spaces as homes and artist's studios.—KVW

55

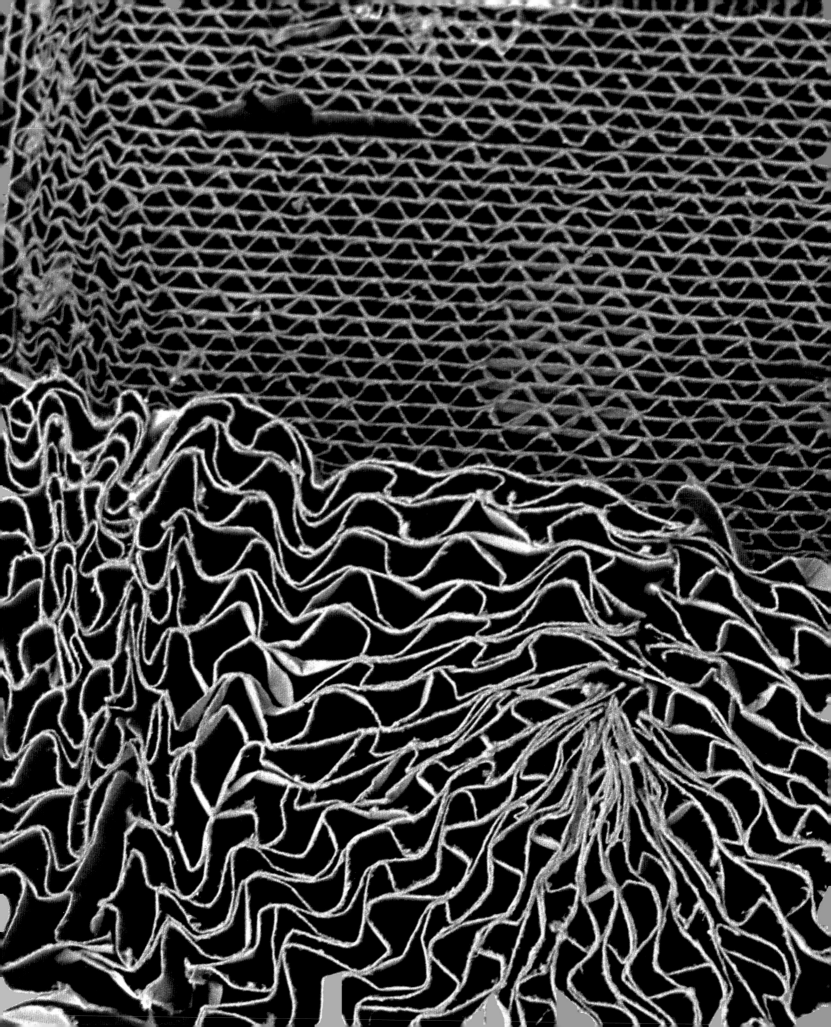

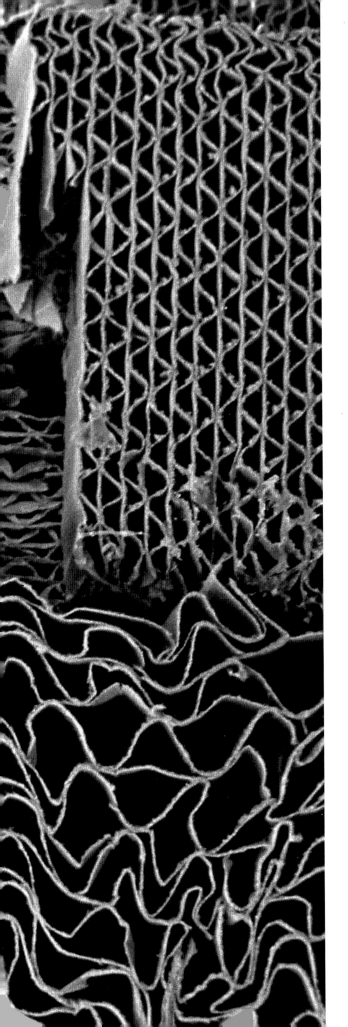

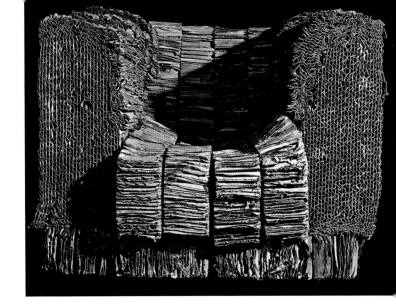

Experimental Edges Cardboard Furniture
1979–82

Gehry considers the furniture and lamps he has developed to be the "quick fix" of his architectural practice: their realization is relatively immediate and low cost, and they provide a satisfying smaller forum in which various design concerns, including those relating to his buildings, may be explored. Like his Easy Edges (1969–73), Experimental Edges furniture was constructed from corrugated cardboard sheets. In contrast to the attenuated lines of the earlier pieces, the Experimental furniture is bulkier, with rough, shaggy edges and an improvisational appearance that is in keeping with the sensibility of Gehry's architectural designs. Given this interrelationship, it seems logical that as the buildings became more substantial during the 1980s, he would develop this second line of furniture based on denser volumes.

For Experimental Edges, Gehry used a thick corrugated cardboard with a pronounced texture to create these larger volumes, manipulating the density of the pieces by combining sheets of varying widths within a single form. Some sheets were intentionally misaligned within the stacks, creating an undulating line and slight ripples within the cardboard folds. Many pieces were developed from 1979 to 1982, and a select few were marketed commercially beginning in the mid-1980s.—KVW

Left: Cardboard detail.
Above: Experimental Edges Grandpa Beaver chair.

Above: Experimental Edges Sherman Lounge.
Collection of Fred and Winter Hoffman, Santa Monica,
California.

Below: Experimental Edges Bubbles Lounge.

Facing page: Experimental Edges Little Beaver chair
with ottoman.

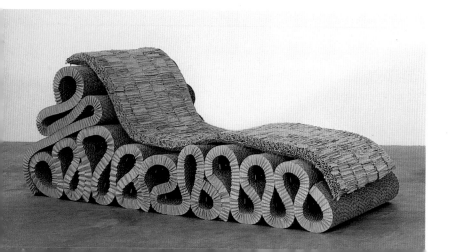

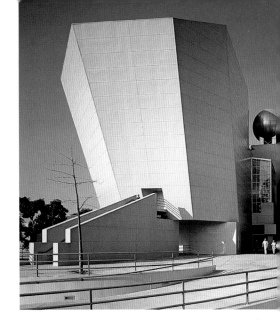

Aerospace Hall, California Science Center
Los Angeles 1982–84

Although now famous for the numerous museums he has designed, by 1982 Gehry had completed only one such facility, the Cabrillo Marine Aquarium (1977–79) in San Pedro, California, which is distinguished by chain link and galvanized metal sheathing. Gehry's second museum commission, the Aerospace Hall at the California Science Center (formerly the California Museum of Science and Industry) clearly demarcates its purpose as an aeronautic exhibition space: a fighter jet is attached, seemingly mid-flight, on the facade. The technological program is further suggested through the industrial materials, including glass, steel, and sheet metal, covering the building's abstract forms, whose irregularity and arrangement mimic its urban context. The building is located on the grounds of Exposition Park and positioned at one end of the armory that housed the previous Aerospace Hall. The original intention was that Gehry's building would function together with new exhibition spaces planned for the armory.

The interior space is practically configured to accommodate airplanes and other large-scale aerospace objects, and an oversized, hangar door makes it possible to easily move them in and out of the building. The hall's underlying structure is exposed and has floor to ceiling openings. Each of three levels offers expansive views of the objects exhibited within a large open space. Abundant skylights bring in natural light, and the soaring ceiling emphasizes the sky and the theme of flight.—KVW

Left: View looking northeast with downtown Los Angeles in the distance. The original armory building is visible at left.

Above: Although in Gehry's original design the interior of this polygonal structure was continuous, it was later subdivided into smaller spaces against the architect's wishes.

This page: Sketch of south facade (above), and final design model, scale unknown (below).

Facing page: A fighter jet, a Lockheed F-104, is mounted on the south facade of the building.

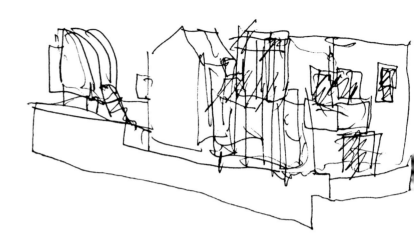

Right: Preliminary perspective sketch. The separate study, which would later assume the appearance of a lifeguard shack, was first conceived as a metal-sheathed structure. Gehry's modification further integrates the house within the surrounding beach landscape.

Below and facing page: The amalgamation of materials and forms that comprise the house's exterior integrate it with its surroundings, as seen looking northwest (below), and from the beach (at far right).

Norton Residence

Venice, California 1982–84

Each of Gehry's buildings is rife with idiosyncrasies, evidence that he adapts his architecture to fit the preferences of his clients. On the beachfront side of the Norton Residence—a modest house on a narrow Venice lot designed for Bill Norton, a screenwriter, and Lynn Norton, a painter—Gehry placed a freestanding structure reminiscent of a lifeguard shack, which functions as a secluded office. The shack is joined to the main house by an extensive deck on the second level. Its height permits picturesque views of the ocean, but the room remains isolated from the activity of the boardwalk below. Aesthetically, it ties the house to the visual mayhem of the beach, while its exposed wood beams and inexpensive waferboard interior remain consistent with the design of the main structure.

The three-story house is covered in a variety of materials, including glazed tile, stucco, and concrete block. In several places, wood beams are visible through glass sheathing. Such details exhibit Gehry's continued interest in the manipulation of wood-frame construction. Externally, the house is an agglomeration of colors and geometries, reminiscent of the Gehry Residence (1977–78) in nearby Santa Monica. The Nortons were intrigued by that earlier project, and it clearly inspired the layering of materials and the manipulation of what might have been a typical box-like residence in the design of their own home. The interior is more subdued, featuring large, open spaces and extensive natural light filtered through skylights and glass doors. In response to the clients' concern that their privacy on the small lot be maintained, Gehry created several private decks on the upper levels and roof, while the street-front facade has only a minimal number of small window openings.—KVW

65

Above: Interior view of the second level. The living area is in the foreground, with the kitchen and dining area at rear.

Facing page: View from the interior looking west toward the beach. Large glass doors open from the living area onto the second floor deck, connecting the office to the main house.

Floor plans of the first level (left) and third level (facing page): 1. Studio, 2. Bedroom, 3. Garage, 4. Study.

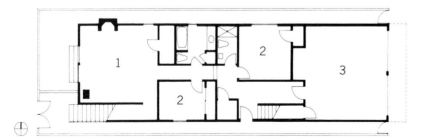

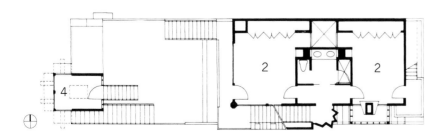

Above and facing page: View of study from boardwalk, and looking west toward the ocean from the second-floor deck.

Above: The guest house, seen from the Philip
Johnson–designed main house, appears as a cluster of
sculptural forms devoid of windows.

Winton Guest House

Wayzata, Minnesota 1983–87

Gehry's primary concern with the Winton Guest House was that the new addition remain distinct from the geometric simplicity of the Philip Johnson design of the main house, while also retaining a tenuous connection to it. Gehry's early models included chain link, a log cabin, and a structure akin to an inverted flower pot—a response to the clients' original suggestion that he conceive of the guest house as a potting-shed complement to the main structure. Emblematic of his skillful adaptation of buildings to their surroundings, Gehry devised an equally spare yet unique solution that is more sculptural than architectural.

Influenced by Giorgio Morandi's still life paintings of bottles and jars, Gehry designed a cluster of rectangular, square, wedge, and cone-shaped buildings, which are nestled between trees and exist independently from the rest of the estate. Exaggerating the concept of a one-room building, Gehry articulates the guest house into individual shapes, which remain connected internally. Each form is sheathed in a single material—brick, Finnish plywood, and sheet metal—that imbues a sleek elegance, which is a departure from the roughness of Gehry's earlier structures. Modulations in shape and color and the absence of windows on the west facade transform the quarters into an absorbing tableau when seen from the main residence. The fragmentation of the structure diminishes the impact of its physical scale and prevents it from overwhelming the Johnson house.—KVW

Gehry's composition of forms lends the guest house an ever-changing character when seen from different vantage points. The living space is located in the metal-clad pyramid; one bedroom occupies the stone-covered wedge; and a second is housed in the painted metal trapezoid. A sleep loft in a galvanized steel box hovers above the plywood-covered rectangle, which houses the kitchen, garage, and service areas. A small brick volume encloses a fireplace alcove.

Below: Preliminary design sketch.

Facing page: The pyramidal roof of the living area is punctuated by skylights that flood the central space with light.

This page: Design process models, scale unknown, and a sketch reveal the evolution from a more conventional rectilinear organization to the final pinwheel plan that has become a frequently recurring motif in Gehry's work.

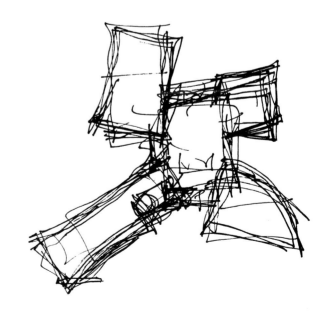

Above: Seen from the trapezoidal bedroom is the interior of the living room, the entrance of which is also visible through the window to the left.

Right: Bedroom interior.

Pages 78–79: Variations in scale and shape integrate Gehry's forms with the surrounding grove of trees. While the elements appear to be separate structures, they are continuous spaces in recognition of the Minnesota climate.

Fish and Snake Lamps
1983–86

The 1983 introduction of Colorcore, a new laminate product of the Formica Company, was launched with an invitation to designers to illustrate the product's distinctive properties. Gehry elected to create a lamp that would highlight the translucency of the laminate's integral coloration. The serendipitous discovery of splintered patterns came after several failed attempts in which one lamp was accidentally broken. Gehry translated the scalelike pattern of the jagged pieces into fish and snake forms. Nearly three dozen lamps were eventually produced by New City Editions.

Fish forms first appeared in 1981 in Gehry's unrealized design for the Smith Residence (a proposed renovation of the Steeves Residence [1958–59], one of Gehry's earliest projects) in Brentwood, California, and in a collaboration with artist Richard Serra for the exhibition *Collaborations: Artists and Architects* at the Architectural League of New York. While Gehry explained his initial use of the fish as a gently mocking response to the postmodern penchant for classical motifs, its continued presence in his work is largely a symbolic allusion to personal childhood memories and a testament to the functional appeal of the form's structural flexibility. In the 1980s, fish were also prominent elements of such diverse projects as the Fishdance Restaurant (1986–87) in Kobe, Japan, and the Chiat Day Temporary Offices (1986–88) in Venice, California.—JFR

Above: *Fish Lamp Study in Paper*, 1984–86. Collection of William and Ruth True, Seattle.

Left: Installation view of *The Architecture of Frank Gehry* (1986), Walker Art Center, Minneapolis.

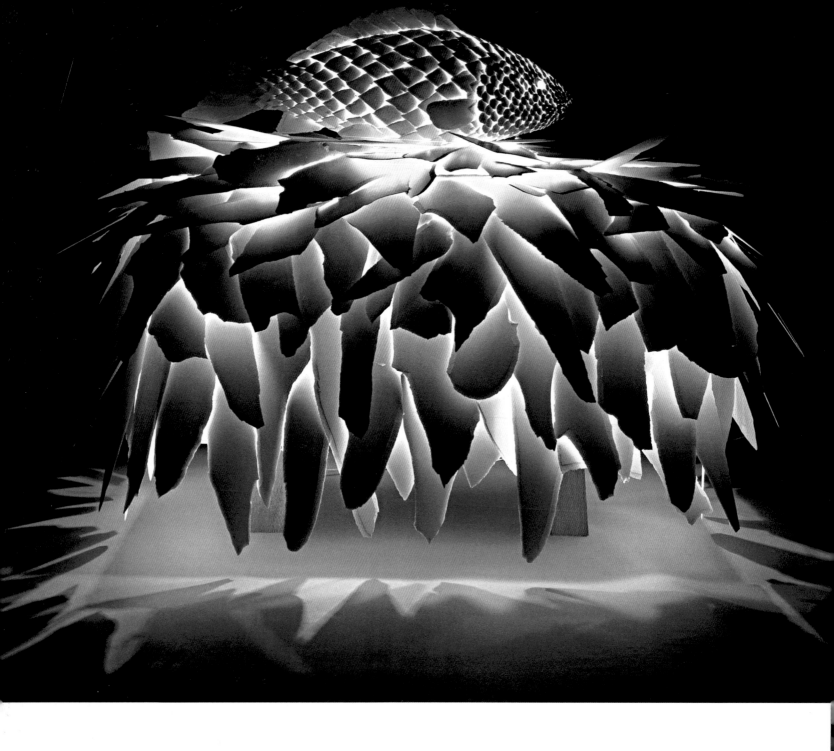

Left: *Low White Fish Lamp*, 1984. Private collection, courtesy of Fred Hoffman Fine Art, Santa Monica, California.

Below: Installation view of fish lamps.

Sirmai-Peterson Residence

Thousand Oaks, California 1983–88

The Sirmai-Peterson Residence derives its unique character from the physical site. Staggered living levels adapt to the uneven topography, while a ravine that previously bisected the lot has been dammed to create a pond behind the house. Vehicles approach the home from above and then descend down a sloping driveway to the entrance. In relation to the surrounding land-scape, the residence appears like an isolated village. Inspired by the layout of a medieval town, Gehry designed the various elements of the house to be oriented around a central courtyard, with the cruciform-shaped main building likened to a church at the center.

Pursuing his interest in one-room buildings, Gehry situated the two bedrooms in separate structures and linked them by passageways to the main structure. Basic building materials are used with new sophistication as wood beams line the ceiling in elegant geometric patterns, and monochromatic cement blocks form the understated interior walls. From the exterior, the three buildings create an interplay of solids and voids, which is heightened by the angles of the expansive windows.—KVW

Above: Final design model, scale unknown.
Left: View of the house looking west across the pond.

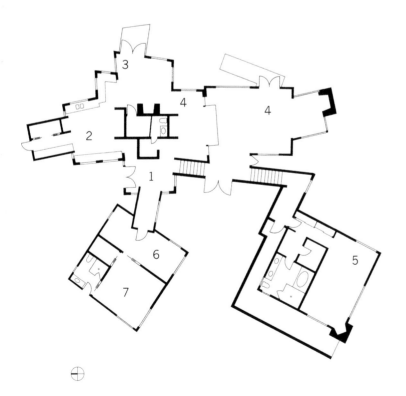

Above: Interior view of the dining area.

Below: Gehry's plan allows for further expansion of the house by the clients. 1. Entry, 2. Kitchen, 3. Dining room, 4. Living and master bedroom, 5. Exercise room, 6. Bedroom.

Above: View from west showing the separate master bedroom, clad in black stucco, and the additional bedroom to its north.

Above: View looking east across Main Street.

Right: Site plan of complex. 1. Parking, 2. Retail space,
3. Courtyard, 4. Restaurant, 5. Theater space.

Edgemar Development

Santa Monica, California 1984–88

For the Edgemar Development complex, Gehry created an enclosed miniature city with a diverse architectural program initially conceived to accommodate an exhibition space, restaurant, retail shops, office space, and parking lot. Facing Santa Monica's Main Street, Gehry's plan employs skewed building orientations and strategically located openings to define and enliven the physical space, the same strategy behind Loyola Law School (1978–) in Los Angeles, but in this case he creates a welcoming public arena in which passersby can shop or dine. Variations in the architectural vocabulary integrate the five buildings and three towers with the surrounding low-level, commercial structures and unassuming residences.

Edgemar's public face is intended to entice visitors to enter its confines. Two angled openings from the sidewalk allow glimpses of the courtyard. A glass-enclosed greenhouse, an open cube of steel beams, and an elevator shaft shrouded in chain link comprise the towers that are visible from the street. Inside the complex, buildings of one and two stories enclose the courtyard, creating an arrangement that is intentionally suggestive of the well-known medieval towers of San Gimignano, Italy.—KVW

Above: Detail of roofscape.

Right: Interior courtyard. The tower wrapped in mesh houses the elevator bank.

Pages 92–93: View from Main Street looking into the courtyard.

Above: View looking east across Main Street.

Chiat Day Building

Venice, California 1985–91

The surprising facade of the Chiat Day Advertising building makes it one of Gehry's most recognizable commissions. Approaching the building on Main Street, one is confronted by a succession of three elements that essentially function as a billboard for the advertising agency. Its literal centerpiece is the monumental form of a pair of binoculars, which functions as an entrance for cars and pedestrians and contains usable spaces within. This playful component is positioned between the hull-shaped building on the north end, and on the south side by a facade of copper-covered rectangular columns and diagonal beams, which has been likened to a group of trees. The binoculars were the result of a collaboration with artists Claes Oldenburg and Coosje van Bruggen and also speak to Gehry's own propensity toward imaginative forms. The involvement of Oldenburg and van Bruggen, with whom Gehry had worked on earlier unbuilt projects, allowed for mutual exchange: the artists were able to modify one of their large-scale sculptures to function architecturally, while Gehry extended his thinking about the potential of built structures to succeed as sculptural objects.

As a starting point for the interior design of the L-shaped, 75,000 square-foot plan, Gehry drew upon his previous configurations for the Rouse Company (1969–74) and Mid-Atlantic Toyota (1976–78). The space is open, and the height of cubicle walls are varied to break the monotony of the interior, also facilitating interaction between departments. Natural light filters through the entire space via a network of skylights located throughout the main office area and within individual meeting rooms. Although the detailing is limited to basic plywood fixtures and standard office furniture, this neutrality gives employees the freedom to personalize their space, thus acknowledging the inventive nature of the company.—KVW

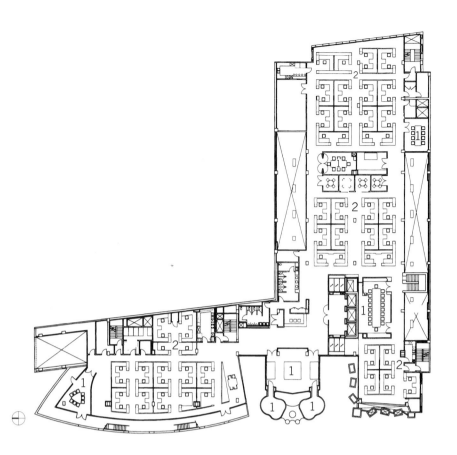

Left: Second floor plan. 1. Conference rooms, 2. Offices.

Facing page, below: Preliminary design sketches of Main Street elevation.

Below and facing page, above: Design process models, scale unknown. Gehry experimented with a variety of forms before serendipitously arriving at the binoculars as the central element in his facade. In the model below the central element is a blank facade, while at right it has been augmented by a container of nails.

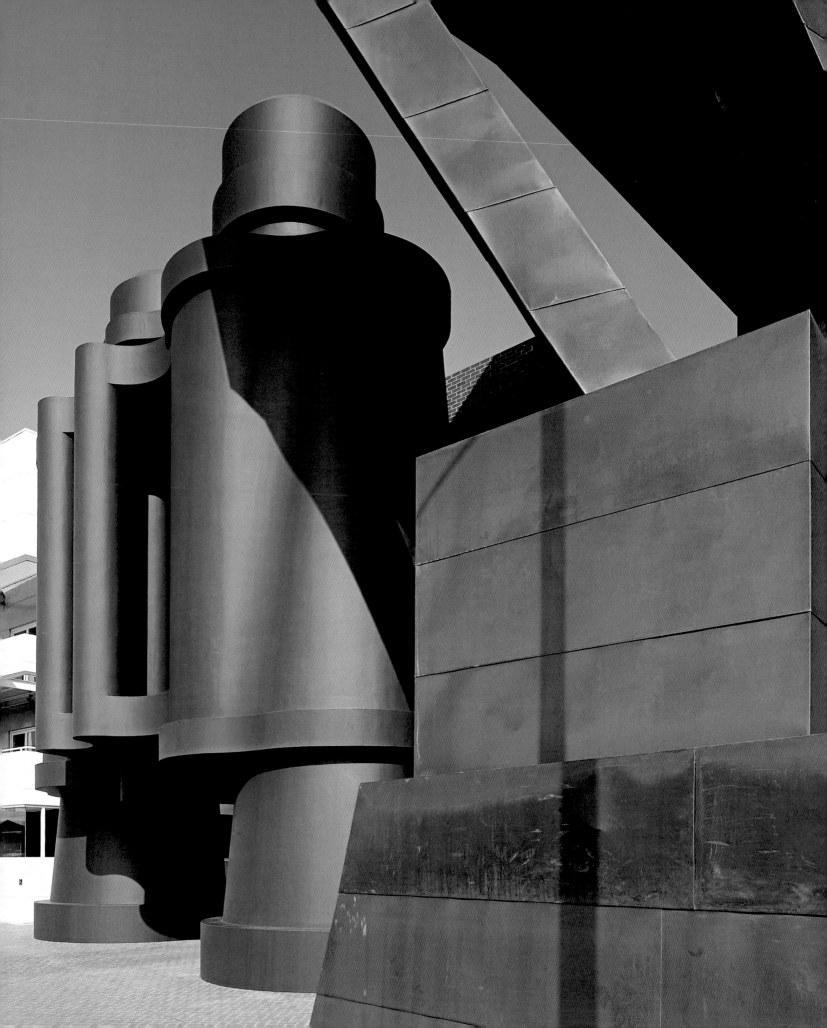

Facing page: Exterior detail of the binocular element. Oldenburg and van Bruggen's form arose as part of a performance piece, *Il Corso del Coltello*, which the artists conceived along with Gehry in 1985. The three first collaborated in their design of the unbuilt Camp Good Times (1984–85), an eleven-building summer camp for children in the Santa Monica Mountains, where architecture and sculpture converged in the camp's fanciful building forms.

Above: Small conference rooms are located within each cylinder of the binoculars. At the uppermost level, they are capped with a skylight that is located in each eyepiece and an exaggerated lightbulb fixture.

Page 98: The facade of the hall-shaped structure functions as a brise-soleil and as circulation space between the three office levels.

Page 99: A conference room is located directly behind the binoculars and is accented with a bentwood fixture designed by Gehry.

Schnabel Residence
Brentwood, California 1986–89

Invited to participate in *Follies, Architecture for the Late-Twentieth-Century Landscape*, a 1983 exhibition at the Leo Castelli Gallery in New York, Gehry began to reimagine an element common to the American suburb—the tract house. His resulting design, intended to break the monotony of the middle-class landscape, eschewed the typically anonymous, blocklike home, and was devised instead as a series of nine rooms broken into nine structures, each with a distinctive architectural presence. While Gehry initially arranged these rooms according to a grid, separating them by pathways, the final design showed them scattered across the plot. While this theoretical proposal for enlivening the American neighborhood was never realized nor exhibited, it directly inspired the design of the Schnabel Residence, located in an elite Los Angeles neighborhood on a relatively undistinguished rectangular plot of land.

The structures that make up the Schnabel Residence draw upon myriad historical influences and visual impressions. The bulbous dome of the office (originally a guest bedroom) recalls Griffith Observatory in Los Angeles, but it also makes oblique reference to the domes of Islamic mosques. The central living space is cruciform in plan, suggestive of medieval church architecture. The master bedroom originally opened onto a Zen-like reflecting pool (since replaced with grass). The buildings vary in scale, manipulating the perception of the lot size, and the site has been extensively landscaped in relation to the buildings. In its architectural diversity, the Schnabel Residence is more reminiscent of a scattered village than of an ordered residential compound.—KVW

Left: View looking east across Carmelina Avenue.

103

Below left: Ground floor plan. 1. Entry, 2. Living area, 3. Dining area, 4. Kitchen, 5. Family room, 6. Study, 7. Bedroom, 8. Study/Guest room, 9. Garage, 10. Covered walkway.

Below right: Inside the entrance gate, the numerous variations in scale and style that occur among the buildings are immediately evident. Gehry retains order amidst the jumble of elements by aligning them along an east-west axis, which is articulated by the path that leads to the main entrance.

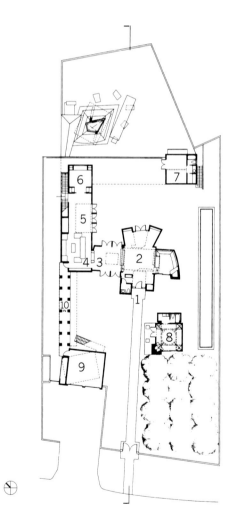

Above: Design sketch.

Left: The master bedroom is located at the rear of the sloping site below grade to provide privacy. It originally overlooked a shallow pool that has since been filled in with grass. Here, copper pylons appear as sculptural elements that seem to float on the water and shade the bedroom from the intense sunlight. Gehry draws upon the reflective surface of water as an architectural element in his designs, using the water garden as a means of engaging a building's surface with the surrounding landscape.

Left: Against the white walls of the living area, the wood joists of the ceiling are exposed, and the lead-coated copper that clads the exterior is used in its uncoated state to accent fireplaces and other architectural elements.

Above: Master bedroom interior.

Vitra International Manufacturing Facility and Design Museum

Weil am Rhein, Germany 1987–89

A palpable shift in Gehry's aesthetic occurred with his first European commission, the design of two buildings for the manufacturing center of the Vitra furniture company. Gehry was asked to create a unified plan for a factory building that would sit adjacent to Nicholas Grimshaw's 1981 factory, as well as a small museum to house company CEO Rolf Fehlbaum's collection of approximately two hundred Modern and contemporary chairs. The resulting design departed from the disparate layering of geometries and informal materials common to Gehry's southern California structures and evidences his incipient desire to produce amorphously sculptural buildings. The impulse behind the Vitra design and the limitations that his firm discovered during the course of the project would drive the search for a computerized solution to engineering complexities.

The angularity of Gehry's previous structures was broken at Vitra by his use of the curve. Baroque arcs and gentle spirals imply collective movement, responding to the dynamic nature of the manufacturing center. Even the rectilinear factory is whisked into the action by the undulating ramps that flank it and visually correspond to the curvilinear museum. The sloping plaster and stucco forms recall Le Corbusier's iconic chapel Notre-Dame-du-Haut (1950–55), an important architectural landmark for Gehry located nearby in Ronchamp, France. The zinc rooftops of Gehry's museum and factory work in tandem with Grimshaw's aluminum-clad building to loosely unify the campus, yet are varied enough in style to work with further architectural additions. In recent years, buildings by Tadao Ando, Zaha Hadid, and Alvaro Siza have been added to the facility's grounds.
—KVW

Right: View of manufacturing facility, at left, and museum, at right.

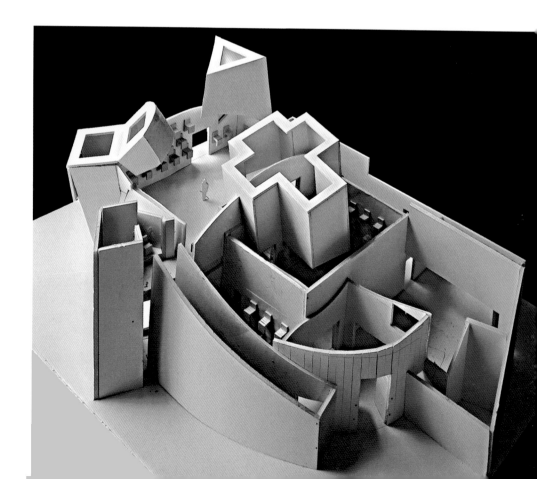

Facing page: View of museum's main entrance.

Above: Presentation model, scale 1:100 m. The curving elements that flank the manufacturing facility function as a backdrop for the museum and visually link the two buildings.

Right: Interior study model, scale 1:50 m.

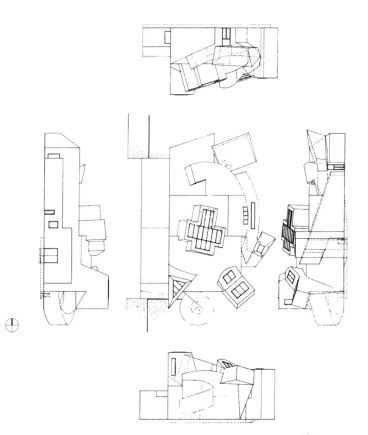

Above and facing page: View of the museum's south facade, and detail of the manufacturing facility.

Left: Roof plan of museum, with elevations.

Pages 116–17: The exhibition galleries are distinguished by a striking architectural vocabulary and dramatic skylights that give each a unique character, while linking them visually.

Team Disneyland Administration Building

Anaheim, California 1987–96

Disneyland's administrative building has a duality that acknowledges both the client's corporate identity and the setting adjacent to the Santa Ana Freeway. The perspective from the parallel freeway prompted Gehry to design an east facade whose low-slung profile and insistent horizontality is best viewed at sixty miles per hour. The sense of speed and energy is enhanced by the highly reflective cladding of blue-green quilted stainless steel. By contrast, the west facade, which faces the amusement park, acknowledges the playfulness of Disneyland. Exuberant curvilinear forms and bold yellow stucco animate this facade, breaking down the building's attenuated length. Despite a limited budget, the design exhibits a vitality that masks its administrative purpose.—JFR

Above: View of east facade.

Right: The main entry is distinguished by curvilinear forms and covered with galvanized metal canopies. The entry plaza is patterned in colored concrete stripes.

This page: The only specific client reference—and the only portion of the interior designed by Gehry—is a large-scale image of Goofy applied to the boldly colored atrium (above). Interior study model, scale 1/4" = 1' (left).

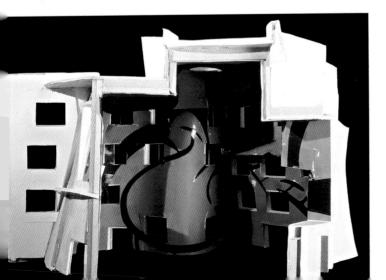

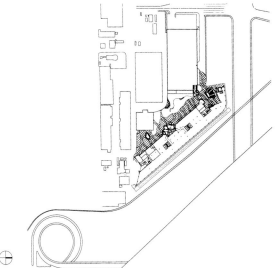

Above: The freeway facade converges in a point and is accentuated by a cowcatcher form that bridges the transition between the vertical and horizontal planes.

Left: Site plan.

Top: View looking north. The central villa houses the public spaces of the complex and is connected to the office building behind it by an enclosed atrium.

Above: Design sketch of east elevation.

Facing page, below: Ground floor plan. 1. Entry, 2. Lobby, 3. Kitchen, 4. Cafeteria, 5. Reception, 6. Offices.

Vitra International Headquarters

Birsfelden, Switzerland 1988–94

Gehry's distinctive corporate structures function as iconic symbols for their organizations. Such is the case with his Vitra International Headquarters in a suburb of Basel, which echoes the Vitra International Manufacturing Facility and Design Museum (1987–89) he designed in Weil am Rhein, Germany. Like the manufacturing facility, the headquarters' rectilinear office building provides a subdued backdrop for a visually separate anterior structure—in this case, a "villa" whose smaller scale and animated arcs recall the museum. The villa is sheathed in zinc, the roofing material used in Weil am Rhein, but its facade is distinguished from the earlier buildings by its brightly painted stucco panels.

As in his earlier designs for the workplace, Gehry structured human relations through the architectural arrangements. The centrally located villa, which houses a cafeteria, meeting rooms, and recep-

tion, functions as the social heart of the organization, its smaller size creating an intimate gathering place. An atrium joins the rectilinear office block to this central core, thereby directing employees to a common point of convergence. The neutral office space counters the more distinctive architecture of the villa, and it recalls the open plans of Gehry's Rouse Company Headquarters (1969–74) in Columbia, Maryland, and his Chiat Day Building (1985–91). Minimal fixed furniture allows for flexibility so that the space might function as both office space and product showroom simultaneously. The unbroken interior, designed to facilitate a sense of community among departments and among all levels of staff, counts upon the daily passage of employees through its central areas. Gehry also negotiates the relationship of the building with the surrounding neighborhood, which ranges from factories to residences: the low-rise office building has an industrial quality, while the miniature villa appears to be an adjoining home. — KVW

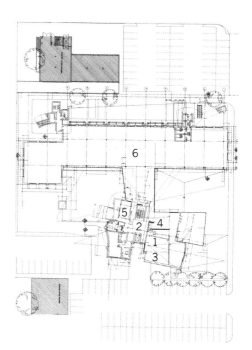

Above: View of one of the highly sculpted meeting rooms located within the villa.

Left: Interior view of the glass-enclosed atrium that leads from the villa to the office building. Bridges on the second and third levels also link the two structures. The primary function of the atrium is to connect the two buildings, and Gehry highlights it as a luminescent space.

Facing page: View looking southwest shows the villa where it is met by the atrium passageway.

Bent Wood Furniture Collection

1989–92 (manufactured 1992–)

The sinuous forms that began to emerge in Gehry's work of the late 1980s and early 1990s are also reflected in the bentwood furniture he created for the Knoll Group during the same period. A workshop next door to his firm's offices gave Gehry the opportunity to conduct a sustained investigation of the material and an appropriate production process. Creating a variety of jigs, he experimented with different configurations of the maple strips.

Gehry's initial bentwood prototypes recall the serpentine lines of the Easy Edges furniture (1969–73), their earlier cardboard kin. And like those furnishings, the structural support and material of the bentwood pieces are seamlessly integrated. Over the next two and a half years, 120 prototypes were produced, from which four chairs, two tables, and one ottoman were marketed. Though derived from the vernacular form of the bushel basket, the twisting elegance of the maple line far surpasses its humble origins. Durable yet remarkably light and resilient, the bentwood furniture quickly assumed a place alongside iconic Modern furniture designs by Charles and Ray Eames and Jens Risom.—JFR

Right: Prototypes in Gehry's workshop.

Page 128: A wall of jigs in Gehry's workshop, above which are stacked prototypes for the Cross Check chair.

Page 129: Prototypes of production pieces in Gehry's workshop. From left the High Sticking chair and the Sit on Me 2 chair, above which is centered the Hat Trick chair. Many pieces in the series are christened with a term deriving from the game of ice hockey, the architect's favorite sport.

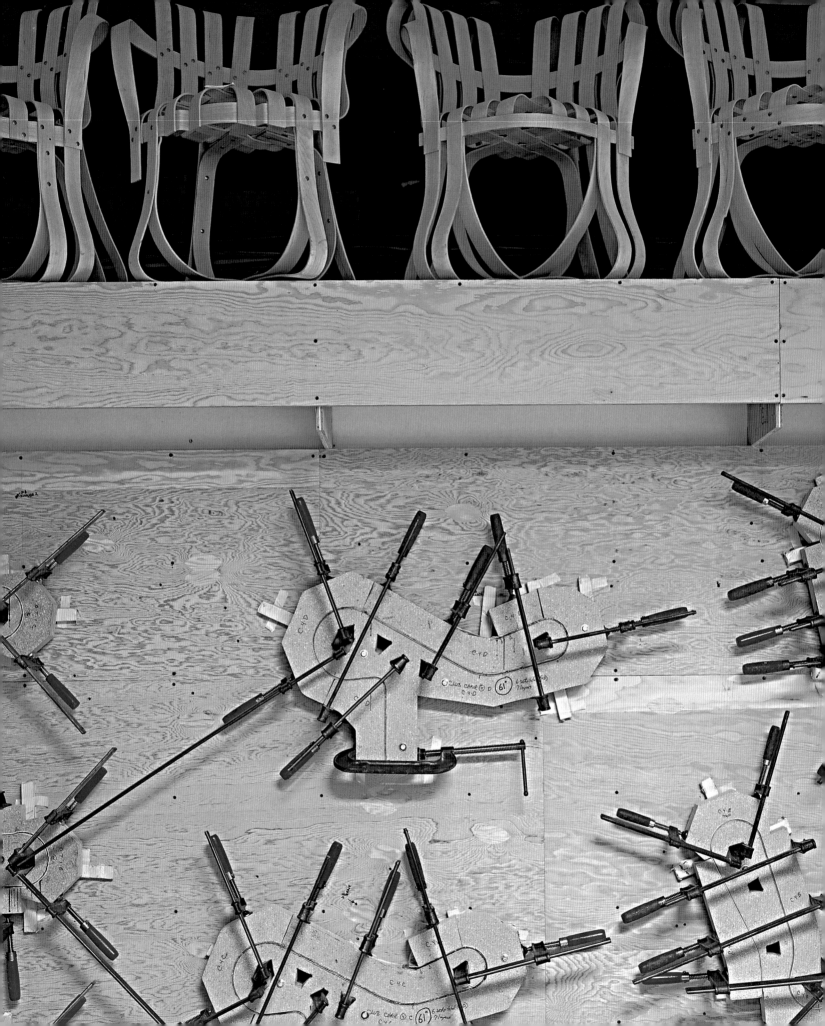

Frederick R. Weisman Art Museum at the University of Minnesota

Minneapolis 1990–93

Gehry has noted that he works as an "artist in architecture." His well-known sympathy for the visual arts has inspired museum designs that evidence a deep respect for the artworks these buildings contain, no matter how provocative they may be as architecture. His exhibition designs demonstrated this same duality: for a 1968 Billy Al Bengston exhibition at the Los Angeles County Museum of Art, for example, Gehry reconfigured the museum's neutral galleries to evoke a motorcycle den, while the shimmering stainless-steel backdrop that Gehry designed for the Solomon R. Guggenheim Museum's 1998 exhibition *The Art of the Motorcycle* resembled a sleeker version of this earlier setting.

In 1990, Gehry received his first commission for a public art museum. The Weisman's 11,000 square feet of gallery space are located on the third floor of a four-story rectilinear building. The galleries are relatively understated, though they are a far cry from the anonymous boxes typical of museum architecture. Austere white walls are cut with geometric details on their uppermost perimeters, and ceilings are punctuated by curvilinear slices, revealing skylights that permit natural light to flood the interior. These idiosyncratic elements complement the Modern and contemporary art housed inside.

The exterior shapes expand upon the sculptural spaces within, announcing the museum's contemporary artistic program to passersby on the nearby Washington Avenue Bridge, and a vermilion concrete echoes the older brick buildings of the campus on which the museum is located. On the west facade, which overlooks the banks of the Mississippi, stainless-steel panels converge in angles that ripple across the surface, mimicking the movement of the water below; the reflective surface transforms the museum into a gleaming landmark when viewed from across the river on a sunny day. — KVW

Right: The two-level Washington Avenue Bridge conducts both pedestrian and vehicular traffic to the museum and campus. The museum's dramatic facade acts as a greeting to approaching visitors.

Above: View of northwest facade. The dynamic stainless steel facade completely masks the rectangular structure of the museum when the building is seen from the west; an entirely different impression of the form is gained when it is viewed from inside the campus.

Right: Longitudinal section. 1. Offices, 2. Lobby, 3. Auditorium, 4. Gallery space, 5. Carpentry shop, 6. Parking, 7. Art storage.

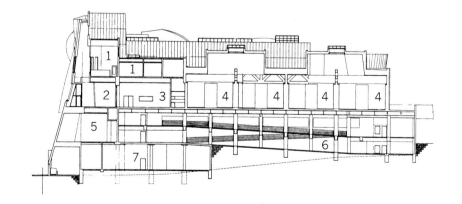

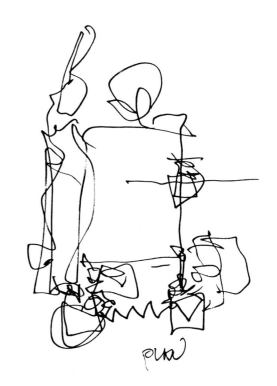

Right: Preliminary design sketch of plan.
Below: Facade study model, scale 1" = 1'.

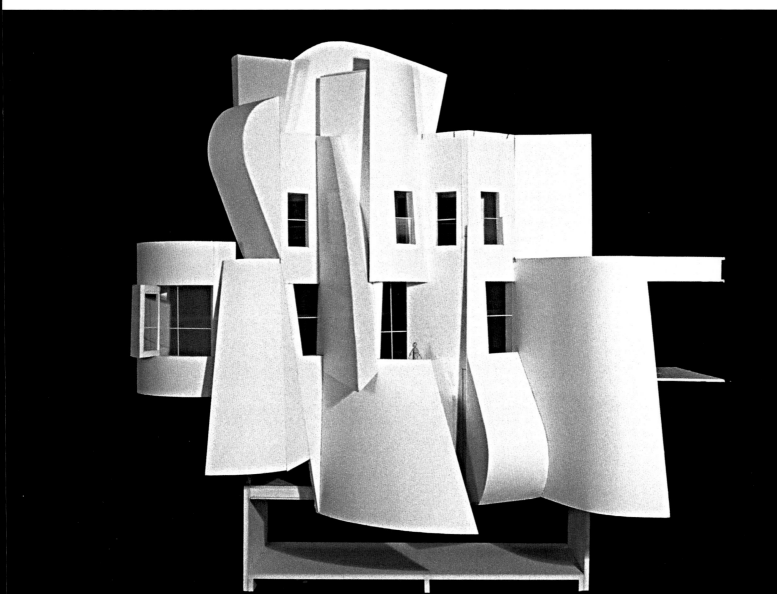

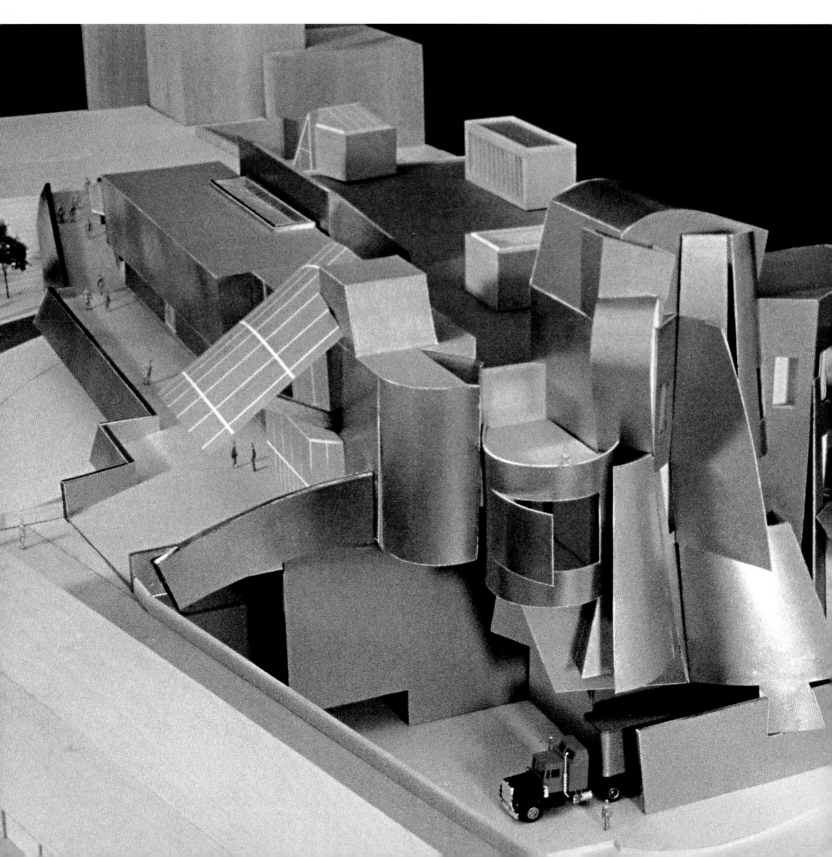

Below: Design process model, scale unknown, showing an early plan to sheath the entire structure in stainless steel.

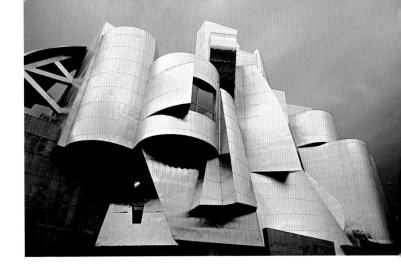

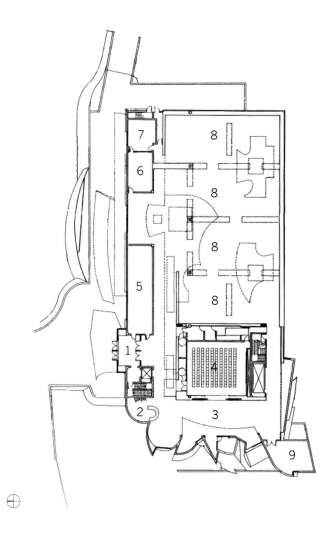

Top: The metallic surface of the west facade takes on dramatically different appearances depending on the time of day and weather conditions.

Bottom: Third floor plan. 1. Entry, 2. Reception and coat check, 3. Lobby, 4. Auditorium, 5. Shop, 6. Office, 7. Print/Study room, 8. Gallery, 9. Seminar room.

Below: Gallery interior.

Facing page: View of main entrance looking west with downtown Minneapolis in the distance. The busy location adjacent to a walkway connecting the campus with the Washington Avenue Bridge further integrates the museum with the university.

Fish Sculpture at Vila Olimpica

Barcelona 1989–92

The fish is a frequently recurring motif in Gehry's work, serving as inspiration and mascot. In Vila Olimpica, a monumental fish sculpture functions as a landmark within a retail complex designed by Gehry. Initiated for the 1992 Olympics, the larger redevelopment site includes designs by Skidmore, Owings & Merrill. This fish sculpture was also a landmark in the history of Frank O. Gehry & Associates, inaugurating the firm's use of computer-aided design and manufacturing. Financial and scheduling constraints prompted James Glymph, a partner of the firm, to search for a computer program that would facilitate the design and construction process, leading to the adoption of CATIA (computer aided three-dimensional interactive application). A three-dimensional modeling program developed for the French aerospace industry, CATIA has design, manufacturing, and engineering applications. A modeler of complex surface geometries, the program analyzes data generated from the digitization of physical models. The results are used to engineer and fabricate complex building systems. The continued use of CATIA by Gehry's firm has enabled the translation of the gestural quality from model to built work and the realization of ambitious designs within established project parameters.—JFR

Left: View looking west. Gehry's fish iconography is ideally suited to the waterfront setting of the complex, while the trellis-like structure provides shading for the retail court and circulation areas below.

Above: Final design site model, scale unknown. While the expressive form of Gehry's sculpture stands in contrast to the rectilinear language of the tower development designed by Skidmore, Owings & Merrill (SOM), his choice of stone, steel, and glass was drawn from SOM's material vocabulary as a means to unify the projects.

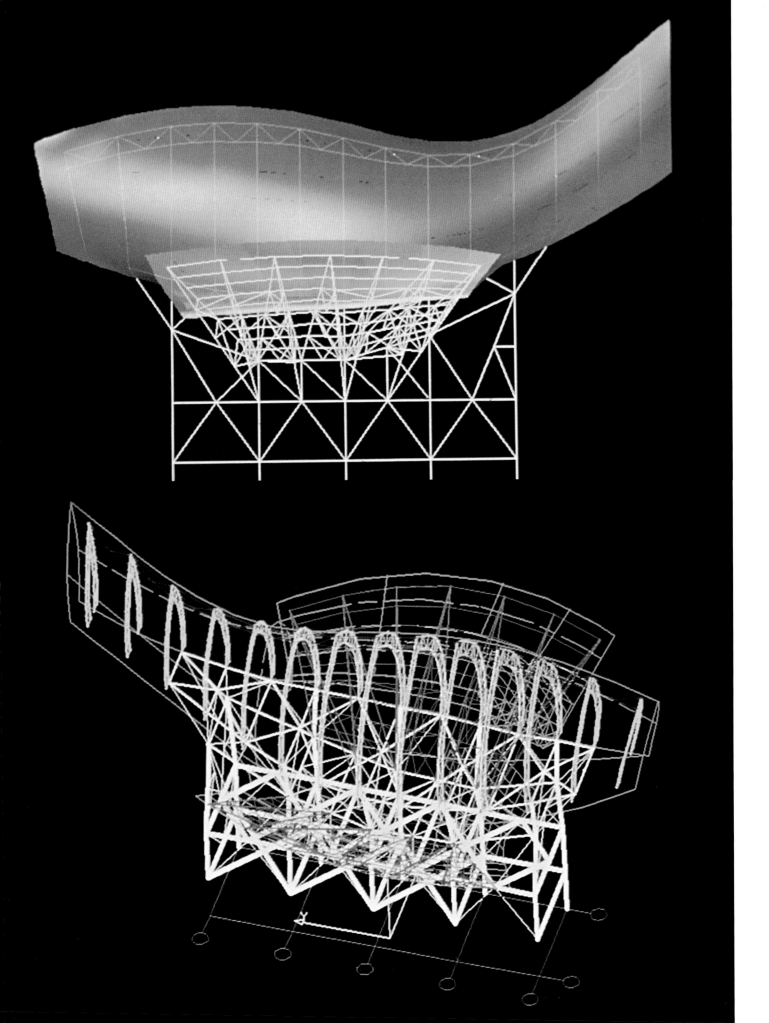

Facing page: CATIA surface model (top), and CATIA
model showing structural ribs in yellow (bottom).

Above: Construction view.

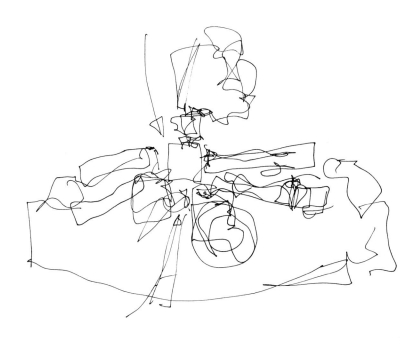

EMR Communication and Technology Center

Bad Oeynhausen, Germany 1991–95

Like Gehry's Vitra International Manufacturing Facility (1987–89) in Weil am Rhein, Germany, the EMR Communication and Technology Center, a power-distribution facility, eschews the strictly utilitarian aesthetic that is typical of industrial architecture. The building is arranged according to a pinwheel plan, with arms fanning out from its center. Gehry first utilized a pinwheel layout in the Winton Guest House (1983–87) in order to reduce the perceived mass of the addition. As in that residential structure, the 43,000 square feet of the EMR building appear to be dispersed among a collection of small, separate forms. Along Mindener Strasse, the thoroughfare that leads into Bad Oeynhausen, the building presents a facade of glass, steel, and plaster—characteristically industrial materials that merge with the adjacent low-rise commercial buildings. Behind this face, the complex unfurls into a garden that overlooks the river and mountains to its north.

As in the centralized arrangement of the Vitra International Headquarters (1988–94) in Birsfelden, Switzerland, the functions at EMR are focused around a central atrium at the center of the pinwheel layout. Meeting rooms and a public exhibition hall branch off this lobby space, and more specialized functions, including the computer room and offices, are located farther away from the building's center. In keeping with the company's focus on natural resources, large windows and skylights set into the narrow arms of the building bring daylight to the indoor spaces. In addition to this use of natural light, the building is structured to employ several other energy-saving elements, including solar panels placed on the roof to harness energy, and ventilation shafts employed during warmer months to assist in cooling the building.—KVW

Left: View looking west toward the EMR Communication and Technology Center.
Above: Design sketch of plan.

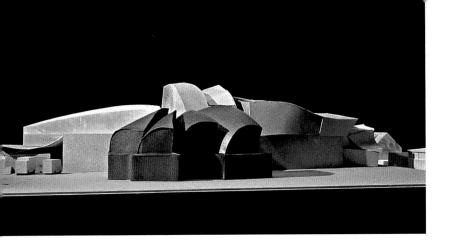

Left top: Design process model, scale 1:200 m.

Left bottom and facing page: Gehry uses natural light throughout the building's interior, an environmentally sound approach to the facility's energy consumption.

Below: Design process model, scale unknown.

Above: The serene pond facing Mindener Strasse is actually a collection facility for surface water runoff.

Right: Ground floor plan. 1. Entry, 2. Lobby, 3. Heat and power plant, 4. Network control area, 5. Processors, 6. Dining room, 7. Break room, 8. Kitchen, 9. Cafeteria, 10. Offices, 11. Garage, 12. Exhibition space.

Facing page: View of main entrance. EMR was conceived during the same period as the Guggenheim Museum Bilbao (1991–97), and the building's more curvilinear forms were some of the first developed by Gehry's firm using CATIA software.

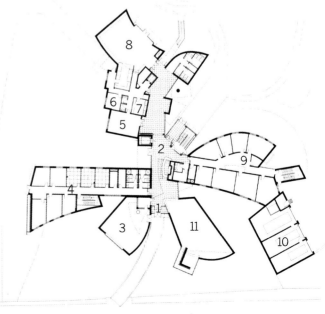

Lewis Residence (unbuilt)

Lyndhurst, Ohio 1989–95

Residential commissions have afforded Gehry the freedom to experiment, occasioning many of his most dramatic formal breakthroughs. His experimentation with this type of building reached its apogee in successive designs created for the unbuilt Lewis Residence. What began as a residential remodeling would eventually consume nearly a decade and generate many modifications and expansions to accommodate the client's changing needs and heightened ambitions. Gehry has described it as the equivalent of being awarded a MacArthur fellowship because of the generous support the client provided for the architect's intense study of materials and methods—an effort yielding a number of ideas that have informed his subsequent work.

The plan to renovate the original house was quickly abandoned in the face of the mounting needs that overwhelmed the structure, and the square footage rose from 18,000 to 42,000 square feet. The final 22,000 square feet were still generous enough to accommodate the commercial-grade kitchen, multiple master bedrooms, gallery space, indoor lap pool, guest and staff quarters, and garages that the client desired. Situated on nine wooded acres, the project was conceived as a partial collaboration with several artists, including Larry Bell and Frank Stella, landscape architect Maggie Keswick Jencks, and architect Philip Johnson.

Above: Design study model, scale unknown (1989).

Right: Design process model, scale 1/8" = 1' (September 1992) with view of east elevation.

From its beginnings as a cluster of relatively conventional forms and motifs organized around a central court, the design became successively more elaborate and fantastic as Gehry stretched physical forms to keep pace with his imagination. An increasingly fluid and organic vocabulary emerged, replete with such zoomorphic configurations as his signature fish shape. To capture the baroque curves of these unconventional architectural structures, working models were rendered with such malleable materials as clay, melted plastic, wax-infused velvet and laminated-paper shapes fabricated by computer.

Despite the fact that it was never realized, the Lewis Residence remains an important milestone for Gehry's firm, tracing a trajectory that begins with the formal syntax of the Winton Guest House (1983–87) in Wayzata, Minnesota, and ends with the ever more complex and unique forms made feasible by the technology of computer-aided design and manufacturing. Ultimately, the Lewis project served as a laboratory for pure invention that spawned a new direction in Gehry's work, and as such is testimony to the importance of residential design in forging new ground within the field of architecture. —JFR

Above and right: Design process model, scale 1/8" = 1' (September 1992).
Facing page, top: Design sketch of south elevation overlooking water garden.

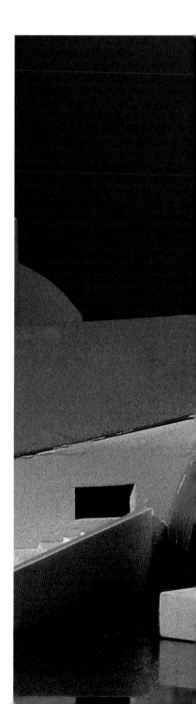

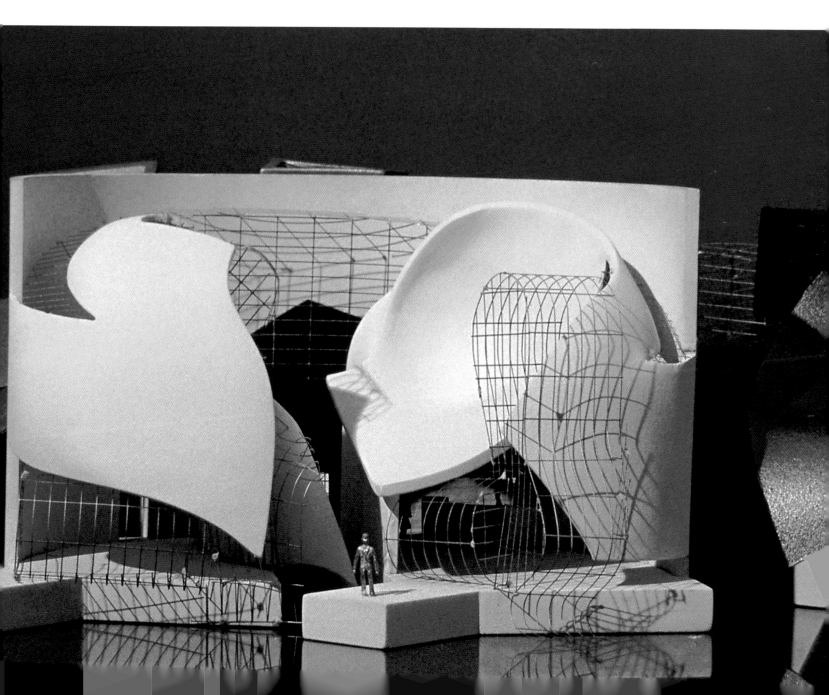

Left, top to bottom: Design process models, all scale 1/8" = 1' (1994).

Facing page, top: Design process model, scale 1/4" = 1' (December 1994).

This sequence of design process models in plan view shows the rapid design development from February to December 1994. An octopus-shaped guest house is by Philip Johnson. Four sentinel forms—housing dining room, living room, study, and master bedroom—overlook water garden.

Above: Design sketch of plan. The house's elements are arranged in the pinwheel layout that Gehry first utilized in his design of the Winton Guest House.

Facing page, bottom: Design process model, scale 1/8" = 1' (November 1994) with view of southwest elevation and garage, fish-shaped guest house, and staff quarters.

Above: Design process model, scale 1/4" = 1'
(February 1995) with view of south elevation and
sentinel forms overlooking the water garden.

Right: Design process model of sentinel, scale
1/2" = 1', housing the study.

Living Room

Above: Design sketch of living-room sentinel on south elevation.

Right: Design process model, scale 1/4" = 1' (February 1995) with view of east elevation and conservatory.

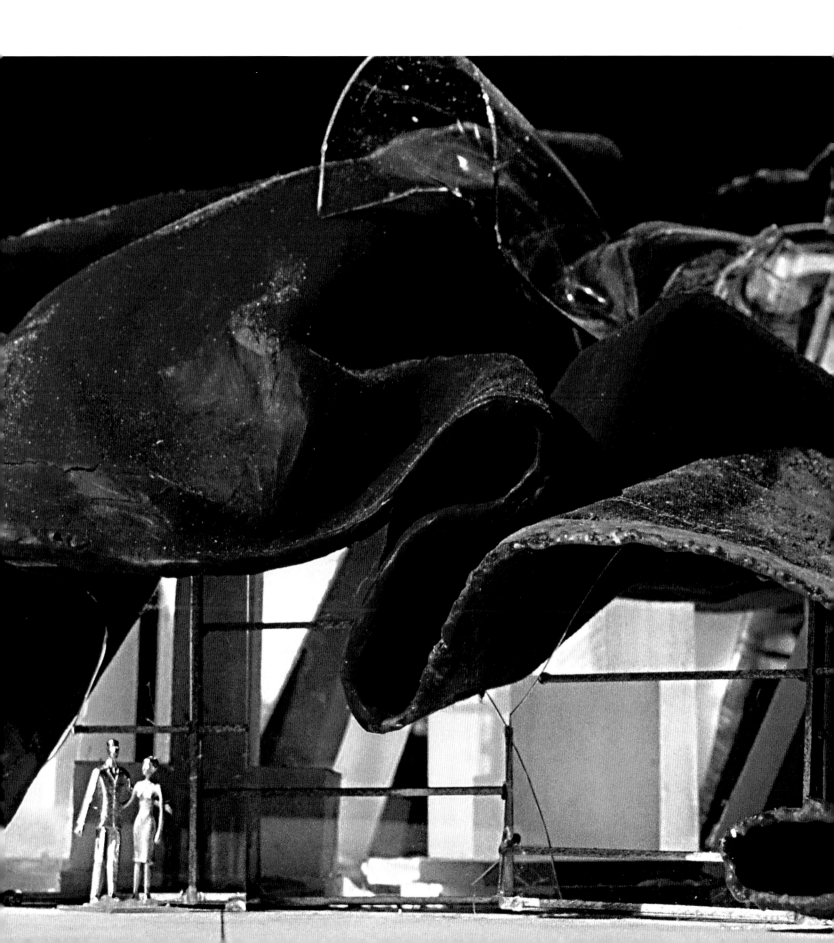

Above and right: Final design model, scale 1/4" = 1'
(February 1995) with view of west elevation and
entrance court and view of conservatory roof.

Below: Final design model of horse-head shaped entry
hall and gallery, scale 1/2" = 1'.

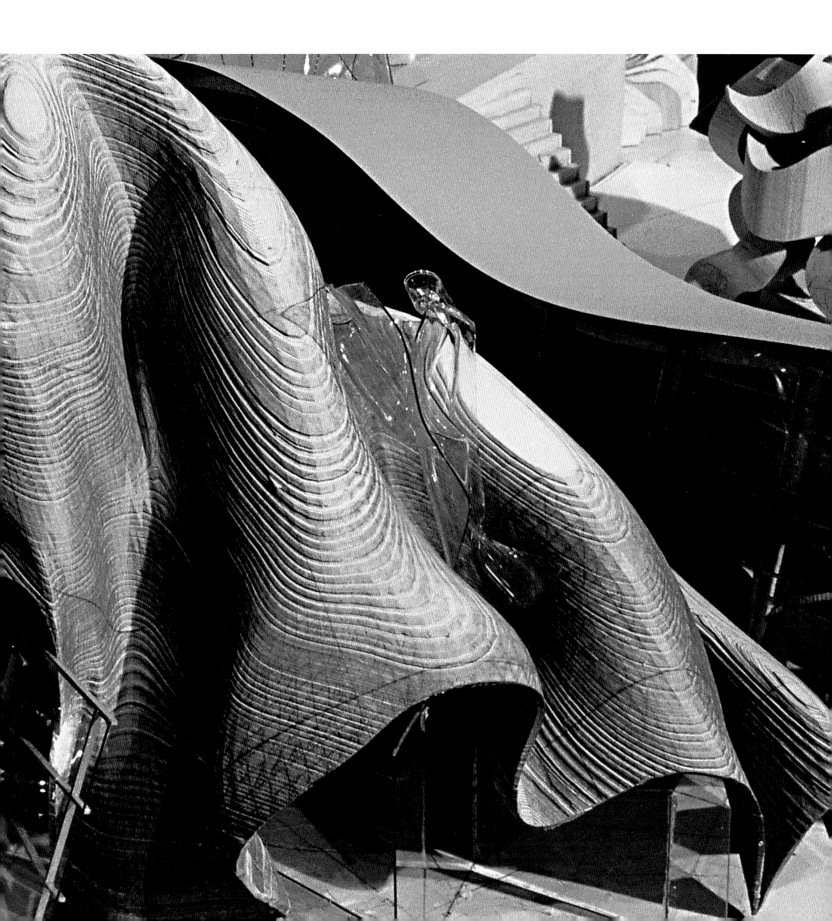

Guggenheim Museum Bilbao

Bilbao, Spain 1991–97

In contrast to proposals submitted by Arata Isozaki and Associates and Coop Himmelblau to the limited competition, Gehry's design for the Guggenheim Museum Bilbao demonstrated a distinct sensitivity to the new museum's surroundings. Located at a bend in the Nervión River on a former industrial site, the museum makes the most of this location by forging a strong visual presence in relation to the Museo de Bellas Artes nearby and to the Universidad de Deusto across the river, as well as to additional points along the river. From this position, the museum serves as a gateway to the city's business and historical districts.

With this building, the gestural quality of Gehry's sketches was captured in built form for the first time. While CATIA software had been in use at his office since the firm worked on the Fish Sculpture at the Vila Olimpica (1989–92), the Guggenheim Museum Bilbao was the first major project in which the full potential of the program was realized. CATIA was of enormous significance from both aesthetic and technical points of view, for not only did it afford greater freedom in the design of Gehry's distinctively organic forms, but it also simplified construction by providing digital data that could be employed in the manufacturing process, thus controlling costs.

This museum leaves the supposed neutrality of the conventional white cube at the door. The galleries are variously configured to accommodate contemporary installations and old master drawings alike, with challenging exhibition spaces to which living artists might respond as well as rectilinear galleries (termed "stodgy" by the architect) for the presentation of easel painting and traditional sculpture. The great strength of Gehry's architecture lies in its response to existing conditions, and in the museum's acknowledgment of both its urban context and the art for which it was intended, it successfully negotiates interior and exterior conditions simultaneously.

A collaborative project between the Solomon R. Guggenheim Foundation and the Basque Government, the Guggenheim Museum Bilbao was conceived as part of an economic redevelopment plan for the largest city in the Basque Country, and has succeeded in creating an iconic identity for Bilbao. The singular economic and cultural impact felt in the wake of its opening in October 1997 (known as "the Bilbao effect") has spawned a fierce demand for similar feats by contemporary architects worldwide. Its success has sparked an increased awareness of the powerful force that architecture can wield.—JFR

Left: View looking southwest. Nestled in a valley along the banks of the Nervión River, the museum adapts to its setting with billowing forms that face the river and evoke marine imagery, and shallow water gardens that visually link it to the river. Extensive plaza spaces surround the museum, encouraging pedestrian activity. The building runs under the Puente de la Salve, and emerges on the other side in the form of a high tower that serves as a visual landmark.

Right: Second floor plan. 1. Vestibule, 2. Bookstore,
3. Restaurant, 4. Terrace, 5. Kitchen, 6. Lobby, 7. Gallery,
8. Library, 9. Lounge, 10. Open to below.

Below: Urban context study, scale 1:500 m, looking west
along the Nervión River.

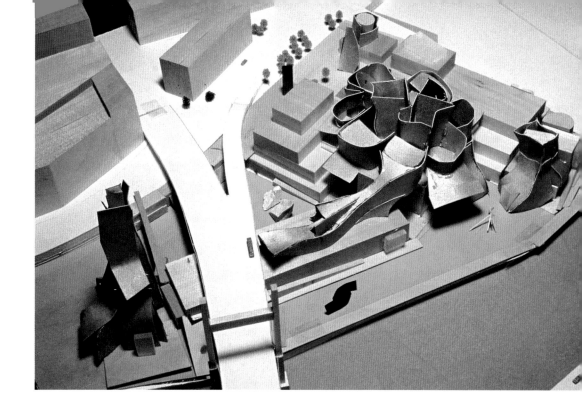

Above: Original competition model, scale 1:500 m.

Right: Design process models, scale 1:200 m. During the course of the design, as seen in the top model the original flower-like roofline of the atrium (visible in the competition model) was replaced by a square atrium surrounded by box-like galleries. Eventually, as seen in bottom model the flower-like roof scheme was resuscitated and the atrium rendered in a more sculptural fashion.

Facing page: Construction view. The Guggenheim Museum Bilbao was the first Gehry project to use a computer database to design, document, and fabricate the steel members of the structure. Both CATIA and BOCAD (a steel detailing program) were used.

Above: Preliminary design sketch of riverfront elevation.

Below: CATIA structural steel model.

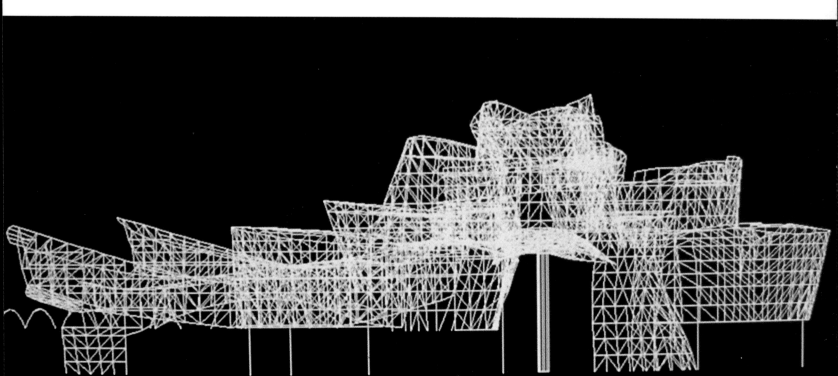

Above: Though metal cladding has long been a hallmark of Gehry's work, the Guggenheim Museum Bilbao represents his first use of titanium. Typically used in smaller applications that exploit the material's strength, here it is used as an exterior finish on a large scale, along with Spanish limestone. In searching for a metal finish that was responsive to changing lighting conditions, stainless steel was rejected as too cold and industrial, while lead-coated copper had been outlawed due to its toxicity. After extended experimentation, during which titanium samples were rolled to varying thicknesses and manipulated with myriad chemicals and oils, a treatment meeting the architect's requirements was identified.

Approximately a third of a millimeter thick, the titanium panels are applied using a traditional locked seam. The material's thinness, together with its application method, results in a pillowlike effect. When a strong wind blows, the titanium flutters slightly and enhances this effect.

166

Right, top to bottom: The museum's undulating curves and nonrepetitive geometries were realized with CATIA software in its first large-scale use by Gehry's firm. The physical design model is digitized to capture points, from which a surface model is created and then shaded. After milling a physical model from this to verify the computer data, the primary and then secondary structures are developed. These are ultimately translated into shop drawings.

Page 168: Approach to the museum from the south along Calle de Iparraguirre.

Page 169: In a reversal of traditional architectural strategies, a processional staircase plunges from the street-level plaza down to the main entry of the museum, simultaneously straddling the sectional drop and making possible the atrium's soaring height which would have otherwise overwhelmed the nineteenth-century scale of the surrounding neighborhood.

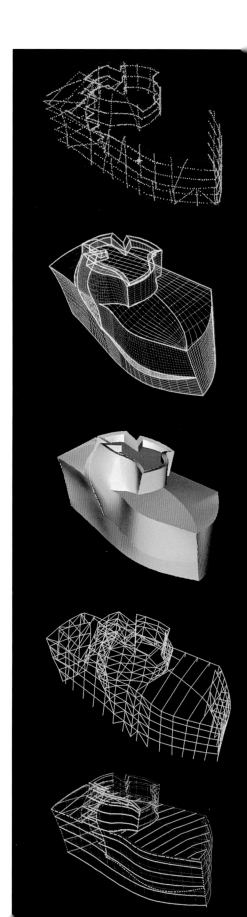

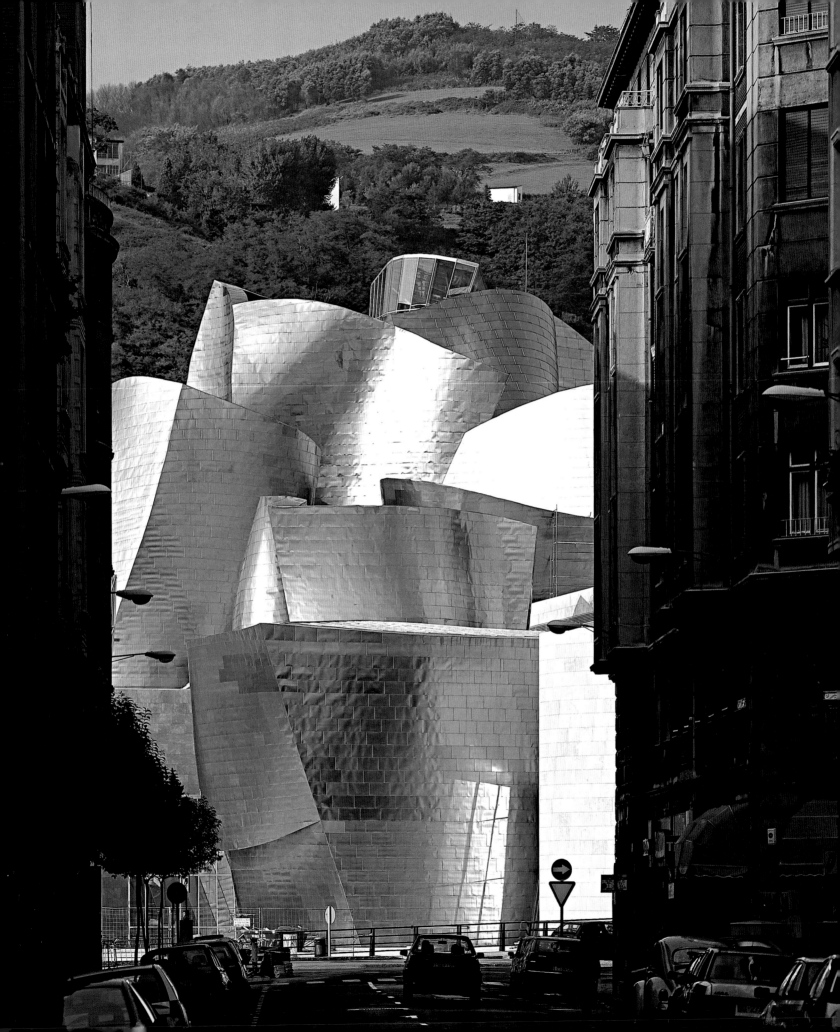

Below: The museum's signature roofline is a composition of twisting, curving forms that unfold like a flower over the atrium.

Facing page: The light-flooded atrium reaches a height of 165 feet and provides a central circulation space around which the galleries are oriented. Although Gehry originally conceived of it as a more rectilinear space that would accommodate art on its walls, he was persuaded by the client to develop a more highly sculpted space in the spirit of Frank Lloyd Wright's Solomon R. Guggenheim Museum in New York.

Above: Richard Serra's monumental ellipses—seen here in the museum's largest gallery, which is referred to as the "boat" or "fish"—meet the challenges posed by the strength of Gehry's architecture.

Facing page, top: Interior study model of classical galleries, scale 1:50 m.

Facing page, bottom: The rectilinear form of the classical galleries—shown here as installed for the inaugural exhibition with works by Eduardo Chillida, Robert Motherwell, and Antoni Tàpies—provides a conventional environment for more traditional work on a smaller scale.

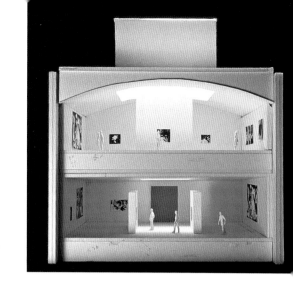

Nationale-Nederlanden Building

Prague 1992–96

Gehry used his customary contextual approach in looking for clues to guide his design of this modest speculative office building. Situated along the Vltava River in the historic district, the building is prominently located on a corner across from a public square and a major bridge. The location and Gehry's observations of Prague's "implied towers" and nineteenth-century predilection for architectural detail were decisive factors.

The fluidity of the riverfront facade smooths the transition between its seven stories and the five stories of neighboring buildings. Moving up and down and projecting away from the facade, the windows take on a distinctive presence in a manner first seen in the original 1977–78 renovation of the Gehry Residence in Santa Monica. Striated patterning further enhances the rhythmic effect across the concrete surface, which is composed of unique precast panels made possible with computer aided manufacturing (CAM).

The "body language" of the two towers earned the building its nickname, "Fred and Ginger," after dancers Fred Astaire and Ginger Rogers. Resting lightly atop slender animated columns, the glass-clad tower—its pinched waist minimizing obstructions to the river view from the adjacent building—leans in toward the cylindrical tower. — JFR

Right: View of west facade. Topped by a sculptural crown of woven steel mesh, the uppermost floor is occupied by a restaurant with spectacular views of the Prague castle and the skyline.

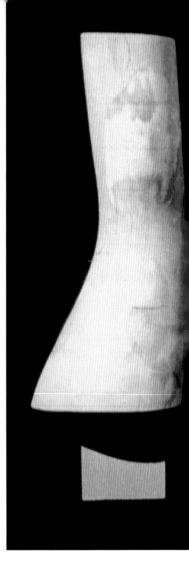

Left top: Design sketch of riverfront facade.
Left bottom: Final design model, scale 1:50 m.

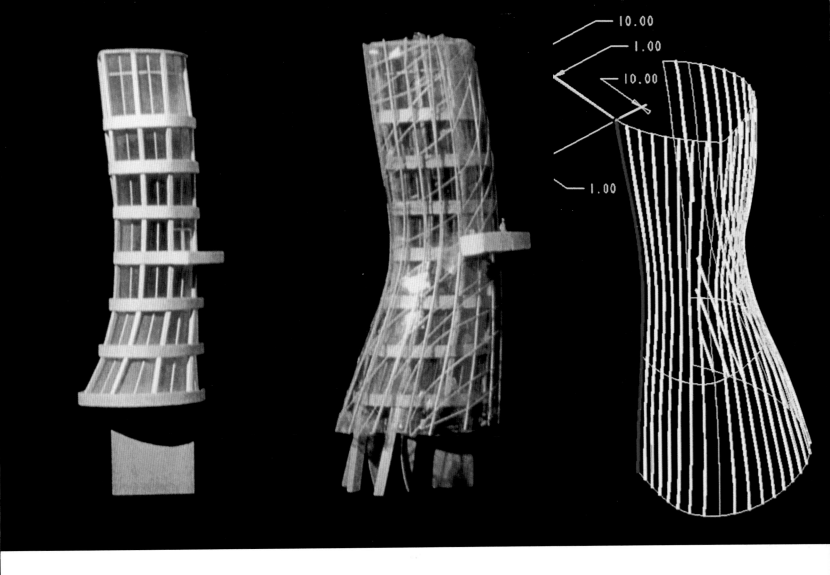

Above left to right: design process model, scale 1:100 m; design process model, scale 1:100 m; tower element of final design model, scale 1:50 m; and CATIA structural study. Numerous models were made in the process of designing a glass tower. This sequence shows the development of the final design, from the process model that reveals the curving form of the tower, to its ultimate resolution in the final design, second from right, and a CATIA structural study of the metal armature that supports the glass.

Page 178: The glass tower, which is occupied by a conference room on every floor, is comprised of two glass layers, with the outermost layer functioning not unlike a "dress" that clads the building beneath. The innermost layer is sealed to the exterior, while the curving effect of the outer layer is created of rectilinear glass shingles that overlap but are open to the weather.

Page 179: Gehry describes the windows along the riverfront facade as "like framed pictures on the wall." They take on a strong presence and actually project away from the facade, rather than following the line of the exterior skin. The mullions are also reversed in every other window in order to further enhance the rhythmic effect. In subsequent projects such as Der Neue Zollhof (1994–99) in Düsseldorf and the DG Bank Building (1995–2001) in Berlin, the windows are elaborated in a similar manner.

Facing page: View of north facade. At its base, the glass-clad tower provides a canopy over the main entrance.

Above: View of glass-clad tower.

Goldstein Süd Housing

Frankfurt 1991–96

This city housing project, located west of downtown Frankfurt, is composed of eight low-rise buildings on an eleven acre site that is bordered by a park and a municipal forest. In contrast to the comparatively somber neighboring housing projects, Gehry's design is oriented to the adjacent greensward spaces and interjects notes of bold color to humanize what could have been a generic, impersonal development.

Gehry's sensitivity to space and scale is particularly evident in this 162-unit complex, which includes retail shops, a community center, and parking. By varying the heights from three to five stories, casually grouping the buildings in slightly off-kilter U-shaped configurations, and engaging the surrounding landscape, the architect creates a townscape rich in variety. Boldly sculptural shapes clad in zinc accentuate the otherwise conventional forms and serve to define entrances, balconies, and freestanding auxiliary spaces such as bicycle garages. The success of Gehry's design suggests that there is a place for exuberance and individuality even within the highly regulated realms of government-subsidized housing. —JFR

Above: View of interior courtyard.

Right: Site plan. The complex is crossed by two main paths; one runs east-west and connects to a tram stop, the community center, and kindergarten, while the north-south path links the development to the nearby park and forest.

Right: Final design model, scale 1:50 m.
Below: Exterior view.

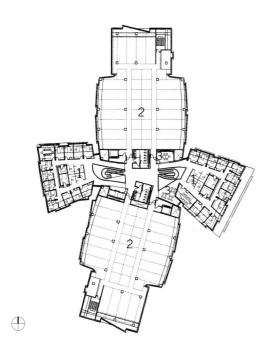

Vontz Center for Molecular Studies, University of Cincinnati

Cincinnati 1993–99

Gehry's laboratory building provides an animated welcome at the main entrance to the campus for the University of Cincinnati Medical Center. Although the brick cladding—quite unusual in Gehry's work—is a link to the staid university buildings nearby, the tilting and bulging forms demonstrate the architect's ability to coax unexpected forms from even the most conservative materials. The building seems to constantly change as one circles it. The striking sense of movement is magnified by the roofline's angled planes, and by the pronounced multistory windows that provide views of the activity inside. State-of-the-art labs are organized along the building's north-south axis; offices occupy the smaller east-west axis. At the center of the cruciform plan, large skylights flood the central atrium, which includes a meeting area for staff. Walkable interstitial spaces above each of the three laboratory floors house the mechanical systems, allowing easy access for maintenance or future changes without disrupting the work of the researchers.—JFR

Above: Second floor plan. 1. Offices, 2. Laboratories, 3. Lounge.

Right: View of south facade along Martin Luther King Drive. Gehry's curvilinear structure contrasts strikingly with the conservative brick boxes on the campus.

Above left: Exterior detail. The multistory windows move in opposition to the sculptural forms of the building.

Above right: Design sketch of west elevation oriented toward the university commons.

Below: Final design model, scale 1/4" = 1', with view of main entrance at corner of First Street and South Grand Avenue.

Facing page: Design sketch.

Walt Disney Concert Hall

Los Angeles 1987–

The Walt Disney Concert Hall—the future home of the Los Angeles Philharmonic under construction adjacent to the extant Music Center—is Gehry's most ambitious large-scale project in Los Angeles. The concert hall is conceived as part of the cultural hub in the center of downtown Los Angeles, an area that is home to the Dorothy Chandler Pavilion and the Museum of Contemporary Art. Like many of Gehry's larger public structures, the hall is intended to establish a sense of place. This is accomplished not only by the building's intriguing design but also by extensive gardens and outdoor performance spaces.

Gehry's design for the concert hall provides striking evidence of his commitment to creating functional buildings that serve his clients. The original proposal—selected in a competition over submissions by Gottfried Bohm, Hans Hollein, and James Sterling and Michael Wilford—defined the central auditorium as a cluster of intimate boxes opening onto the performance area. This initial design underwent significant modifications as the architect consulted with acousticians, several prominent classical musicians, and the music director of the Los Angeles Philharmonic, Esa-Pekka Salonen, and visited some of the best concert halls around the world. Further design produced an auditorium that is shaped like a convex box, bowed in the middle and raised on either end, a structure tailored to convey orchestral sound as effectively as possible. Gehry conceived of all aspects of the interior, which bear his signature focus upon simple materials. Clad entirely in wood, the 2,300-seat auditorium recalls the warm surfaces of a violin. The seats rise from the stage front to the back of the room and wood strips billow from the ceiling and fall in a cluster around the tiller-like pipe organ behind the stage. The curved wooden pipes of the instrument, designed by Gehry and organ builder Manuel Rosales, integrate it into the environment of the hall, where a conventional organ would have looked out of place in relation to the dynamic interior elements.

The movement in the surfaces of the auditorium crescendos in the building's exterior, where the boxy hall is enveloped by a stainless-steel wrapper that flutters and swoops around its perimeter. The most profound impact upon the exterior of the hall has been made by Gehry's use of CATIA software, which enabled the design and construction of the Guggenheim Museum Bilbao (1991–97). CATIA significantly reduces projected construction costs and, most important, makes such unconventional, spectacular forms an engineering possibility. —KVW

Above: Competition model, scale 1/16" = 1'. In Gehry's first conception of the project, the building was oriented toward the Museum of Contemporary Art and was accessed by a plaza off of South Grand Avenue. With the entrance now rotated to the corner of First Street and South Grand Avenue, the concert hall more openly engages pedestrian traffic.

Facing page, top: Design process model, scale 1/8" = 1'. Gehry considered a combination of limestone and steel sheathing for the exterior.

Facing page, bottom: Design process model, scale 1/8" = 1', with view of main entrance.

Above: Final design model of hall interior, scale 1/2" = 1'.
The platform stage is surrounded by 360 degrees of seating. By blurring the physical separation between audience
and performer, Gehry assigns the space an intimacy that is
unusual for a hall of such a large capacity.

Left: Acoustical study model, scale 1:10 m. Of primary
importance in the new building was that the auditorium convey exceptional sound quality. With the assistance of
acousticians, a large-scale model of the interior was built,
and tests were conducted in which musicians played their
instruments inside the space in order to determine the path
of the sound. The interior space and elements were then
adjusted accordingly.

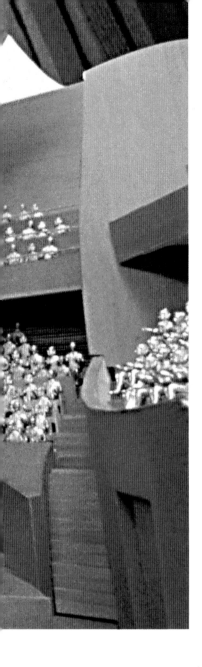

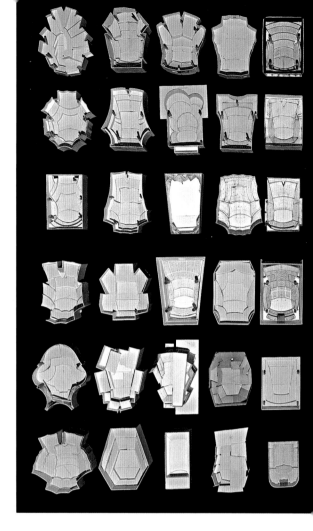

Above: Thirty hall-shaped study models, each scale 1/16" = 1'. After making a small-scale model of his desired hall shape, Gehry would solicit acoustician Yasuhisa Toyota's critique of the design's acoustical properties, and he would then incorporate Toyota's structural suggestions in a new model iteration. Over 50 models were produced to achieve the desired effect. The final shape reconciles the strict symmetry that Toyota advised to produce a warm sound with the curvilinear form that Gehry preferred.

Above: Design process model, scale 1/4" = 1', with view of main entrance at First Street and South Grand Avenue.

Right: Perspective sketch.

Facing page, bottom: Final design model, scale 1/4" = 1', with view of staircase at corner of Second Street and South Grand Avenue, ascending to outdoor garden plaza.

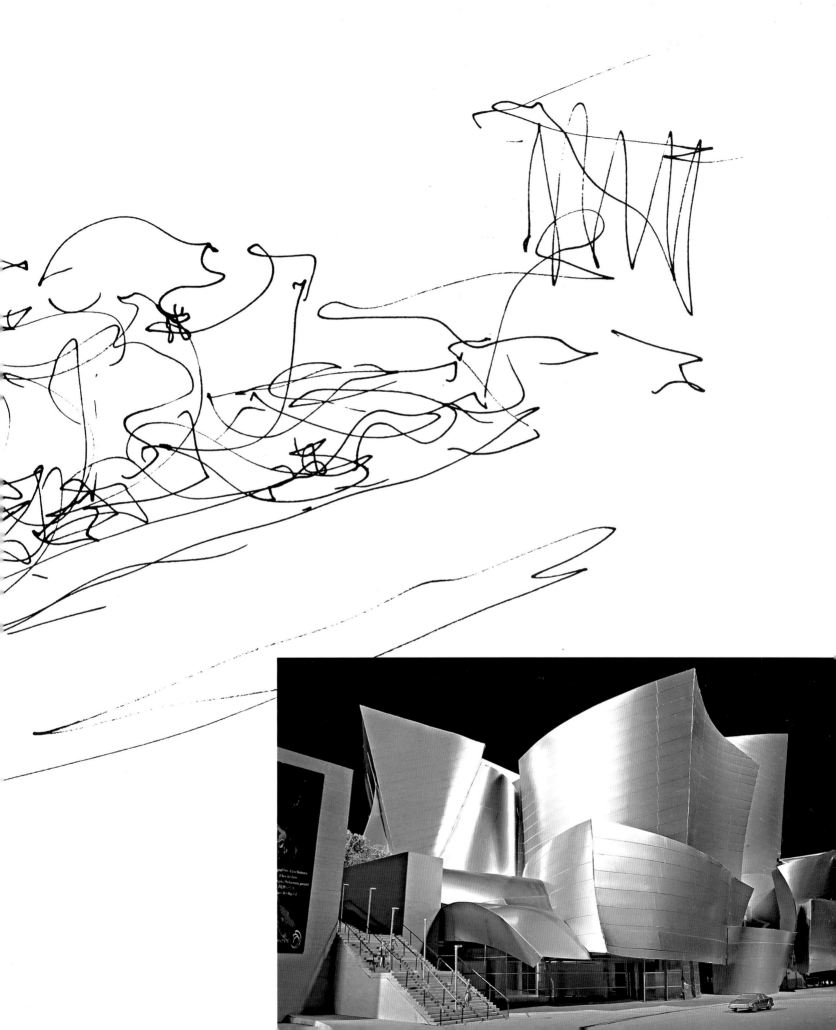

Left: Final design model, scale 1/4" = 1', plan shows boxlike form of the interior hall and the extensive public gardens that will surround the building.

Below: CATIA model of structural steel.

Facing page: Final design model, scale 1/4" = 1', Second Street elevation, shows limestone-covered parking facility that will be located beneath the hall.

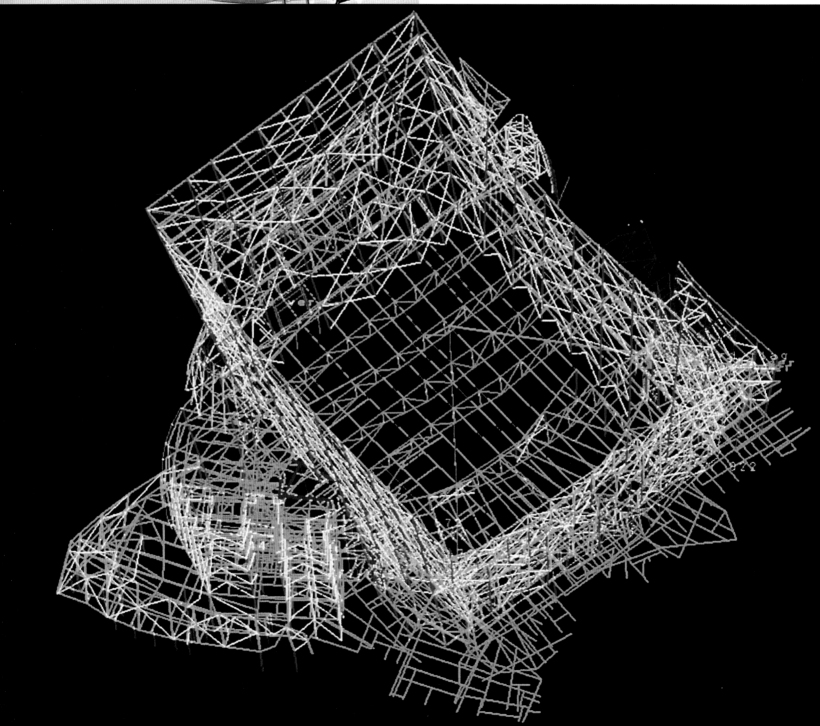

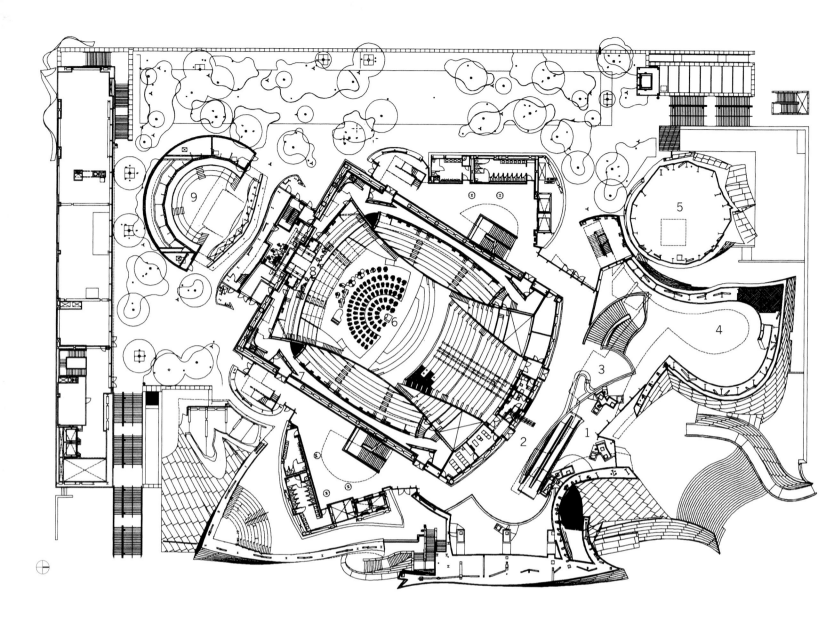

Above: Plan of third level. 1. Entry, 2. Lobby, 3. Concession, 4. Pre-concert room, 5. Founder's room, 6. Concert hall, 7. Antechamber, 8. Organ, 9. Mechanical room.

Facing page, top: View of interior model showing lobby along South Grand Avenue side of building. Gehry has located circulation areas, small rooms, a café, and retail space in the pockets between the outer building facade and the auditorium structure.

Facing page, below left: Final design model, scale 1/4" = 1', with view of main entrance.

Facing page, below right: View of interior model, scale unkown.

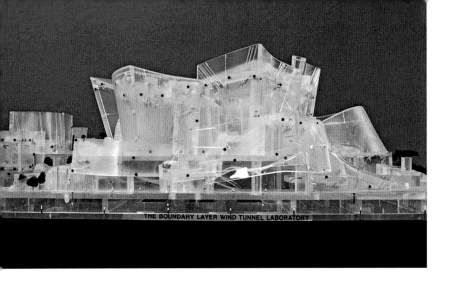

THE BOUNDARY LAYER WIND TUNNEL LABORATORY

Left: Gehry broke new engineering ground with the unconventional form of the concert hall. In order to confirm that the building was structurally sound, an outside firm constructed a three-dimensional model of Gehry's design. The model was run through a number of intensive wind tunnel tests to analyze its structural soundness.

Below: View looking south from the corner of First Street and Hope Street.

Facing page: During the design process, Gehry tested the possibility of casting projections onto the reflective exterior during the evenings.

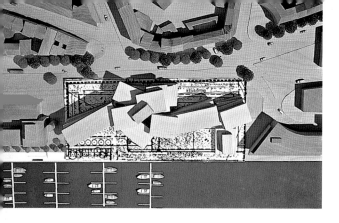

Der Neue Zollhof

Düsseldorf 1994–99

Commissioned to design a speculative office building in a redeveloping waterfront area of downtown Düsseldorf, Gehry chose to create a trio of structures rather than a single large structure in order to maintain visual and pedestrian access to the Rhine River. This strategy takes into account the waterfront promenade and the traffic arteries that converge near the site while maximizing the number of offices with river views and, since each building has a separate identity, facilitating leasing. The staggered massing prevents the buildings from overwhelming their surroundings, although they are significantly taller than many other structures in the adjacent neighborhood. Instead, they provide vertical punctuation to the prevailing horizontality of the harbor area.

Each structure has a unique material and formal identity. The westernmost building is clad in red brick, the central building in mirror-polish stainless steel, and the easternmost building in plaster. Their geometries subtly respond to the sculptural potential of the external finishes, brick being the most angular of the three and stainless steel the most fluid. Though visually distinct, the trio is unified by a similar massing of bundled towers and highly sculptured exteriors with pronounced fenestration.

The complex advances many of the design ideas and technical strategies first explored in Gehry's Nationale-Nederlanden Building (1992–96) in Prague, also a speculative office building. The bundled volumes recall the Prague building's double towers, as do the animated lines of the windows. Perhaps most significantly, the potential of the precast concrete panels first used for Nationale-Nederlanden is here fully realized in the construction of the undulating stainless-steel building. In its urbanistic gestures, technical innovations, and reconsideration of commercial space, Gehry's Düsseldorf project far exceeds expectations for a speculative development.—JFR

Above: Massing study model, scale 1:500 m.
Right: View looking northwest toward harbor.

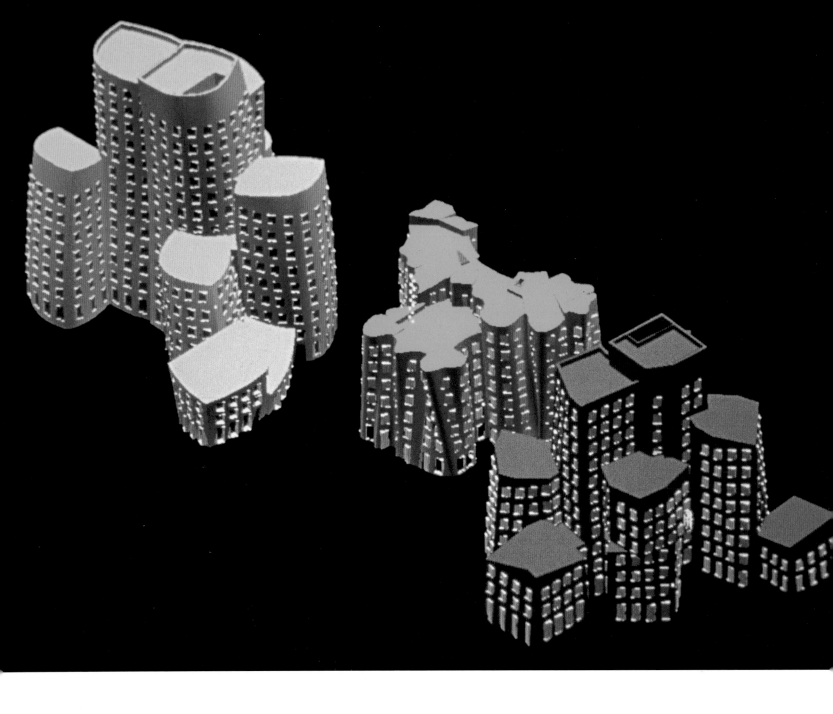

Facing page: CATIA surface model of each structure.

Above: CNC (computer numerically controlled) milled
model, scale 1:200 m. A laminated-paper model of the
easternmost building was generated using CATIA data
in order to verify the accuracy of the CATIA model
against the final design model. This type of verifica-
tion using milled models is no longer practiced by the
Gehry office.

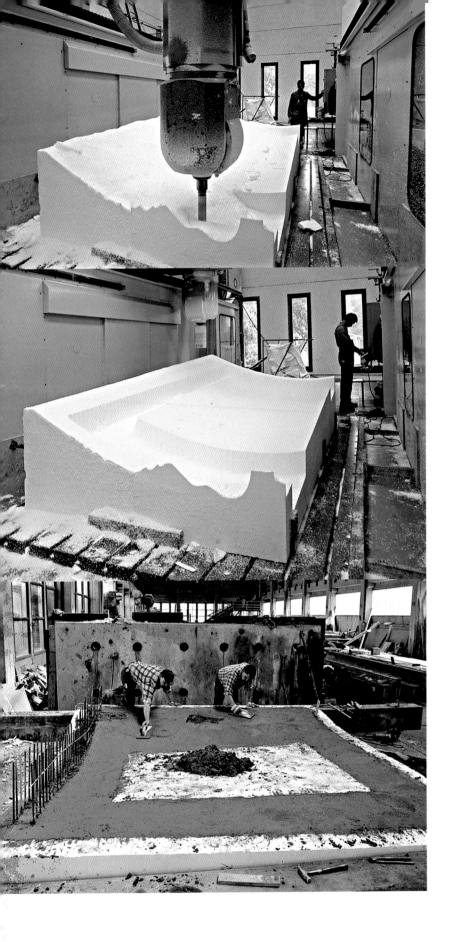

This page: The central metal-clad tower is built of precast concrete panels molded from computer-milled Styrofoam blanks that are eventually recycled. Computer data derived from the design model is used to mill the full-scale Styrofoam blocks, which are fitted with rebar and poured with concrete. As the individually cast panels are assembled, the undulating form of the exterior wall takes shape. While more expensive than building rectilinear shapes using wood forms, each piece fits exactly despite the complex surface geometry.

Facing page: Punching holes to create recessed windows would have compromised the sculptural expression. Instead, windows were developed to move in opposition to the perimeter plane and to introduce a striking angularity that contrasts with the largely curvilinear language of the towers. By breaking free of the exterior plane, the complex's distinctive windows add to the highly animated character of the buildings.

Facing page: View of harborfront facade of east building.
Below: View of harborfront facade of west building.

Facing page and above: Application of stainless-steel
cladding to central building and view of completed
harborfront facade.

Below: Sketch of harborfront elevation.

DG Bank Building

Berlin 1995–2001

Like many of Gehry's projects, this mixed-use building—including the Berlin headquarters of DG Bank—is sited along an urban gateway. The zoning restrictions of the site dictated a design premise that is somewhat atypical for Gehry in its conventionality. In an effort to respect the surrounding architecture on Pariser Platz, which is dominated by the Brandenburg Gate, the sculptural drama is hidden inside and cloaked in front by a subdued five-story facade of thick limestone. Gehry's design was selected from a field that included entries by Tadao Ando and Arquitectonica.

Inside, the bank's offices are arranged around a wood-paneled atrium topped by an elaborate curving skylight. This elongated space is anchored by an element that Gehry retrieved serendipitously while creating the competition entry: the horse-head form of the entry hall and gallery from his design of the unbuilt Lewis Residence (1989–95). Translated into a conference center for DG Bank, the structure commands the wood-paneled atrium, capped above and below by skylights, mitigating what would otherwise be a conventional corporate interior. At rear, the building rises to ten stories for residential units and has an undulating facade that reinforces an orientation away from the front's historic crossroads.—JFR

Left: Aerial view of Pariser Platz with DG Bank Building at upper left and Brandenburg Gate in center.
Above: View of Pariser Platz facade from Brandenburg Gate.

Above: Competition model, scale 1:200 m.

Facing page, top: Perspective sketch of atrium.

Facing page, bottom: Conference center final design model, scale 1:20 m.

Right: CATIA surface model of conference center indicating cladding pattern. The conference center is clad with stainless-steel panels, each approximately 2 x 4 meters. Working with contractors who specialize in building the hulls of ships, a method was developed to press the 4mm-thick panels using the computer data in order to accommodate the form's complex curves.

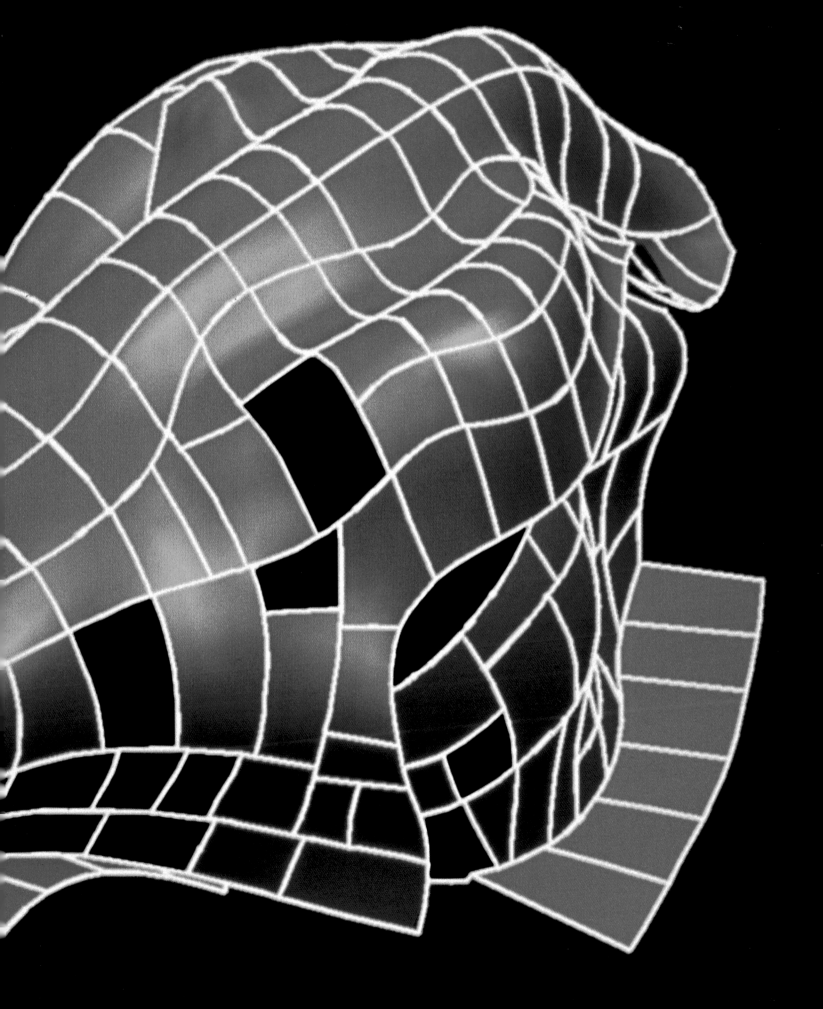

Left: Final design model, scale 1:50 m. An interior skylight caps the cafeteria area on the lower level to prevent noise from filtering through the building.

Below: Ground floor, third floor, and ninth floor plans.
1. Main entrance, 2. Offices, 3. Residential entrance,
4. Entrance to underground parking, 5. Loading dock,
6. Conference center, 7. Apartments, 8. Open to below.

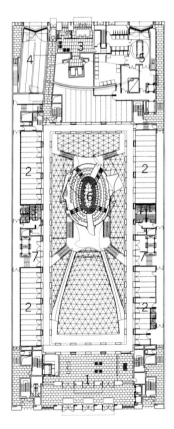

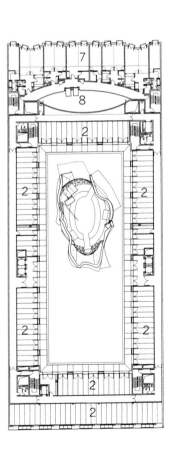

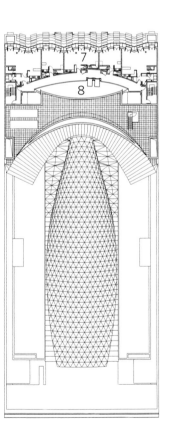

218

Above: Construction view of atrium. The skylight that
extends the length of the structure fills the atrium
with light on sunny days. Since the building will eventually be sandwiched between new construction on two
sides, the east and west facades are devoid of windows. The skylight was thus the only way to bring daylight into the majority of offices.

Facing page: The unusual sculptural quality of the atrium skylight, which is suggestive of a fish, is the result of a collaboration with structural engineer Jorg Schlaich.

Above: With its rhythmic curves and pronounced fenestration, the residential facade along Behrenstrasse is markedly different from the Pariser Platz facade. On the interior, an oval-shaped atrium permits light into both sides of the thirty-nine residential units.

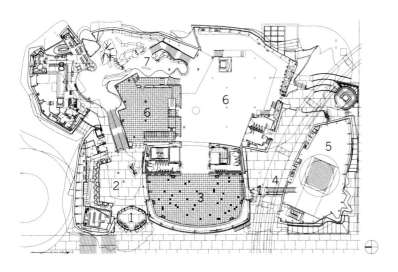

Experience Music Project (EMP)

Seattle 1995–2000

Experience Music Project (EMP) derives its name from the Jimi Hendrix Experience. The client approached Gehry to design a "swoopy" building dedicated to the celebration of popular music. The architect captures the vibrancy of the subject while also reflecting the cacophony of the Seattle Center and a neighboring amusement park. EMP's site at the Seattle Center is adjacent to the Space Needle, the landmark structure from the 1962 World's Fair. Like Gehry's Aerospace Hall (1982–84), which is also located in an exposition park, EMP's exterior—with its exuberant forms and vibrant colors—communicates the program of the exhibitions inside. An existing monorail that sweeps through the building to the Seattle Center enhances the sense of movement that has long been a hallmark of Gehry's work.

The curvaceous forms were sparked by the client's admiration for the horse-head shaped conference center at the DG Bank Building (1995–2001), and grew out of the architect's experiments with broken guitar pieces. The allusion to a shattered Fender Stratocaster is carried through in a glass sculpture that rides the crest of the building, suggesting the strings and frets of a guitar neck. The colors—a riot of gold, pale blue, purple, red, and silver—are symbolic references to various songs and events from the history of rock and roll, including Hendrix's song "Purple Haze."—JFR

Above: First floor plan. 1. Plaza entry, 2. Main lobby and ticketing area, 3. Sky Church, 4. Monorail, 5. Artist's Journey, 6. Exhibition space, 7. Open to below, 8. Restaurant.

Right: View looking south with downtown Seattle in the distance. The EMP is located at the foot of the Space Needle.

222

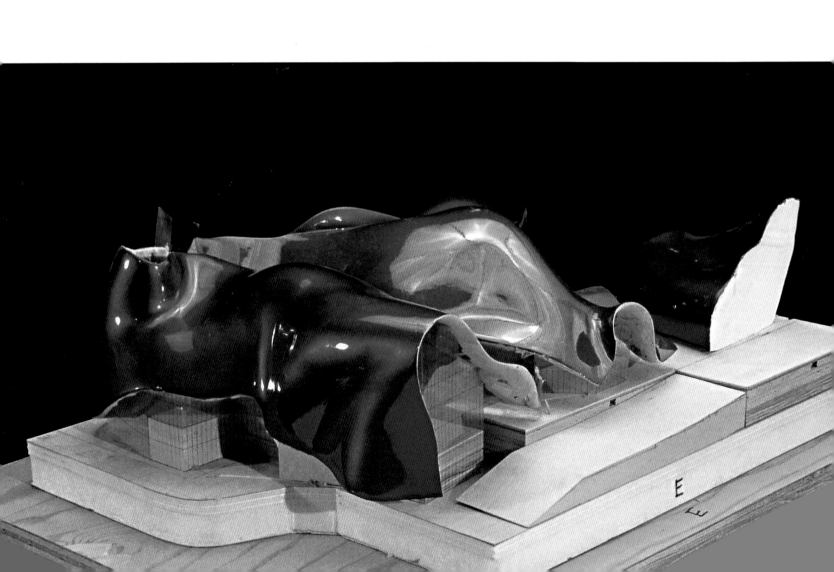

Left and above: Design process models, scale 1/8"=1',
were created with bondo and elaborate paint and
lacquer finishes before arriving at the final design.

Above: Final design model, scale 1/4"=1', Fifth Avenue elevation. The monorail track is visible to the left.

Facing page, below: Design sketch.

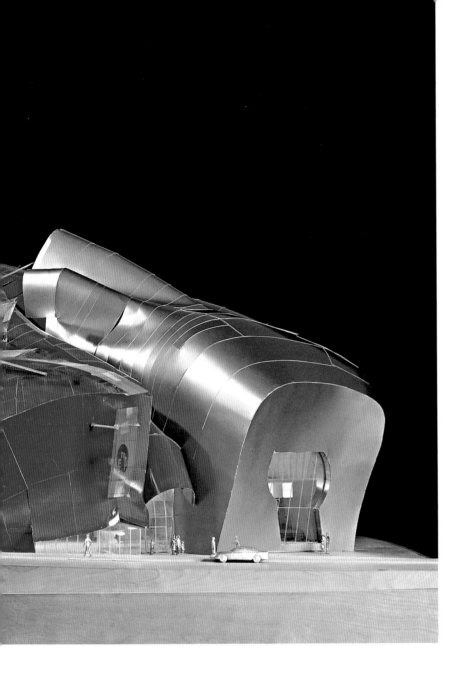

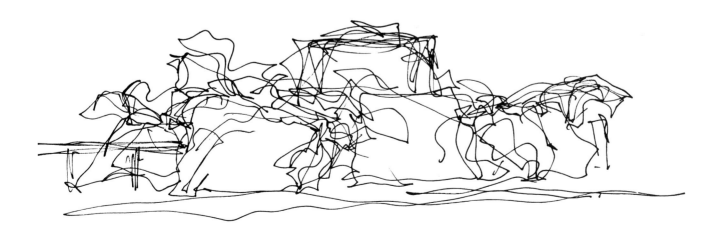

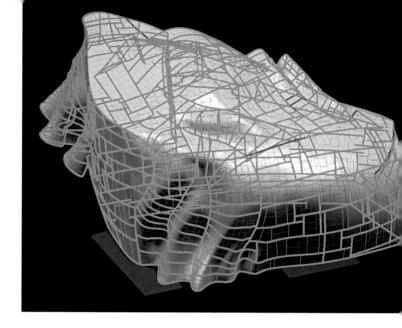

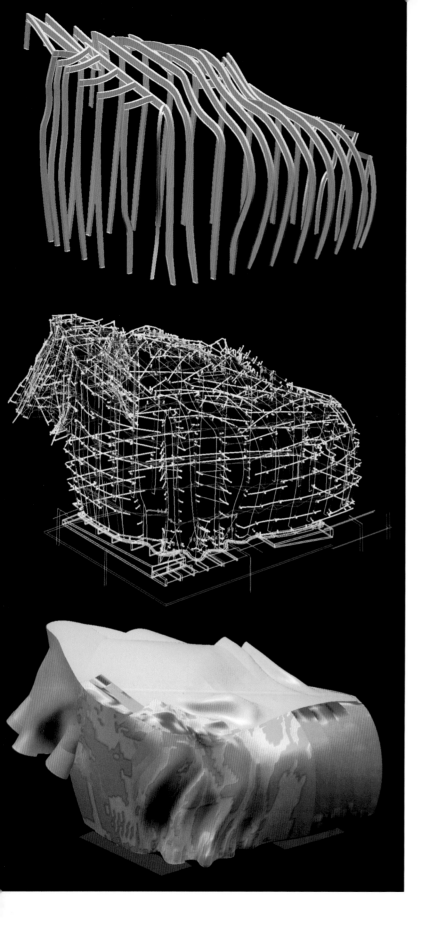

This page: CATIA models of the development of the curvilinear exterior. To generate the extruded structure model (top left), an offset surface is created from the final design model. The secondary structure that supports the exterior cladding is subsequently developed (middle left). Once the form of the surface has been developed, it is analyzed to evaluate the curvature of the sheet metal forms (bottom left): green represents optimal conditions, blue and yellow reflect acceptable conditions, and dark blue and red reveal areas where the surface curvature must be modified. Another program is used to generate a panelized model of the random cladding pattern (above). The perimeter of every shingle is outlined, and can be subsequently isolated, flattened into a planar shape, and used to generate a template with which to individually cut each shingle by computer.

Facing page: The exterior cladding is the uppermost of many layers that comprise the structure and skin of the building. There is a secondary steel structure comprised of pedestal pipes—extending from the primary steel structure through a waterproof membrane—and additional framework to support the cladding. A layer of shotcrete (sprayed concrete) rigidizes the steel frame and provides a surface to which waterproofing and insulation are applied. The more than three thousand panels are comprised of approximately seven shingles each and are clamped to the pipe with extruded aluminum shoes. The gold and purple colors of the stainless-steel shingles are created by dipping each one in an electrically charged acid bath; the gold shingles are treated with a beaded-glass finish to enhance their reflectivity.

Above: This aerial view reveals the building's individually colored components woven together by the glass sculpture that cascades down the roofline along Fifth Avenue.

Facing page: The building's highly animated exterior is amplified by its reflective surfaces and the existing monorail, which seems to cause the exterior to billow out as it rushes past.

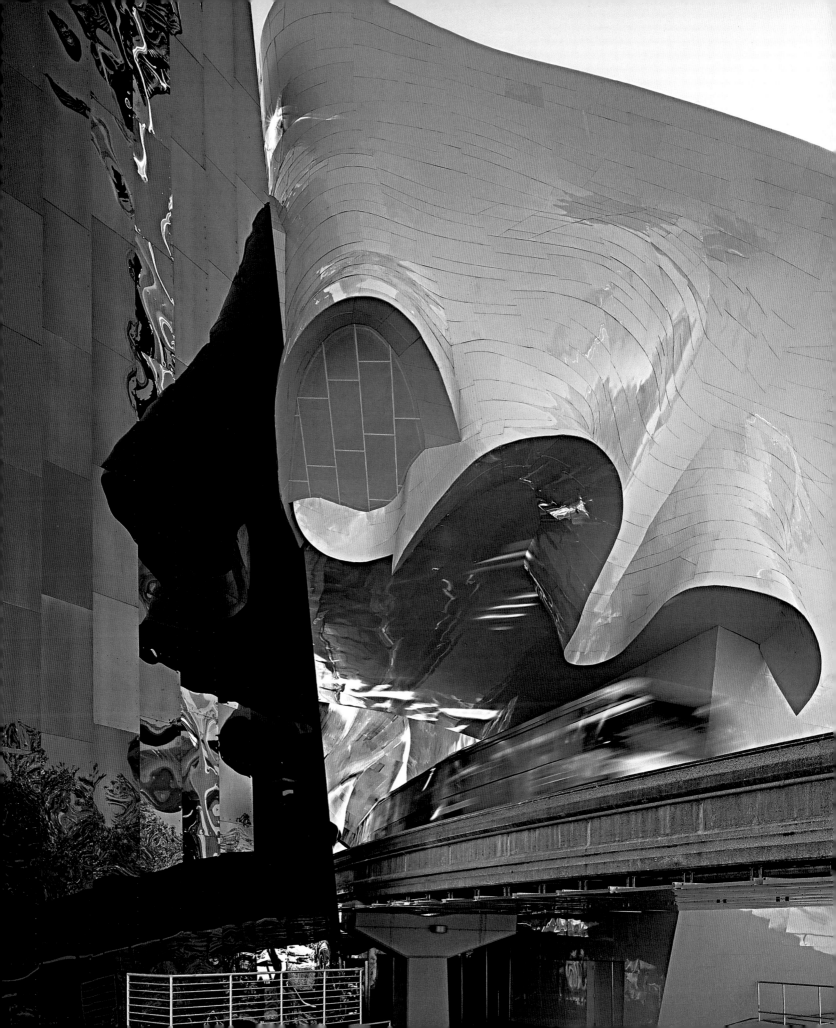

Left: A corridor runs through the building from the plaza-level ticket lobby to a second entrance along Fifth Avenue. The only interior space of the EMP designed by Gehry, it includes various public amenities, such as a restaurant and bookstore.

Facing page: A polished stainless-steel form housing the Sound Lab (an interactive exhibit where visitors participate in making music) hovers over the ticket lobby and reflects the buzz of activity below.

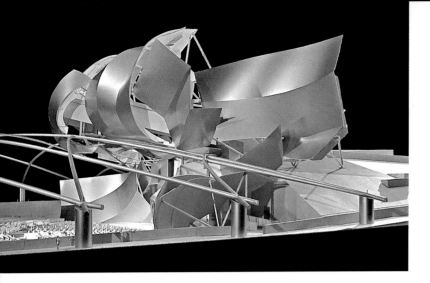

Millennium Park Music Pavilion and Great Lawn

Chicago 1999–

This development in the heart of downtown Chicago relates to a series of Gehry's open-air projects that includes the Merriweather-Post Pavilion (1966–67) in Columbia, Maryland, the Concord Performing Arts Center (1973–76) in Concord, California, and numerous renovations to the Hollywood Bowl (1970–82) in Hollywood, California. Prominently located in a new park along Michigan Avenue next to the Art Institute of Chicago, the Millennium Park Music Pavilion and Great Lawn is part of Gehry's contribution to an ambitious larger plan that includes a theater and extensive gardens. He also designed a serpentine footbridge that provides pedestrian access to Grant Park, located to the west, and is a buffer against street noise.

As with the Experience Music Project (EMP) (1995–2000) in Seattle, the Millennium forms suggest musical qualities. The projecting forms of the stainless-steel orchestra shell are reminiscent of brass horns and push sound out toward the lawn. A trellis-like structure emanates from the shell and arcs over the great lawn while its form suggests sound waves washing over the audience. Its design was prompted by the client's desire to avoid the typical forest of speaker towers, which would otherwise obstruct the audience's view of a performance. Rather, a sound system mounted on the trellis allows the music to float above the audience. —JFR

Above: Final design model of band shell, scale 1/4"=1'.
Right: Current design model with bridge, scale 1/8"=1'.

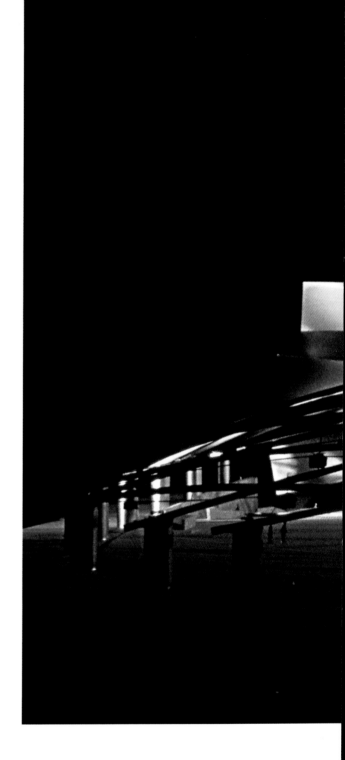

Preliminary sketch of interior and chair design.

CONDÉ NAST. '97 apr.

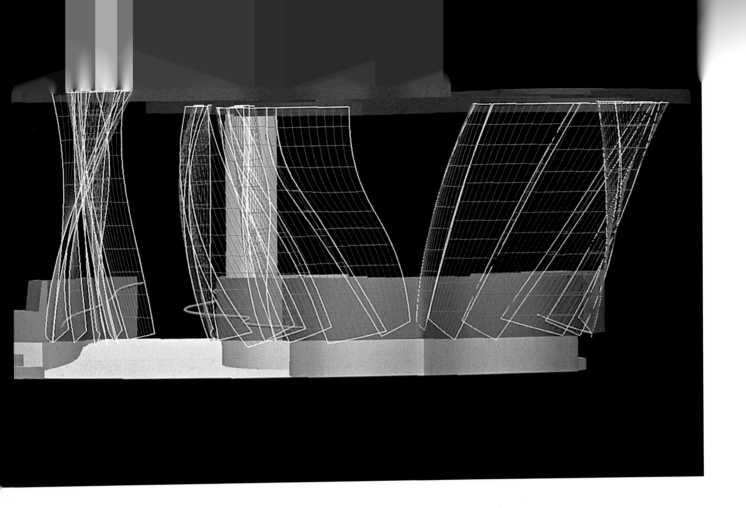

This page: Glass study model, scale 1 1/2"=1' (left), and a CATIA model (above). Models using actual glass were made to study the twisting forms, and a CATIA model was created to precisely calculate the surface curvature of each panel.

Facing page: The glass was fabricated by CTEK, a Santa Ana, California–based company that specializes in complex engineering and fabrication projects. Each laminated panel is unique, and is formed over a computer-milled mold to achieve its complex curves. The maximum dimension of the panels—each weighing between 700 and 800 pounds—was dictated by the capacity of the furnace in which the glass was slumped.

In addition to developing full-scale mock-ups of the titanium paneling at the fabricator's facility in Treviso, Italy, the elements of the cafeteria—including the banquettes, wood platforms, and the framing for the titanium—were preconstructed there, disassembled, and shipped to New York for installation in the interior.

Left: The thick profiles and exposed wood grain of the tables are distinctively Gehry, and, according to the architect, the yellow laminate surface was chosen to "keep the place from looking like a nightclub."

Below: Employees exiting the café walk down an undulating corridor lined on one side in mirror-finish stainless steel. The fun-house effect injects a note of whimsy as well as caution in an environment known for its figure-conscious employees.

Performing Arts Center at Bard College

Annandale-on-Hudson, New York 1997–

Housing a performance theater and small teaching theater on the Hudson Valley campus of Bard College, the Performing Arts Center references the continuum of Gehry's previous work. The design employs the undulating forms and reflective surfaces typical of the architect's more recent large-scale projects. A dramatic canopy, formed from a layer of brushed stainless steel, shelters the entrance to the main theater, while billows of soft steel wrap around the exterior of the entryway. The smaller theater is also roofed in curvaceous brushed steel. Despite these artistic flourishes, which visually mark the building as a cultural hub for the campus, the structure is appropriately humble in other aspects of its design. Covering the building in plaster and concrete, Gehry revisited his early emphasis on simple materials and his ongoing interest in obtaining an unfinished aesthetic is captured in the exposed support system of the spectacular canopy, which is visible from inside the lobby and beneath the canopy itself. The center's simple construction and intimate size create a sensibility that is entirely fitting to the campus and its rural setting.

Inside, the center's two theaters are structured to accommodate acoustical requirements, with the exterior facade—as with the Walt Disney Concert Hall (1987–) in Los Angeles—serving as a mask for the predetermined interior forms. Gehry responded to the flexibility required of a building featuring orchestral, dramatic, operatic, and dance performances by designing the smaller theater's four hundred seats to be entirely removable. The larger theater, whose standard seating capacity is eight hundred, can seat an additional two hundred visitors on the stage. The lobby is illuminated by skylights that permeate the steel cladding, and it is intended that this area might also function as an amphitheater for small lectures or performances. —KVW

Right: Final design model, scale 1/4"=1'. The main performance space is at right, and the smaller theater at left. The metal roofline serves to link the exteriors of the two spaces.

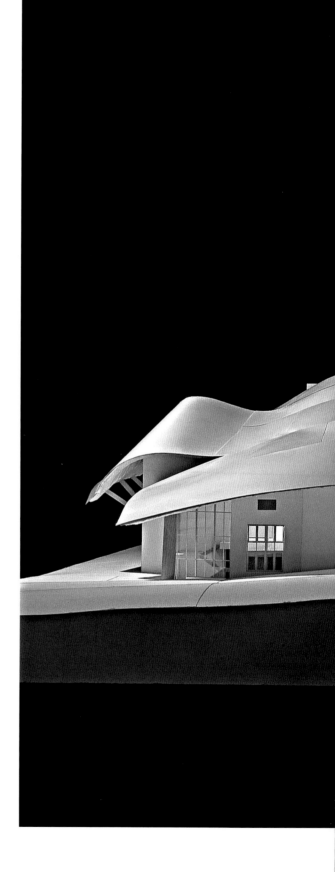

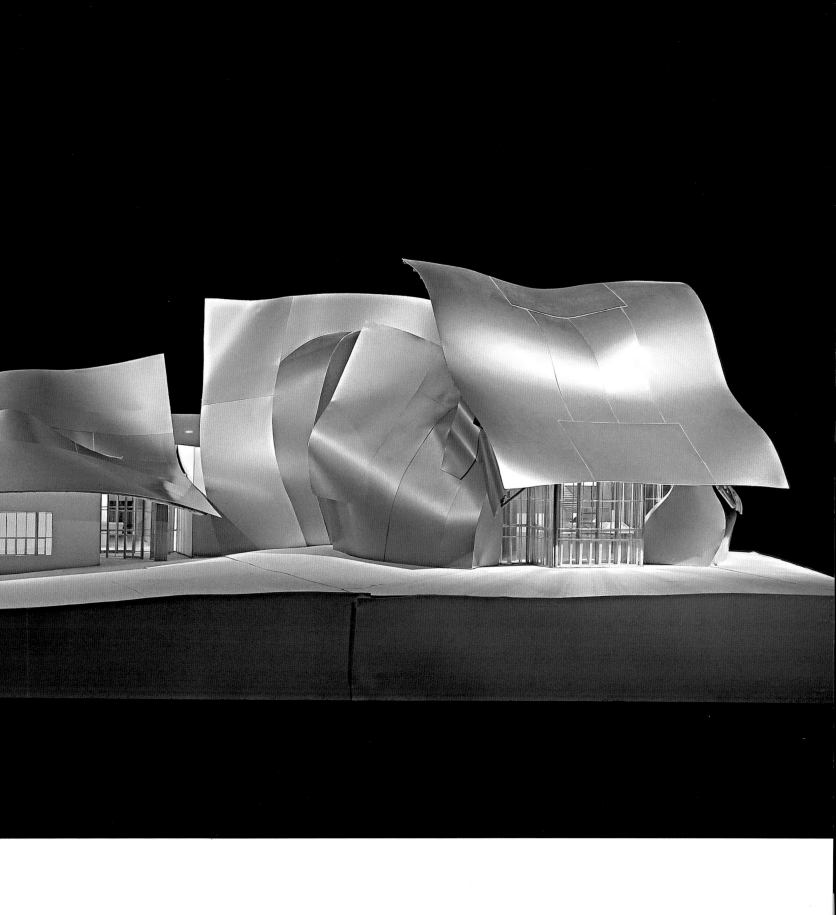

Right: Longitudinal section of main theater. 1. Lobby,
2. Orchestra seating, 3. Balcony, 4. Stage, 5. Fly tower,
6. Dressing rooms and backstage areas, 7. Mechanical
rooms.

Below: Structural model, scale 1/4"=1'.

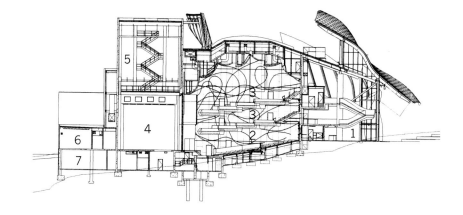

Above: Final design model, scale 1/4"=1'. This interior view of lobby just outside the main theater shows the underlying support for the exterior cladding that will be visible from inside.

Right: Design sketches.

247

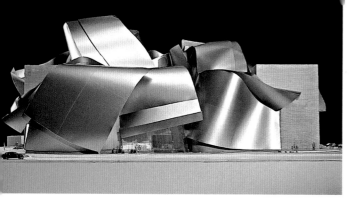

Peter B. Lewis Building,
Weatherhead School of Management,

Case Western Reserve University

Cleveland 1997–

Asked to design a building representative of the ingenuity of the Weatherhead's student-centered curriculum, Gehry responded by exploding the standard Modernist box. Two towers emerge from a rectilinear brick building, with cascades of metal falling from the towers to the street and, in places, puncturing the brick volume. Gehry's design is partially a response to the need for the substantial building to extend upward rather than horizontally due to the limited size of its lot. To avoid overwhelming the low-lying campus, Gehry divided the required floor area between two towers, with the metal cascades serving in part to disguise the height changes between the building's forms. This fluid aesthetic stems directly from Gehry's unbuilt Samsung Museum of Modern Art (1995–97), in which a sculptural metal exterior eases the transition between height variations.

The interior is equally unconventional. The two towers rise from the atrium like paired sculptures on stilts, providing intimate spaces within a soaring interior—much like the horse-head shaped conference center in Gehry's DG Bank Building (1995–2001) in Berlin. Classrooms are centrally located in the towers, and offices and meeting spaces along the perimeter. Circulation paths within the interior are designed to encourage interaction between students and faculty, while the classrooms, each off-center and unique in shape, reconfigure traditional academic seating arrangements.
—KVW

Above: Interior section model, scale 1/4"=1', Bellflower Road facade.

Right: Final site model, scale 1/8"=1'. A solid brick face meets the campus to the northwest, while the sculptural facade of the building greets visitors approaching on Bellflower Road.

248

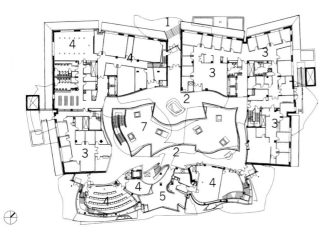

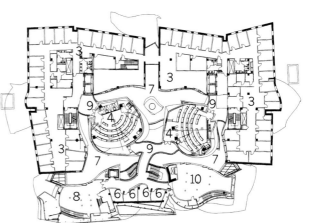

Facing page, top: Interior view of the final design model, scale 1/4"=1'. The centrally located classroom towers are elevated one floor above the atrium on tall supports, thereby facilitating circulation throughout the main level.

Facing page, bottom: First and second floor plans. 1. Main entrance, 2. Lobby, 3. Offices, 4. Classrooms, 5. Café, 6. Study areas, 7. Open to below, 8. Reading room, 9. Atrium bridge, 10. Student lounge.

Right: Classroom tower, study model, scale 1/2"=1'. Each tower contains two classrooms. The tower forms are referenced within Gehry's office as "buddhas," and bear some resemblance to the sentries that Gehry first developed for the unbuilt Lewis Residence (1989–95). Peter B. Lewis is a major donor to the Weatherhead project, and it was his earlier involvement with Gehry that prompted the architect's commission for the building.

Below: Site model with final design, scale 1/8"=1'.

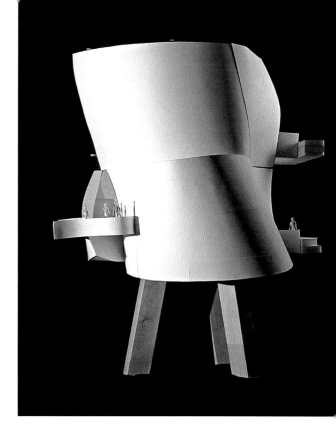

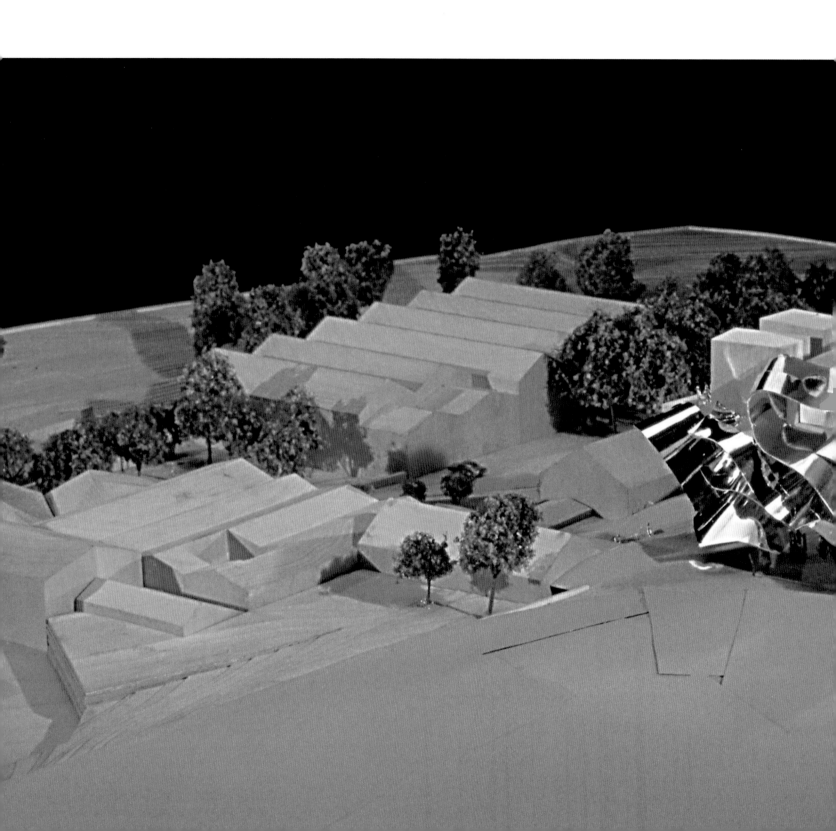

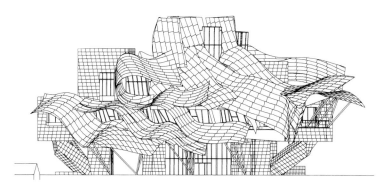

Hotel at Marques de Riscal

Elciego, Spain 1998–

At Marques de Riscal, the oldest winery in the Rioja region of the Basque Country, Gehry explored a new facet of the material used to dramatic effect in the Guggenheim Museum Bilbao (1991–97), layering ribbons of colored titanium in a canopy adorning a hotel building of natural-colored stone. His ebullient structure is a response to the unbroken landscape of lush vineyards surrounding the building. The hues of the colored metal are inspired by the rich tones of the sky and vineyard, while the facade suggests the stone church of San Andres in the town of Elciego.

The techniques Gehry employed to integrate his contemporary structure with its traditional setting are common to his earlier projects. The building's radical departures from the winery's existing architecture, which includes two sandstone structures dating from the nineteenth century, are mitigated by the traditional stone blocks used in its facade. A similar approach is seen in the Frederick R. Weisman Art Museum at the University of Minnesota (1990–93) in Minneapolis and the Peter B. Lewis Building (1997–) at the Weatherhead School of Management in Cleveland, where the appropriation of ordinary materials assists in integrating the buildings' more uncommon metallic elements with the surroundings. Gehry further synthesized the sleek building with its historical setting by exposing the structural support of the canopy—an admission of the building's unpretentious nature. Despite this, the glimmering sculpture, which houses a hotel that includes an exhibition area, a wine tasting room, and a restaurant, is intended to animate the previously undistinguished vineyard with a design that is itself an attraction.—KVW

Left: Site model, scale 1:200 m. The colored metal facade of the reception building dramatically punctuates the unassuming production facilities that surround it.

Above: South elevation.

253

Above: Programming model, scale 1:200 m. At an early stage in the design process, models are built using wood blocks that specify the function and square footage of each interior space in order to insure that the building development meets the client's needs.

Below: Design process model, scale 1:200 m.

Facing page, top: Design process model, scale 1:200 m.

Facing page, bottom: CATIA model of canopy structure with stone, glazing, and floor plates.

Below: Final design model, east facade, scale 1:50 m.

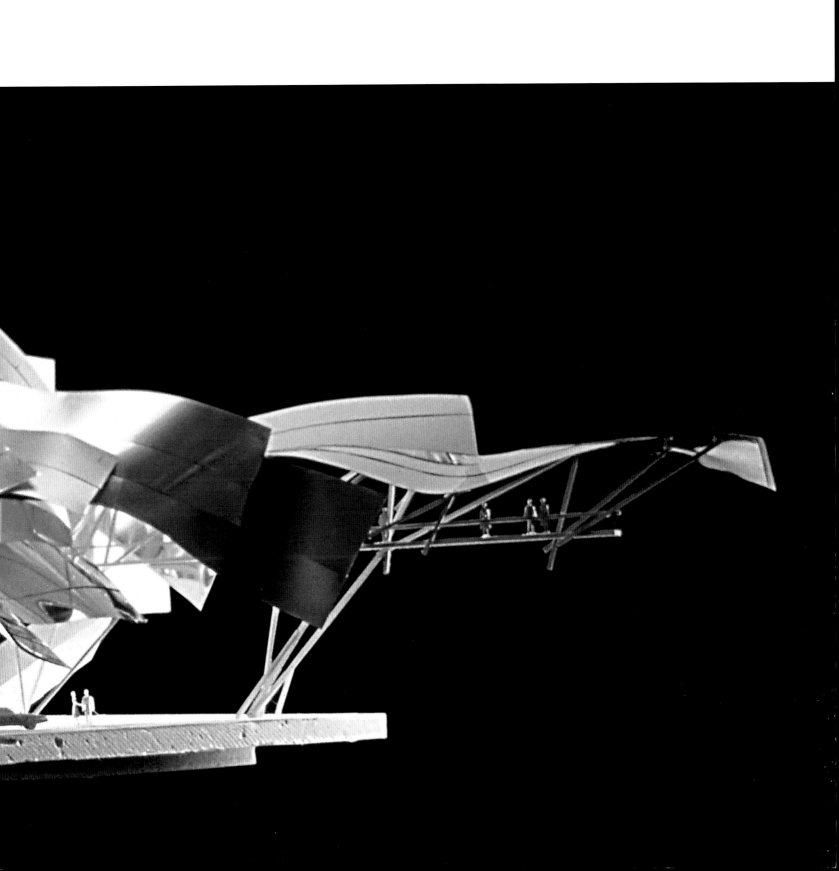

Guggenheim Museum New York

New York 1998–

The iconic structure Gehry has designed for a new Guggenheim facility in New York is the outcome of an extensive process of refinement that began with an initial design for an unspecified location. In its preliminary stages, the building's aesthetic was drawn from the cascading metal facade planned for the unbuilt Samsung Museum of Modern Art (1995–97). In 1999, once a potential location on the site of three piers in Lower Manhattan was identified, the design underwent significant revisions that led to its current dramatic form. In its present iteration, the building responds to the urban landscape that serves as its backdrop and to the East River, which faces it. The rigid forms characteristic of a skyscraper—the quintessence of New York architecture—are fractured and recombined with a curvilinear body suggestive of the water's fluid movement and the energy of the city. The twisting tower is encircled by rolling metal, evoking the image of a skyscraper jutting through a whirling cloud.

The museum's public function on the waterfront is central to its design. In a radical maneuver, the main body of the museum hovers above the river, allowing pedestrians along the Wall Street corridor uninterrupted views of the water. A promenade and extensive park space provide a much-needed gathering place and access to the river, and are supplemented by a sculpture garden and additional public amenities. Gehry's design implies that museums of the future might act not only as repositories for art objects, but as forums for civic engagement.—KVW

Above: Current design model, scale 1:100 m.
Right: Site model looking north with current design, scale 1:1000 m.

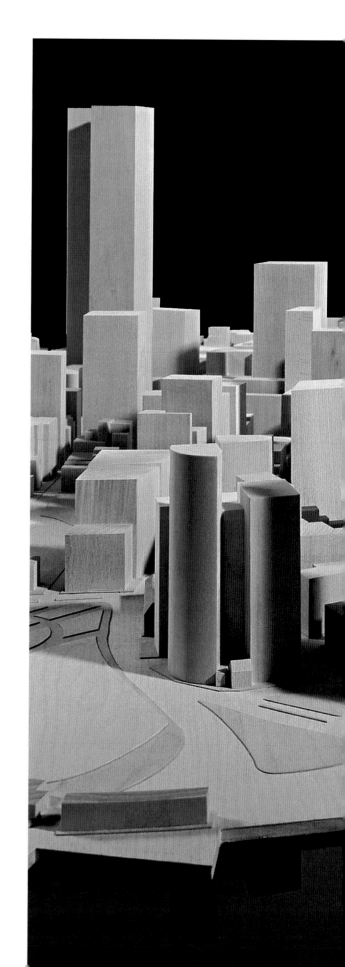

Left: Installation view of current design model, scale 1:100 m.

Above: Design sketch.

This page: Current design model showing the public outdoor plaza at the base of the museum (right). Amenities will include a sculpture park and a water garden that is transformed into an ice rink during the winter months. Large openings bring sunlight down to the plaza (above).

262

Ray and Maria Stata Center

Massachusetts Institute of Technology

Cambridge, Massachusetts 1998–

This center will unite the laboratories for Computer Science, Artificial Intelligence, and Information and Decision Systems and the Department of Linguistics and Philosophy in a 424,000-square-foot facility in the northeast quadrant of the Massachusetts Institute of Technology (MIT) campus. The temporary status and warehouselike spaces of the center's predecessor—the historic Building 20 in which radar was developed during World War II—permitted its occupants free reign in adapting the spaces to their needs, and in designing the new facility Gehry sought to recapture this spirit of flexibility and accommodation.

The center's complex program and myriad user groups considerably amplified Gehry's characteristic process of engaging his clients in dialogue. Drawing on various models, including his Rouse Company Headquarters (1969–74) in Columbia, Maryland, the firm devoted an extended period to conceptualizing responses to the requirements of the various departments, and the center's external relationship to the MIT campus and its system of underground tunnels. His sensitivity to the urban context is here translated to the interior of the building, which is transformed into a sequence of neighborhoods designed around the rather unique needs of each department. Two winglike towers are oriented toward the campus and shelter both a public plaza for students and an upper terrace for research scientists. Both inside and out, communal areas between departments serve as the center's connective tissue.

Gehry's lively design for the Ray and Maria Stata Center aptly symbolizes the invention that takes place within. In acknowledging the center's multiple identities, he has created a facility that provides a great degree of flexibility without sacrificing either client needs or the architect's conception.—JFR

Left: Massing model and future development of surrounding area, scale 1:50 m, looking north toward Charles River. The Ray and Maria Stata Center is the first phase in a master plan for the northeast quadrant of campus developed by the Gehry office. The dark and light blue blocks represent different departments of the center, while future plans for an extension of a biology lab, and a new teaching and learning center are represented by yellow and white blocks, respectively.

Above and facing page, below: Design process models,
scale 1/16"=1'.

Facing page, above: Sketch of south elevation.

Left: Final design model, scale 1/4"=1'. In addition to the four main departments and their related research labs, the building is the home to numerous facilities, including classrooms, an auditorium, boardrooms, a library, lecture halls, several cafés, and a childcare center. The Artificial Intelligence Laboratory occupies the mirror-finish stainless-steel form, the childcare center is located in the blue form, and the yellow structure houses a lecture room.

Below: CATIA shaded surface model.

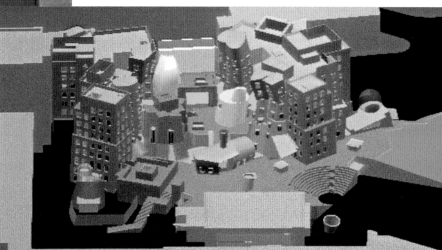

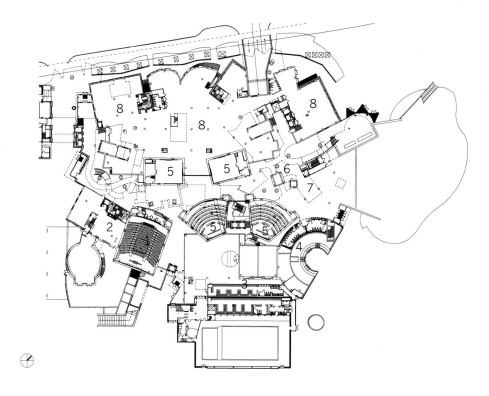

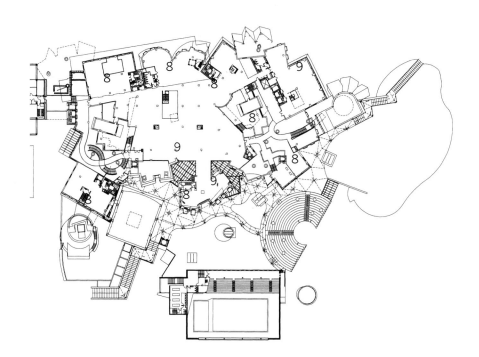

Above: First and third floor plans. 1. Lecture hall,
2. Childcare center, 3. Athletic facilities,
4. Amphitheater, 5. Classrooms, 6. Cafeteria,
7. Incubator, 8. Research space, 9. Offices.

Facing page: Final design model, scale 1/4"=1',
with view of central terrace and Artificial Intelligence
Laboratory.

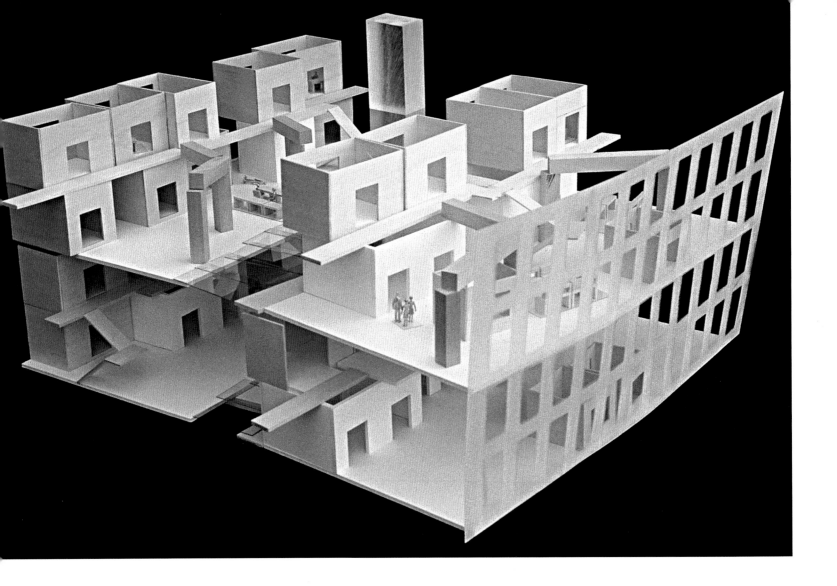

Above: Office study model, scale 1/4"=1'.

Right: Longitudinal section. 1. Machine shop,
2. Loading dock, 3. Laboratories, 4. Parking facilities,
5. Pool, 6. Athletic facilities, 7. Classroom, 8. Raised
garden, 9. Artificial intelligence laboratory, 10. Upper
terrace, 11. Roof terrace, 12. Student street.

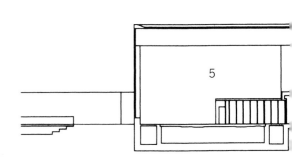

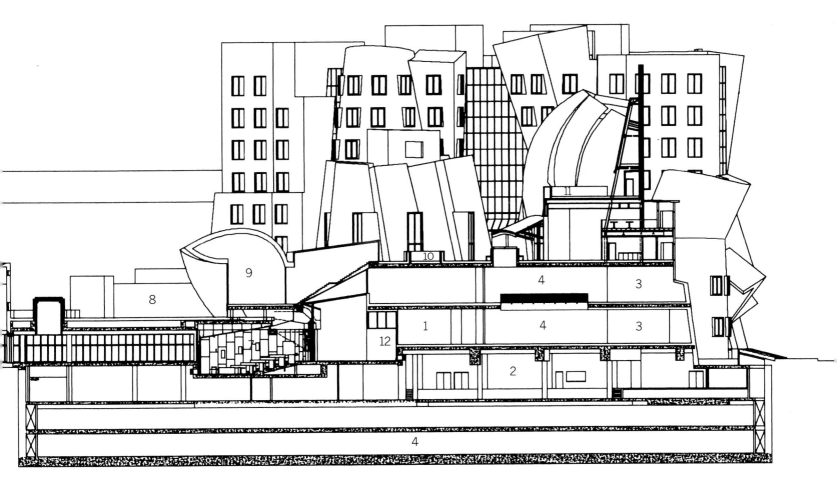

273

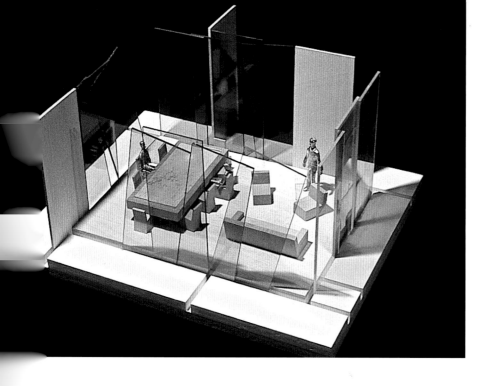

Left, above and below: Office study models, scale 1/2"=1'. In working with the diverse needs of user groups, a number of configurations for the offices and their relation to more communal spaces were developed. The schemes derived from behavioral models of various human and animal cultures and were effective in eliciting responses from the client committee. Based on a traditional Japanese house, in which sliding screens permit maximum flexibility, one design (top) opens up the offices to create a larger public space, but was rejected as providing too many options and requiring too much neatness on behalf of the occupants.

Facing page: Office study model, scale 1/4"=1'. This office model based on the behavioral patterns of an orangutan village was initially met with a less than favorable reaction. Here, researchers were afforded maximum privacy in their office spaces, but emerge from them to join with their colleagues in more public settings—much like primates who live up in the trees and venture down onto the savannah to engage in collective activity.

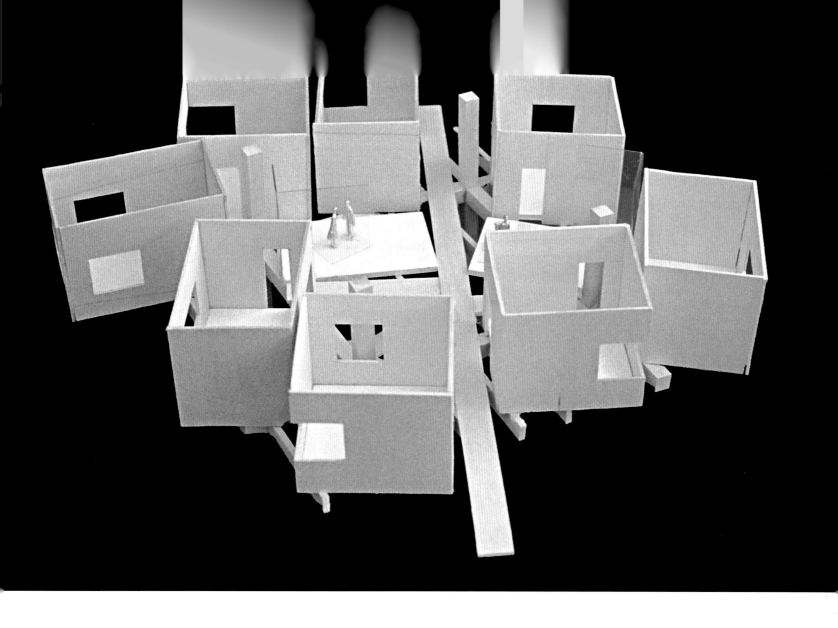

Left and facing page: Final interior design model, scale 1/2"=1'. A lecture hall (left) is capped by a skylight while extensive use of glazing is limited to circulation spaces (facing page) in order to bring light into the building while avoiding myriad problems associated with direct sunlight in the offices and labs, such as glare on computer screens.

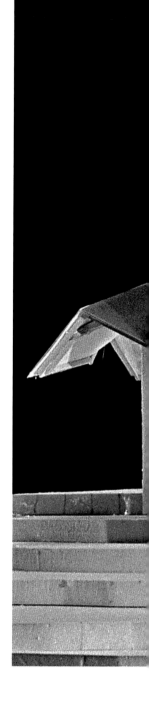

Maggie's Centre Dundee
Dundee, Scotland 1999–

Gehry's first building in the United Kingdom is a modest cancer care center on the grounds of Ninewells Hospital. It is named for the architect's close friend the late Maggie Keswick Jencks, who founded a patient-support program (whose first center is in Edinburgh). The center is a facility where cancer patients from the nearby hospital, as well as their friends and families, can meet to share experiences and to obtain information for services that complement medical treatment.

Gehry has designed a stimulating and uplifting building—a "friendly little clubhouse," as he calls it—for the quiet site overlooking an estuary. The small tower that dominates the project was inspired by lighthouses and has a large space upstairs for a lounge; it also recalls the sentinel forms of the unrealized Lewis Residence (1989–95). The roof with its accordionlike folds is clad in stainless steel to glisten in the sunlight.—JFR

Above and facing page, left: Final design model, scale 1:25 m. The roof structure (left) was developed in a manner that would permit construction by local boat builders in order to minimize costs.

Right: Design sketch.

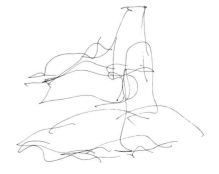

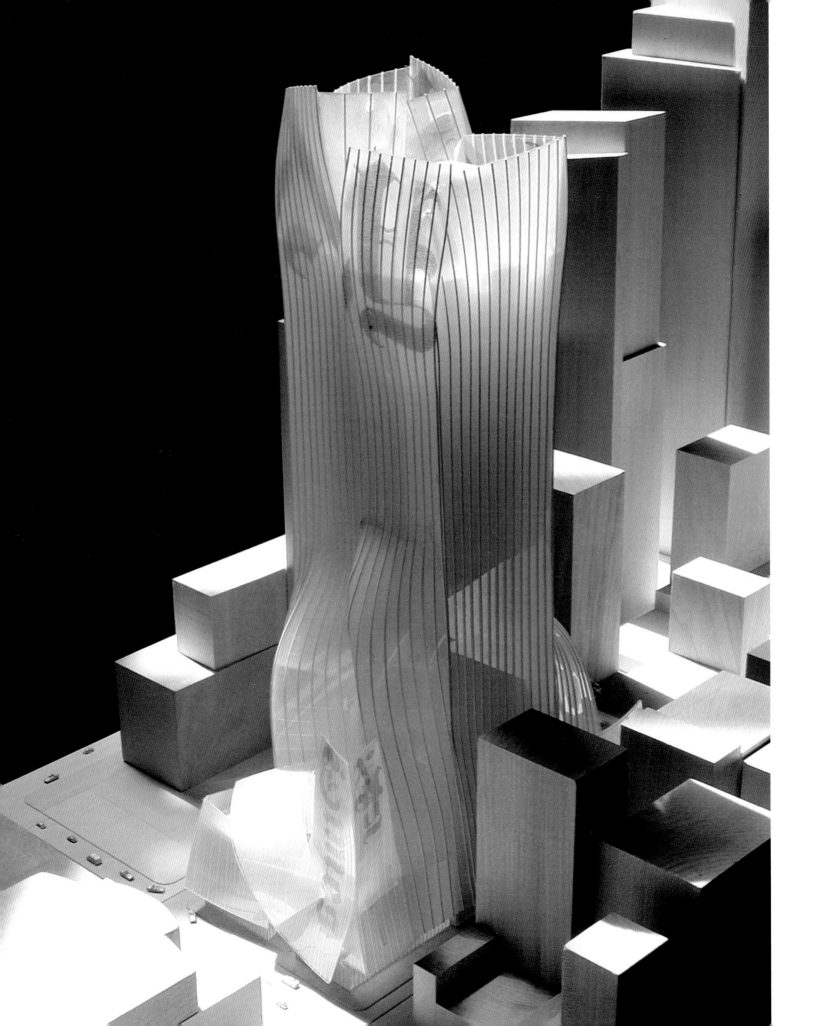

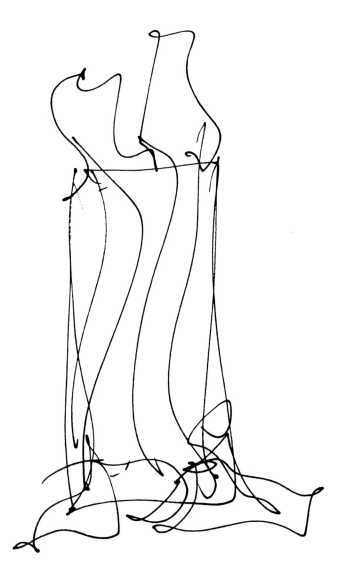

New York Times Headquarters (unbuilt)
New York 2000

It is perhaps not unexpected that the skyscraper—a quintessential emblem of Modernist architecture—has not been a part of Gehry's realized works. In the summer of 2000, however, Gehry in association with David Childs of Skidmore, Owings & Merrill accepted an invitation to participate in a competition for the New York Times Headquarters; the other participants were Norman Foster, Cesar Pelli, and Renzo Piano. The requirements for a new forty-five-story building—with its site bound by Fortieth and Forty-first Streets on Eighth Avenue, across from the Port Authority Bus Terminal—included office space for the New York Times Company at its base and speculative space for commercial and retail tenants.

In the highly congested real estate of midtown Manhattan, the Gehry/Childs design manages to contest the normative vocabulary of the high-rise and break out of the rigid straitjacket that constrains the neighboring buildings. Their glass tower is graced at the top by sculptural forms—based on an abstraction of the *Times* logo—which creates a visual identity along the skyline. Halfway down, the slender high-rise gently begins to twist and erupt in a cascade of molten forms.

The Gehry/Childs team withdrew from the competition shortly before the project was awarded to Piano in association with Fox & Fowle.—JFR

Facing page: Site with final competition model, scale 1/32"=1'.
Left: Design sketch.

Design process models, scale 1/32"=1'. Numerous models—just a selection is shown here—were developed as the design evolved.

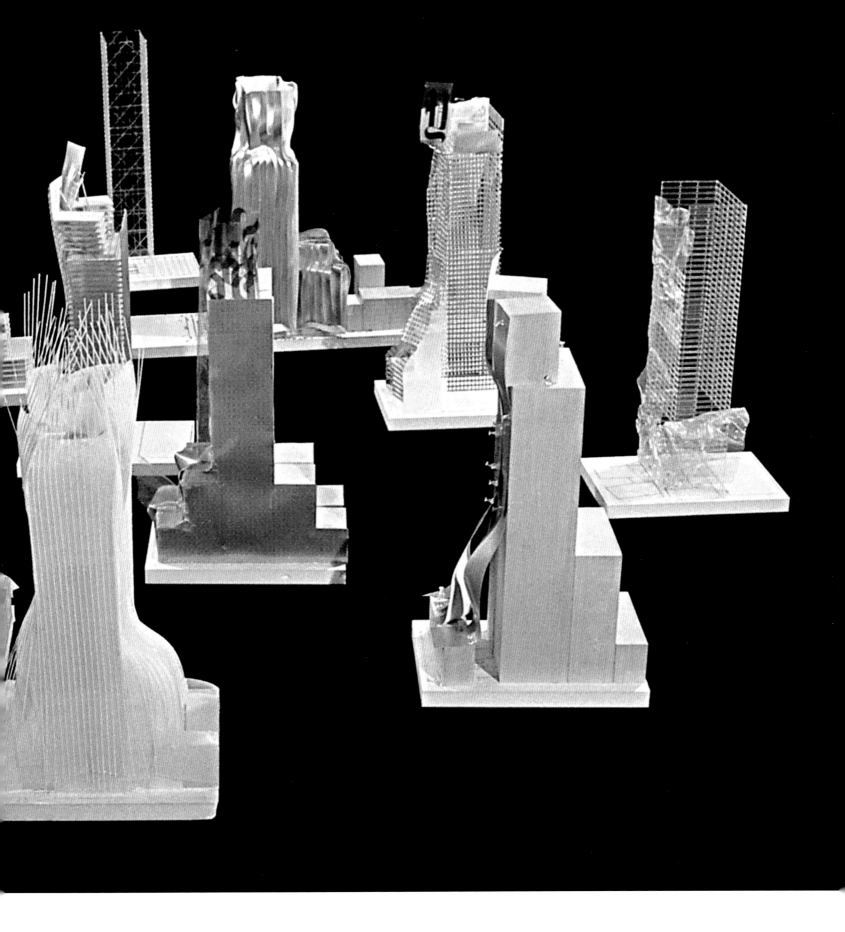

Left: Interior model with view of atrium, scale 1/8"=1'.
Right: Site with final competition model.

Pages 286–87: Site with final competition model,
view looking northeast, scale 1/32"=1'.

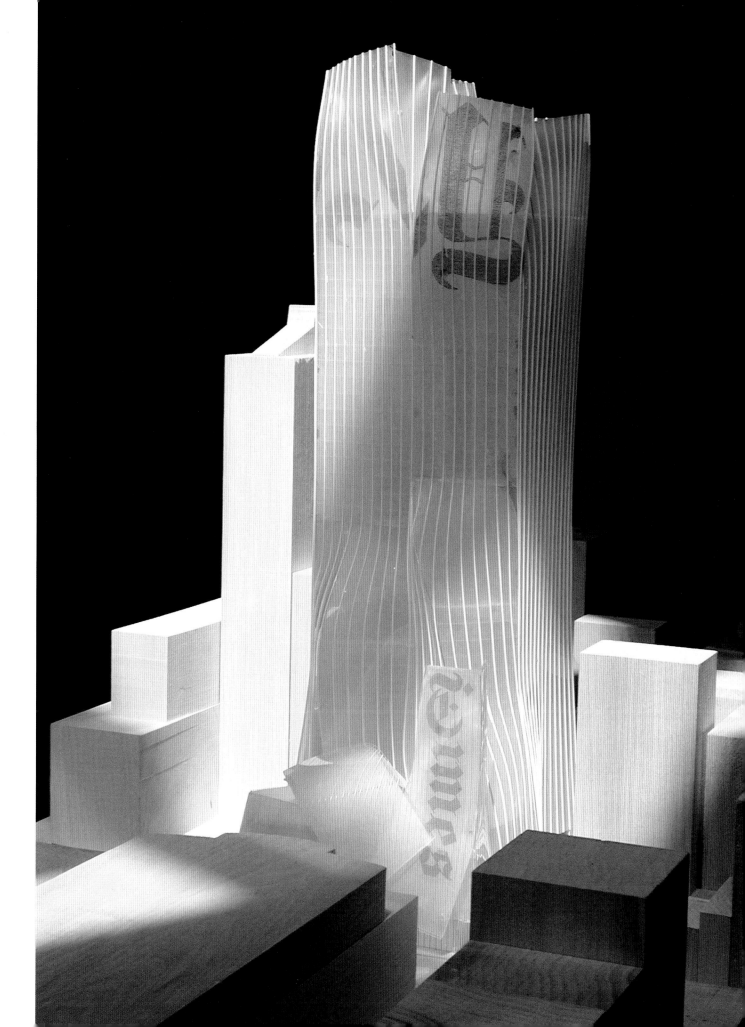

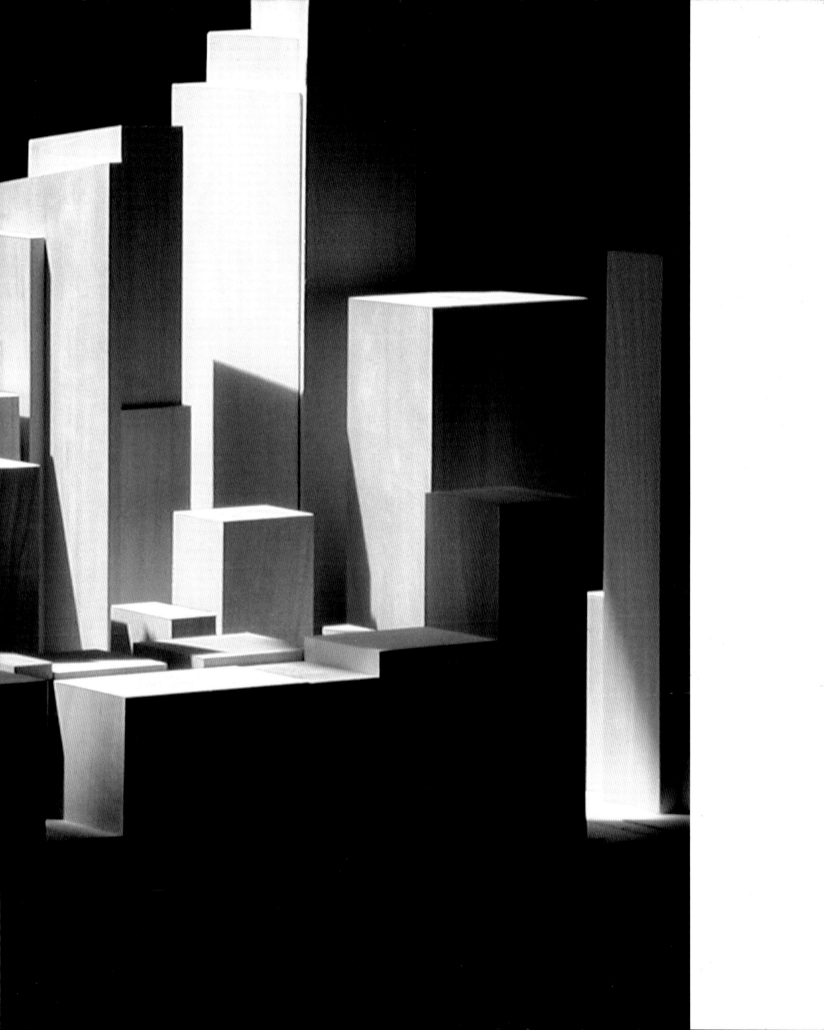

Architecture in Motion

Mildred Friedman

*It's modern life, the real experience of living in this world, that's fueled my work....
The real world today comes hurtling at you like a runaway truck, and either you can freeze
up and let it run you down or else you can jump to the side, take a flying leap, clamber
on board, and struggle your way through the window and into the driver's seat, where you
can try to wrest control of the steering wheel and the brakes. That's the energy I try to
harness in my work. I guess you can say I'm intrigued by the sense of movement.*

Frank Gehry[1]

For more than forty years, Frank Gehry has brought a freewheeling, wide-ranging substance
to the architecture of his time. Born in Toronto, he immigrated to Los Angeles with his family
in 1947, at the age of seventeen. Except for a few intervals during his studies and early career,
Los Angeles has remained his home base. Trained as an architect—at the University of
Southern California and Harvard's Graduate School of Design—in the Modernist tradition, he
eventually designed his way out of its constraints. Gehry's earliest projects were undoubtedly

inspired by the southern California architects
he most admired—Harwell Hamilton Harris
and Rudolph M. Schindler—and secondarily
by Russian Constructivism[2] and, via Frank
Lloyd Wright, the Japanese post-and-beam
tradition. By the early 1970s, Gehry had
become a vital presence in the community of
Los Angeles architects and artists, and his
singular hand emerged. Without reverting to
historic innuendo, he went on to create idiosyncratic, humane spaces filled with surprise,
nuance, and power.

Danziger Studio and Residence (1964–65), Hollywood.

In such early Los Angeles projects as the
studio/residences for the graphic designer
Louis Danziger (1964–65) in Hollywood and the painter Ron Davis (1968–72) in Malibu,
Gehry demonstrated concerns that remained central to all of his subsequent work—for

Experience Music Project (EMP) (1995–2000), Seattle.

example, materials employed in unusual ways: galvanized metal for the Davis walls and roof, and rough stucco ("tunnel mix") for the Danziger exterior walls. Gehry's understanding of the modeling of form with daylight became a key aspect of his work, and in both studio/residences, brilliantly designed skylights incorporated daylight in extraordinary ways. Fundamental to the design of each is the creation of forms that shape space in unexpected, innovative ways. As exemplified by these projects, the most important aspect in Gehry's approach has been his interaction with the client and the work's relationship to place: "I can't do it alone. I need to fall in love with the people, the client, the site. Establishing that trust gives me time to explore. Place is the crucial starting point."[3]

It was not until the first remodeling of his own Santa Monica residence in 1977–78 that Gehry's work came to the attention of the wider architectural cognoscenti. He exposed the bones of the building process in this small two-story dwelling from the 1920s. The layered enclosures of the remodeling, particularly where the angled window/skylights greatly expanded the sense of space in the kitchen and dining areas, created a cubistic collage. He used the kinds of materials—chain-link fencing, plywood, corrugated sheet metal—that gave him a lasting reputation as a maverick whose work does not comply with the accepted canons of architecture. In 1991–92, to accommodate his family's changing needs, Gehry remodeled the house a second time. It became more comfortable and elegant, the site more enclosed and private through the use of new garden walls and extensive planting. But by Gehry's own admission, the residence has lost some of the edge that he captured in the initial experiment.

In 1978, Gehry was commissioned to create homes for the Familian, Gunther, and Wagner families, all in the Los Angeles area. The studies for the three unbuilt residences examined in some depth the possibilities inherent in balloon-frame construction, and further explored the iconoclastic materials and forms that Gehry investigated during the first remodeling of his own house. The Spiller Residence (1978–79), located in Venice, California, again gave Gehry the opportunity to use the rough wood framing and corrugated metal exterior that so intrigued him at that time. In these projects, there was a concern for the art of the everyday. There was a feeling of gestural painting in Gehry's rough carpentry, and one could discern parallels with Robert Rauschenberg's large-scale paintings and sculpture of the same period. Gehry maintains, "I keep a certain rawness through the detailing. I work hard at making it nonprecious."

Another important focus during the late 1970s and into the 1980s was Gehry's concept of separate one-room buildings arranged in a village-like setting. An early example of that schema was the 1981 proposal for the Smith Residence in Los Angeles's Bel Air neighborhood. The project would have allowed Gehry to renovate one of his earliest commissions, his Wright-influenced Steeves Residence (1958–59), which was sold to the Smith family in 1981. In Gehry's proposed addition, eagle and fish columns mark the entrance, and the added rooms are articulated but attached to the existing structure. Unfortunately, the design was not approved by the Bel Air Fine Arts Commission, whose members maintained that it did not look like a house.

Perhaps the most accomplished of Gehry's early objects-in-a-landscape groupings is the Loyola Law School (1978–), a work still in progress. Located in an inner-city neighborhood,

Loyola Law School (1978–),
Los Angeles.

just three blocks from Gehry's parents' first Los Angeles home, it demonstrates the architect's singular ability to evoke history without succumbing to it. "You can't redo old ideas," he explains, "you can learn from the past but you can't continue to be in the past. I cannot face my children if I tell them I have no more ideas and I have to copy something that happened before. It is like giving up and telling them there is no future for them."[4] Because the client asked for a design that would refer to classical traditions, Gehry decided to create "a pileup of buildings, like an acropolis. I was exploring disparate sculptural forms placed beside each other."

Professor Robert Benson, who was a member of the Loyola selection committee in 1978 when Gehry was chosen as the school's architect, has explained how what started as a new building became an entire campus with "a sense of place."[5] Among the seven architects interviewed, Gehry was undoubtedly the most radical, boasting that he was "the cheapskate architect," relishing the "unfinished construction" look.[6] After the first phase was completed, some obdurate faculty wanted to find a different architect whose aesthetic was less demanding, less revolutionary. But the naysayers were soon outvoted when positive reviews began to come in and visitors from around the world came simply to experience the architecture of the new campus, which was often compared with Jefferson's exemplary design for the University of Virginia in Charlottesville. For more than twenty years, Gehry has worked to develop the Loyola campus, and an addition is currently in the design phase.

Another variation on the village idea is the Winton Guest House (1983–87), in Wayzata, Minnesota. Its four interconnected structures clad in Finnish plywood, limestone, brick, and sheet metal create a pinwheel plan that settles comfortably into the rolling green of the landscape and beckons to the presiding 1952 Philip Johnson–designed house across the lawn. "We said we didn't want another villa on the hill," Penny Winton remembers. "We wanted it to be amusing to children so that they would want to keep coming to visit grandma and

Final design model, Lewis Residence (1989–95, unbuilt).

grandpa." Mike Winton says that "the thing that keeps coming to me about the work is how self-assured it is, and how convincing and real, although totally unique." In design for close to four years, the house was slow to gel, but when completed, its serene sculptural forms—reminiscent of Giorgio Morandi's paintings of bottles and jars arrayed like buildings along an avenue—were well worth the wait.

The village concept continues to occur in Gehry's work. Perhaps the most significant late project in this vein is the unrealized Lewis Residence (1989–95), designed for a site in Lyndhurst, Ohio, near Cleveland. Peter B. Lewis, who owned a suburban house he wanted to remodel, gave the architect free rein in his unprecedented search for new ways to create a domestic environment. Gehry has compared this project to a MacArthur fellowship, because it allowed him the support and time to carry out an in-depth exploration of materials and forms that have influenced many succeeding works. Innumerable models tell the story of the project's complexity. Even the final models include paper modifications that suggest further possible emendations to the scheme. In order to add to his own invention, Gehry invited several friends to participate in the design of the Lewis property. Philip Johnson designed a guest house in the shape of an octopus, Maggie Keswick Jencks created landscape elements, and Richard Serra and Larry Bell made proposals for sculpture. But perhaps inevitably, the house was not built.

Francesco Borromini, S. Carlo alle Quattro Fontane (facade, 1665–67; interior, 1638–41), Rome.

Although Gehry's early projects were rectilinear—because, he maintains, "we have to take small steps"—the recent work has become what can best be described as sculptural architecture. He maintains that architecture's most significant quality "is that it encloses space. The manipulation of the enveloping surface is what distinguishes architecture from painting or sculpture."[7] In the Guggenheim Museum Bilbao (1991–97) and the Experience Music Project (EMP) (1995–2000), Seattle, the roofs and walls flow into one another in a series of baroque, rolling forms. According to historian Spiro Kostof, "Roman Baroque is an urban style. The curved facades step outward into the street; their gesticulating statues engage the passerby directly. Wings extend from the buildings to encompass a public space."[8] The words "Frank Gehry's baroque" could replace the term "Roman Baroque" without changing the accuracy of the statement.

In recent projects, Gehry has taken the risks that the seventeenth-century architects of the Roman Baroque, such as Francesco Borromini, inspire. Gehry has created the organic shapes that are aspects of a new baroque vocabulary involving the mutability of light and form, a vocabulary that makes the Guggenheim Museum Bilbao and the EMP so expressive. Metal cladding has been one of his hallmarks, beginning with corrugated metal and continuing through to recent stainless-steel and titanium applications. The shapes and colors of the electric guitar together with the sounds of rock and roll were absorbed into the forms of the EMP, which is dedicated to the great guitarist Jimi Hendrix. The building's metal skin has over twenty thousand shingles, cut and shaped with the aid of the computer program CATIA.

Guggenheim Museum Bilbao (1991–97).

The painted red metal is designed to fade until it resembles an old truck. The sense of motion in the EMP's curved walls is enhanced by the incorporation of the monorail, which brings visitors directly from downtown, through the building, to the Seattle Center.

Gehry's work has developed alongside that of the many artist friends he admires, and with whom, as in the Lewis project, he has occasionally collaborated. Two architectural collaborations with Claes Oldenburg and Coosje van Bruggen are particularly memorable. Camp Good Times (1984–85), an unbuilt project in the Malibu mountains, was an effort by the three friends to bring wit and playfulness to an environment for children with cancer. Imaginative structures were proposed in the shape of milk cans, an inverted ship's hull, and a wave form. And there was their realized collaboration: the Chiat Day Building (1985–91) in Venice, California, in which Oldenburg and van Bruggen's folly in the form of binoculars created a surprising entrance at street level and housed two soaring conference rooms above.

A proposal for the Financial Times Millennium Bridge Competition (1996) in London—for a footbridge connecting the new Tate Modern in the former Bankside Power Station to St. Paul's Cathedral across the Thames River—was a collaboration with sculptor Richard Serra. In this work, the two men created a singular curving form that is a remarkable melding of their minds. Earlier, Gehry and Serra had designed a bridge for a 1981 exhibition, *Collaborations: Artists and Architects*, held by the Architectural League of New York. In that case, they envisioned a connection between the World Trade Center and the Chrysler Building, with anchors in the East and Hudson Rivers.

On a number of recent large projects, Gehry has collaborated with other architects to create agglomerations that he believes produce richer environments than those designed by a single practitioner. When he became the architect for the Vitra International Manufacturing Facility and Design Museum (1987–89) in Weil am Rhein, Germany, he proposed that—instead of having a master plan of stylistically similar works—the company, whose site included a 1981

Model, Financial Times
Millennium Bridge
Competition (1996, unbuilt),
in collaboration with
Richard Serra.

factory by Nicholas Grimshaw, should take a pluralistic approach. Gehry encouraged company head Rolf Fehlbaum to hire a number of architects to create an urbanistic campus for the growing furniture company. As a result, in addition to those by Gehry, Vitra now has buildings by Tadao Ando, Zaha Hadid, and Alvaro Siza, and has a large outdoor sculpture by Oldenburg and van Bruggen. The ongoing Arena Centre (2000–) in Prague is a joint effort with the distinguished French architect Jean Nouvel. It is a large-scale redevelopment project commissioned by the same client who commissioned the Nationale-Nederlanden Building (1992–96), Gehry's collaboration with the Czech architect Vlado Milunic.

In the same spirit that characterizes his work with artists and other architects, Gehry shares responsibility with his colleagues in Frank O. Gehry and Associates. With partners Randy Jefferson and James Glymph, senior associates Edwin Chan and Craig Webb, and a group of young architects, he works collaboratively on each project—ever sensitive to their input.

For many years, Gehry was undervalued in his home state, where important institutional commissions went to such outsiders as Mario Botta, Hardy Holzman Pfeiffer, Arata Isozaki, and Richard Meier. While he did not receive the commission for Los Angeles's Museum of Contemporary Art, which went to Isozaki, he did remodel a warehouse structure for that museum called the Temporary Contemporary (1982–83; now the Geffen Contemporary). With this project, Gehry demonstrated the potential for the exhibition of art within many deserted industrial buildings. And he undoubtedly influenced later major renovation/conversions of industrial sites such as those by Bruner/Cott & Associates for MASS MoCA in North Adams, Massachusetts, which opened in 1999, and by Herzog & de Meuron for the Tate Modern, which opened in 2000.

Not until he received the commission for the Walt Disney Concert Hall (1987–) in Los Angeles did Gehry achieve the recognition he deserved at home. Outside of the visual arts, Gehry's other great love has always been music. One of his oldest friends is Ernest Fleischmann, former Executive Director of the Los Angeles Philharmonic Association, who initiated their friendship when he commissioned Gehry to renovate the Hollywood Bowl (1970–82). In order to improve the acoustics, retrofitting of the orchestra shell was done in two stages, first with sonotubes and later, and more successfully, with fiberglass spheres. Gehry shares with Fleischmann admiration for Hans Scharoun's Berlin Philharmonic Hall (1956–63), a building he visited a number of times before receiving the 1987 commission to design the Walt Disney Concert Hall. Fleischmann explains, "Scharoun Hall is a very intimate building, because the various sections are rather small, little villages in which the audience sits. It's very much of a piece, and acoustically it's superb. I was concerned to create a similar intimate space in Disney Hall, where no one would feel out of touch with the performers."

The lessons learned from the long evolution and complex problems of this project will pay dividends for many years to come. For example, the CATIA computer program — which includes CAD (computer aided design) and CAM (computer aided manufacture) applications — helped make the realization of the Walt Disney Concert Hall technically possible. Now used for all projects in the Gehry office, CATIA allows the architect to control a building's form and costs, working in collaboration with the contractors.

Hans Scharoun, Berlin Philharmonic Hall (1956–63).

Another Gehry project related to music, as well as theater and dance, is the Performing Arts Center at Bard College (1997–), now under construction in Annandale-on-Hudson, New York. Leon Botstein, the school's president, has talked about this building as small in comparison to the Guggenheim Museum Bilbao and other recent Gehry designs. He contends that as the college is a "client of poor artists," its project attests to Gehry's ongoing effort to work for smaller institutions, rather like the architect's commitment to the Loyola Law School campus. Yet when the project started, the school wondered if working with Gehry was "the route to bankruptcy." Not only is that not the case, but the Gehry office has been extremely flexible and helpful, especially given the change of site that was thrust upon them in midstream. The building has now become part of a group of existing buildings by other architects that creates a small, welcoming compound at the campus's entrance.

In addition to his Bilbao triumph, Gehry has received a number of significant European commissions. Among them, the DG Bank Building (1995–2001) in Berlin is particularly interesting because its relationship to its surroundings is remarkable in a different way from most of his recent projects. In a unique reversal, its interior is organic, its limestone exterior Cartesian. This was the result of an effort to harmonize the exterior with the neo-classical limestone buildings on this historic square, where the Brandenburg Gate is also located. The offices for the DG Bank, the building's primary occupant, overlook a glass-enclosed wood atrium that contains a conference hall in the shape of a horse's head. (The interior form is similar to one first seen in studies for the Lewis Residence.) The south side of the building contains thirty-nine apartments arrayed around a second smaller atrium that brings natural light into every apartment.

Kurt Forster believes that "Gehry manages to free his projects from typological constraints, enabling his buildings to assume shapes of unprecedented kind and configuration."[9]

Characteristic of his inventive approach, Gehry's 1998 proposal for a new Guggenheim Museum in New York does not conform to the city's typical architecture. To be built on an East River site at the edge of the Wall Street financial district, the project pays homage to the city's cultural and economic power, and to the popular conception of New York as a city in constant movement. Writing about this project, Herbert Muschamp maintains that "New York's most vital tradition is its ethos of change.... This is the city's greatest paradox."[10] Although, by and large, this ethos has rarely been captured in specific buildings. Just as Frank Lloyd Wright's Solomon R. Guggenheim Museum brought unexpected form to upper Fifth Avenue, Gehry is proposing to bring an unfamiliar form to Lower Manhattan, one that sets new precedents for New York's architecture to come.

Change requires a special kind of courage. Looking at a model of his Ray and Maria Stata Center (1998–) in a Massachusetts Institute of Technology (MIT) site plan model, Gehry remarked, "The part that doesn't look like the rest of the campus is mine."[11] The center is a large project that, on its completion in 2004, will house a thousand people in a group of buildings. Two towers on either end of a raised platform cradle the smaller structures that are the heart of the complex. MIT linguists, philosophers, and cognitive scientists who deal with computers, artificial intelligence, and robotics were actively involved in the evolution of the program. They were determined to have green systems in the buildings. Thus, for example, the lab windows are operable. The project, divided into a series of "neighborhoods," includes a student street with teaching areas, social spaces, and a café. It also contains a gym, a child-care facility, and an amphitheater. This intricate work will create a welcoming new front door to the MIT campus in Cambridge.

Gehry's overriding concern with client needs and desires, as expressed in the MIT project, underscores the fact that he is more architect than artist. His early studies in urban planning at Harvard have served him well in large-scale urban interventions, such as that at MIT and at Der Neue Zollhof (1994–99) in Düsseldorf. When Gehry went to Germany to start the process for the latter project he arrived with a box of wood blocks, explaining that each one represented 500 square meters. The blocks were piled one on top of the other to achieve the required 30,000 square meters of space. The client, advertising executive Thomas Rempen, explains that "right then, we decided not to build Rockefeller Center!" In the end, Gehry created three office buildings instead of one, which would have cut off the view of the Rhine River for the occupants of the buildings farther from the river's edge. As Gehry asserts, "It allows the city to breathe." "I always build two models, one big, one small, which show a project's program in relation to its city, because if you only work with one scale you become fascinated with the forms for their own sake. You have to force yourself to change scale and go back and forth. It keeps you honest." The three Neue Zollhof buildings create a neigh-

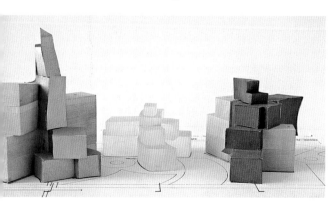

Massing model, Der Neue Zollhof (1994–99), Düsseldorf.

borhood, and encourage additional compatible development along the riverfront.

One building type whose realization has eluded Gehry is the tall building—the skyscraper. The Neue Zollhof buildings are the closest he has come. Several skyscraper projects have been in early stages of design—but none has been realized. The competition proposal for the New York Times Headquarters in 2000, in collaboration with David Childs of Skidmore, Owings & Merrill, was the most recent and perhaps the most exciting example of Gehry's examination of this building genre. He recognizes that "there is not much wiggle-room in the design of a

center-city high rise, so in thinking about a tall building I'm looking for the subtleties, the subtle freedoms." Although unrealized, the New York Times project is again an example of Gehry's in-depth investigations into the potential of a material. In this case glass is used in an entirely new way to create a sculptural, translucent curtain wall that resembles water in motion. This research into glass as a sculptural medium followed on Gehry's design for the Condé Nast Cafeteria (1996–2000) in New York, in which laminated glass panels are a major component.

Condé Nast Cafeteria (1996–2000), New York.

Although the design of the furnishings for building interiors is not always part of an architect's commission, Gehry has created a number of memorable interiors for his own buildings and a few for buildings by others. The staff cafeteria he designed for the Condé Nast Building by Fox & Fowle Architects was given a generous budget that enabled Gehry to match the challenge posed by Condé Nast's chairman, S. I. Newhouse, Jr. Typical of Gehry's approach to a new problem, he decided to use this opportunity to experiment with shaped glass in combination with titanium and ash wood, which were both significant components of the Guggenheim Museum Bilbao interior. In order to control the main room's acoustics, the perimeter walls are lined with perforated blue titanium. The room includes serpentine-shaped banquettes surrounded by individually shaped, laminated glass panels, each held at top and bottom by stainless-steel connectors. Contrasting with the blue titanium and the green tinted glass, the banquettes are upholstered in tan leatherette and the tabletops are yellow.

Gehry also modified his new aluminum FOG Chair (manufactured by Knoll) for the Condé Nast project, by upholstering the seat and back. This chair, to be part of a collection of indoor-outdoor pieces, is the most recent example of Gehry's uncommon furniture designs, which began with his Easy Edges (1969–73) cardboard furniture. For that first collection, seventeen pieces—including a variety of chairs, tables, and desks—were stained and joined, using the same techniques that are applied to wood. The cardboard sheets were built up in the same way that plywood—another material beloved by Gehry—is constructed: the grain of each sheet alternates direction. The artist Robert Irwin was a partner in this endeavor and a collaborator on the design of several pieces. The line, which was inexpensive and durable, was successfully sold in department stores, such as Bloomingdale's in New York. But after only a few months on the market in 1972, Gehry withdrew the furniture. He did not like dealing with the commercial aspects of the retail world and was concerned that too much time would be lost from his architectural practice.

However, Gehry continued to be intrigued with the potential of cardboard and went back to furniture design in 1979, in an informal partnership with the architect Richard Wurman. This time, however, he used big chunks of loose cardboard in fluted, rough shapes. These pieces, Experimental Edges (1979–82) cardboard furniture, were made by artisans in small quantities, by hand, and were essentially useful works of art. They were sold initially through the Max Protech Gallery in New York. Gehry believes that "chairs are contextual — related to what's going on. Designing a new chair is a Talmudic question, not just four legs and a seat."[12] The bushel basket, with its lightweight wood strips, inspired his bentwood furniture (1989–92) and solved a problem that had fascinated him for many years: how to create a chair whose support structure and seat are formed of the same material? The solution freed bentwood furniture from its earlier rigidity. In addition to their light weight, and comfort, Gehry's bentwood chairs are available to a broad public, manufactured by Knoll.

He also designed spectacular fish and snake lamps (1983–86). In a curious way, the lowly fish has long been Gehry's mascot. Childhood memories of carp swimming in his grandmother's bathtub inspired his figurative response to the Formica Corporation's request for designs using Colorcore, a translucent laminate introduced in the early 1980s. (His grandmother would buy a carp on Thursday and keep it in the bathtub until using it to make gefilte fish for Friday evening's Sabbath meal.) Inspiration hit when Gehry accidentally broke some Colorcore pieces, thus creating the fish-scale elements he subsequently used to shape his lamp forms.

In such designs as the Fish Sculpture at the Vila Olimpica (1990–91) in Barcelona, the horsehead shaped structures in the Lewis Residence and DG Bank Building projects, and the fish and snake lamps, Gehry has played with figuration in a variety of materials and stages of abstraction. Recent references to forms in nature have become increasingly abstract — especially in the Guggenheim Museum Bilbao and the proposal for the Guggenheim New York — evoking the movement of water or clouds. These projects continue Gehry's attempt to capture motion with an ever-expanding vocabulary of forms that promise an architecture still to come.

Notes

1. Lawrence Weschler, "Talk of the Town," *New Yorker*, January 31, 1994, p. 30.

2. In 1980, Gehry designed a remarkable installation for the Los Angeles County Museum of Art's exhibition *The Avant-Garde in Russia, 1910–1930: New Perspectives.*

3. Unless otherwise noted, all quotations from Frank Gehry and his clients are taken from interviews with the author in the years 1997–2000.

4. Gehry, quoted in Charles Jencks, *FOG Individual Imagination and Cultural Conservatism* (London: Academy Editions, 1995), p. 33.

5. Robert Benson became a private client in 1979 when he commissioned Gehry to design his own house, completed in 1984, in Calabasas, California.

6. Gehry, quoted in Robert Benson, "How Loyola Law School Selected Frank Gehry as Its Architect" (Los Angeles: McLaughlin, Loyola Law School, 2000), pp. 78–79.

7. Gehry, quoted in Alejandro Zaera, "Conversations with Frank O. Gehry," *El Croquis* 74/75 (1995), p. 23.

8. Spiro Kostof, *A History of Architecture* (New York and Oxford: Oxford University Press, 1985), p. 516.

9. Kurt Forster, "Architectural Choreography," in *Frank O. Gehry: The Complete Works* (New York: Monacelli, 1998), p. 9.

10. Herbert Muschamp, "Living Up to the Memories of a Poetic Skyline," *New York Times*, August 13, 2000, Arts and Leisure section, p. 32.

11. Gehry, quoted from author's notes of Gehry and Paul Goldberger conversation presented at *The New Yorker Festival*, May 7, 2000, Condé Nast Building, New York.

12. Frank Gehry, "Up Everest in a Volkswagen," *Design Quarterly* 155 (spring 1992), pp. 17–19.

Gehry Residence, after 1991–92 renovation.

The House That Built Gehry

Beatriz Colomina

The cook: "I saw only what you wanted me to see."
The wife: "Of course. How could I know it was real unless someone saw?"
> Peter Greenaway, *The Cook, the Thief, His Wife and Her Lover*, 1989

Even though I often put as much detail work into what I do as anyone, it always appears
casual. That's the edge I'm after. For people to see what I want them to see, but for them
not to be quite sure if it was designed or if it just happened.
> Frank Gehry[1]

What can one say about Gehry's house that has not been said already? What is there to add
to the discussion of one of the most discussed houses of the postwar period? What is left
to say, after so many articles, in so many venues, from newspapers and popular magazines to
architectural tabloids, airline magazines, art journals, professional reviews, museum catalogues,
real-estate sections, publications, and monographs? The question seems to have puzzled
Gehry himself as early as 1986, when on the occasion of a major retrospective he said:

> *My house. I'm afraid so much has been said about it that it is very difficult for me to add*
> *anything except that living there is very comfortable. It does leak a little and we are working*
> *on fixing that.*[2]

The architect of a notorious object can only point to its most basic ability to provide shelter.
All the talk comes down to a leak or two. Yet for all of Gehry's reluctance to engage in any
intellectual discussion of his work, practically everything that has been written about his
house can be traced back to apparently casual, off-the-cuff statements repeated by him over
the course of the years. The suspicion with which critics, reasonably enough, usually regard
the statements of the most theoretically minded architects is suspended. As if Gehry could
only be telling us the truth, as if there was no reason to suspect his statements, no need to
question the casual posture, despite the obvious clichés, the systematic repetitions, and the
calculating intelligence of it all. The critics see only what Gehry wants them to see.

Gehry Residence, before 1977–78 renovation.

Time and again, from museum catalogues to *People* magazine, Gehry is presented as "childlike," "ingenious," "nonverbal," "intuitive," "visceral," "naïve," "lighthearted," "uninitiated," "unrefined," "prelogical," "primitive." The viewer is dumbed down too, encouraged to become a child when facing the work: "It is important to see all of Gehry's work from a perspective of blissful ignorance, to observe his structures from the childlike viewpoint of one who has no preconceptions about what architecture must be," says the *Los Angeles Times*.[3] The work, it seems, falls outside traditional modes of judgment. Critical viewing and discourse are abandoned. "It's so far out of normal expectations that it defies traditional criticism," says Philip Johnson.[4] Terence Riley, Chief Curator of Architecture and Design at New York's Museum of Modern Art (a position deemed responsible for determining the legitimacy of styles), declares it "outside the 'style wars' of the last thirty years."[5] Charles Jencks, the reigning master of categorization in architecture, claims that it fits every label and is therefore "unclassifiable."[6]

The difficulty in pinning Gehry down is often traced back to his refreshing lack of theorization: "He wrote no papers and advanced no theories. The only consistent direction in his work was an increasingly sculptural approach to architecture."[7] But is sculpture outside theory? Can one still pretend that objects simply stand in front of us, exuding certain qualities independently of the way they are framed by countless discourses, including those of the artists? Can one really ignore the way Gehry frames his own work?

Gehry himself feeds the view that architecture can be practiced outside theory: "I think that it's nice to be able to master verbal gymnastics and exercise your head too, and it may not have anything to do with the work of art. The expert, the majordomo of that game is Peter Eisenman. His talk has nothing to do with his work. It does and it doesn't; I think the good stuff that he does is intuitive."[8] But if Eisenman hides his intuition behind theory, could it be that Gehry, who insistently presents himself as an intuitive architect, is in fact hiding his intellect behind folksy stories? He is, of course, not as innocent as he pretends to be. We see only what he wants us to see.

So what does Gehry want us to see? Many things. Gehry has not just one theory regarding his house, but many well-thought, persuasive, provocative, captivating, irresistible theories. This collage of theories is like the collaged structure of the house itself, in which fragments fly off in independent directions. Gehry's architecture always has many channels. As he once said:

What I like doing best is breaking down the project into as many separate parts as possible.... So instead of a house being one thing, it's ten things, it allows the client more involvement, because you can say, "Well, I've got ten images now that are going to compose your house. Those images can relate to all kinds of symbolic things, ideas that you have liked, places you've liked, bits and pieces of your life that you would like to recall." I think in terms of involving the client.[9]

But in the age of mass media, the client is not simply the one paying for the building, or the one living in it. The client is also the critic, the reporter, the neighbor, the reader, the politician—in short, the wider audience. Just as Gehry tries to involve his traditional clients by presenting ten different possibilities for identification, so he tries to involve this new client, literally designing the response to his house by presenting an attractive range of precooked readings. He targets every possible respondent, providing many enticing narratives, one appropriate for every occasion. Critics cannot stop them-

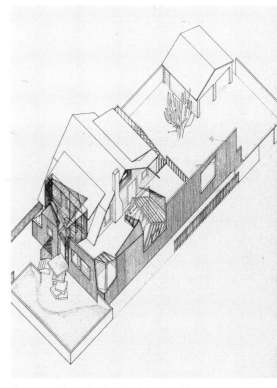

Axonometric projection of Gehry Residence for 1977–78 renovation.

selves from repeating them. Part of what makes Gehry's narratives so appealing is that they are not presented as theories. They slip under the radar and into the head of the critic. The architect weaves a whole series of intersecting narratives that form a fabric, an open structure through which the house is seen and not seen at the same time. The architecture of his theory has all the complications and seductive force of his house.

Let us follow ten stories, ten threads of Gehry's web.

Outrageous House

Even before Gehry's 1977–78 renovation of his house was completed, it was controversial. An article appeared in the *Los Angeles Times* at the end of 1977, describing Gehry as an instigator of conflict. "Radical stuff: a house deliberately left unfinished, with posts and beams standing naked to the world,...a porch enclosure made of chain-link fencing."[10] A group of architecture and journalism students had just visited Gehry's studio and argued about his work. It seems, in retrospect, like a dress rehearsal for the polemical wars that would be waged on the pages of newspapers all over the country. The architecture students were "delighted" with what they saw, while the journalists were "contemptuous." The journalists considered the architects to be isolated in their own world, speaking their own, incomprehensible language. One of them even suggested that "architects need a translator."

The first real critics of the house were the neighbors while the house was still under construction, and Gehry's first account of the house came in response to their complaints. The neighbors became the vehicle for his first spin. Symptomatically, it was again the *Los Angeles Times*, rather than an architectural magazine, that provided the coverage. "Gehry's Artful House Offends, Baffles, Angers His Neighbors," blared the headline. The author describes the building as "shocking," "like no house ever seen before," and quotes the neighbors' account of it as "offensive," "anti-social," a "monstrosity," a "prison," a "dirty thing to do in somebody else's front yard," while at the same time declaring it a "strange, exciting, thought provoking building of highly sophisticated beauty" that would be "sure to attract national attention."[11] Little that he knew! This pattern is repeated in article after article. Descriptions of apparently shocking violations of traditional norms give way to praise and celebration. What is celebrated in the end is the shock.

Most of this shock seems to stem from the unconventional use of materials: the corrugated steel, the plywood, and particularly the chain-link fencing. Even Gehry says he dislikes the latter: "I hate chain-link too. People were always ruining my buildings by putting it up."[12] It is as if he wanted to ruin the old house, to offend it.

What really offends is not simply the artistic use of unconventional materials, but the ongoing presence of the original house, trapped as if it were inside a foreign body. Far from being removed, or simply assaulted, the house is being tortured in public. That it remains on display is what aroused the anger of those who lived in similar houses. They felt themselves under attack. Their reaction was intense. There were protests and hecklers from the neighborhood, phone calls and letters to the mayor and to the newspapers; a lawyer down the street tried to sue Gehry; an architect tried to get the building department to put him in jail; Paul Lubowicki, a recent graduate working with Gehry on the project, says the neighbors used to shout at him;[13] an architecture critic would walk his dog on the lawn; and on two occasions, someone fired a bullet through a window.[14] Neighborhood war.

Gehry is no stranger to violence. Or at least he wants us to believe that he is tough, reminding us that he used to be a truck driver, that he worked out through middle age as a boxer

and even earned a belt in full-contact karate.[15] More recently, he took up ice hockey, "rough ice-hockey, on a team he organized himself, with his two sons and some ex-college hot shots thirty or forty years younger than he is."[16] Then there are the stories of his friendship with some Mafia guys and the prank he once played with them on Peter Eisenman.[17] And when told that a Basque sculptor, Jorge Oteiza, was so upset about the Guggenheim Museum Bilbao that "he threatened physical violence against the architect," Gehry responded, "I could relate to that. I feel sort of the same way when I. M. Pei builds something in Los Angeles."[18]

Le Corbusier boxing with his cousin Pierre Jeanneret.

The architect as street fighter. Gehry had role models. Le Corbusier made the boxer the paradigmatic inhabitant of his interiors (modern man as sportsman and fighter), and he appeared in an early photograph boxing with his partner and cousin Pierre Jeanneret on the beach. The boxer exemplifies the image of the avant-garde artist as a provocateur, brutally reconfiguring everyday life.

Gehry's house is intended as an aggression. As he used to say, "it's tough." Its architecture is calculated to produce the desire for a counterattack. The neighbors' shock and anger, designed and taken advantage of by Gehry the fighter, are institutionalized by the critics and transplanted into architectural discourse. The house is presented by even some of the most knowledgeable historians as subversive and anti-architecture, as if these critics of Modern architecture were suburban neighbors astounded by the renovation of a modest house on a corner in Santa Monica. Gehry celebrates: "I wish we had sold popcorn," he says in reference to the continuous stream of visitors.[19]

Striptease House

> It was just a dumb little house with charm and I became interested in trying to make it more important. I became fascinated with creating a shell around it…[that would] define the house by only showing parts of the old house in an edited fashion.… I was trying to build a lot of ideas and when I got caught in the game of the old house, it became serious. I began to engage the house in a dialogue by cutting away from it, exposing some parts and covering up others.[20]

More than anything else, Gehry wants us to see his house as a sex act, a striptease. His most insistent descriptions of what he was trying to do with this house involve voyeurism. He even declares, "I am a voyeur. I like to see what other people do."[21] When asked, "Is anything falling apart?" Gehry answers:

> Oh you think I do falling aparts. It is an act. Do you know where I learned that? You know those vaudeville acts where the guy pulls the string and his clothes all fall off? I used to go to a lot of dirty vaudeville shows when I was a kid in Canada.[22]

Others also see it this way, as if following his lead. Stanley Tigerman speaks of the house as "undressing, as seeing through a building."[23] David Gebhard expresses "embarrassment" at the sight of "its inner workings."[24] Tim Vreeland describes how he had tried to "stay away from the house for as long as I could," as if resisting some lurid temptation.[25] Barbara Goldstein speaks of the "half-built" house as if it were a half-dressed woman Gehry was in love with.[26] And Sharon Lee Ryder (in an article aptly titled "Brutally Frank") says, "It is the quintessential house in drag, appearing to be what it is not, while at the same time being all the things it pretends not to be: a conventional house dressed up in the clothing of another genre."[27] Even the neighbors, its first audience, see the house as an offensive act: "It is a dirty thing to do in somebody else's front yard."[28]

Reviews are dominated by the sexualized metaphor of stripping, littered with phrases such as "undressing," "naked," "exposure," "peeking," "hard shell—soft core," "SM house," "view of raw building," "perversity," "disturbing kind of satisfaction," and so on. But the sexual act they describe is carefully choreographed. It is precise and controlled. The original structure is "tenderly undressed," in Gehry's own words. One critic expresses amazement that Gehry's wife "willingly" allowed the old house to be "stripped then swathed in tin clothes."[29] Exposed, then partially, more seductively, concealed. Simultaneously revealing and concealing, the architectural act is at once more attractive and more provocative. No wonder it aroused so much.

Cozy House

Do we really need to know, as every critic is fond of repeating, that Gehry has married twice, that he has two daughters from the first marriage, two sons from the second, that he loves his beautiful Panamanian-born wife, Berta Isabel Aguilera? When asked about his house, Gehry always responds with folksy domestic stories, starting with the discovery by his wife of an old, little house:

Kitchen, Gehry Residence, after 1977–78 renovation.

Diamonstein: Can you tell us what your intentions were there?
Gehry: It had to do with my wife. She found this nice house—and I love my wife—this cute little house with antiques in it. Very sweet little things.[30]

My wife went out and bought it. She said "come see it" and I said "aw, go ahead." Of course she knew I'd do some-thing to it.[31]

Everything continues in this way, from the "dumb little house" to "my little addition," which is also described in a folksy way, as in a fairy tale or a folk song:

My wife, Berta, found this beautiful … anonymous little house, and I decided to remodel it, and … since it was my own building … explore ideas I'd had about the materials I used here: corrugated metal and plywood, chain link. …. And, I was interested in making the old house appear intact inside the new house, so that from the outside, you would be aware always that the old house was still there.[32]

While generations of historians have dug into Le Corbusier's archives to find the smallest clues about his enigmatic relationship with his wife, Yvonne Gallis, Gehry leaves it all hanging out. We can even make out what he eats. In photographs, the glass doors of his kitchen cabinets, which are an extension of an old bay window, prominently display ordinary packaged food, as if to insist on the ordinariness of the house's inhabitants: Lipton Cup-a-Soup, Morton salt, Ronzoni spaghetti, Glad bags, Ala mashed potatoes, Kikkoman soy sauce, Manischewitz matzos, Crisco shortening, Folger's instant coffee, Taster's Choice decaffeinated coffee, Bertoli olive oil, and so on.

Le Corbusier, Villa Stein–de Monzie (1926–27), Garches, France.

A photograph of Le Corbusier's Villa Stein–de Monzie (1926–27) shows an open-mouthed fish, an electric fan, a pottery jug, and a metal oil jar arranged on the kitchen counter as in an avant-garde still life, like those painted by Le Corbusier. Photographs of the Eames House (1945–49) show it filled with what the designers called "functioning decoration": kachina dolls, shells, baskets, blankets, buttons, pebbles, driftwood, Japanese wooden combs, English pillboxes, Mexican masks, Chinese kites, Indian fabrics, and so on. And Gehry displays through the glass doors of his kitchen cabinets the everyday products of American food culture. Unlike Le Corbusier and Ray and Charles Eames, he has the objects arranged with no regard to classical artistic compositional guidelines. It may have some relation to Pop—Gehry has expressed his admiration for Andy Warhol's *Campbell's Soup Can* series—but it is not high art and it is not beautiful. It is a declaration of ordinariness, as if to say, "I am the all-American middle-class boy with the all-American split family and we eat all-American food." The wooden grid employed in both the kitchen cabinets and the glass wall that opens onto the backyard suggests that, for Gehry, cabinets and wall are both understood as windows framing key views.

Other photographs of the house demonstrate a similarly self-conscious casualness. It is easy to imagine people living there, even though they do not appear in the photographs. No avant-garde lifestyle here. The breakfast table is set as though awaiting the family, each plate a different color. The backyard, with its toy dump trucks, looks as though it was recently abandoned after an active play session. The vegetables on the counter look as if they have just been pulled out from the refrigerator. Two half-empty glasses of water sit there, as if the children have just run out. The mobile storage units are left ajar. A lived-in house with a little messiness.

Master bedroom, Gehry Residence, after 1977–78 renovation.

There is a systematic effort to present an image of normal domestic life within an abnormal house. The strident polemical

Charles and Ray Eames's Eames House (1945–49), Pacific Palisades, California, under construction.

exterior gives way to an easygoing interior. Gehry insists that the house is very "comfortable." In photographs of the house—the home of a famous furniture designer—there is no designer furniture in sight. Everything, aside from an isolated cardboard chair that may have just been put there for the photo, is distinctly ordinary: flower-patterned couches, decorated bedspreads, ornamental houseplants. Familiar comforts. The coziness serves to make the radical qualities of the house even more dramatic. And again, critics follow Gehry's lead:

> It has another unexpected quality—once you are inside, it is very pleasant.... This house jerry-built in appearance, straining to stay together, turns out to be, of all things, cozy. And thus it goes back to the basic task of building—to provide shelter from the storm. [33]

As the same stories are repeated again and again in different interviews and articles, it is as if time was not passing, as if Gehry's children were not growing, as if life was not moving. For years and years, we kept hearing about Gehry's two "young sons," a narrative that only changed when the house was renovated in 1991–92, when all of a sudden we started hearing about two adolescents. Change in the project produces change in the story, a new version of the same cozy domestic scene.

The generation of historians brought up on TV, with its endless display of the private realm in public, digs into the archives to find traces of the personal, carefully hidden by the architect, and previous generations of critics. The TV generation of architects provides their own script. But isn't this another form of hiding?

Construction-Site House

> I am interested in finishing work but I am interested in the work not appearing finished, with every hair in place, every piece of furniture in its spot ready for photographs.... I prefer the sketch quality, the tentativeness, the messiness if you will, the appearance of in-progress rather than the presumption of total resolution and finality. [34]

Time and again, Gehry insists that he likes the look of unfinished buildings, that they are "more poetic," "fresh": "Most frame buildings look great under construction, but when they are covered they look like hell." [35] And critics have echoed this theory, describing his house as a "well-stocked lumberyard

Ludwig Mies van der Rohe, standing in front of his Farnsworth House (1946), Plano, Illinois, under construction.

viewed from a telescope"[36] or a "perpetual construction site,"[37] and the architect as a "one-man demolition crew."[38]

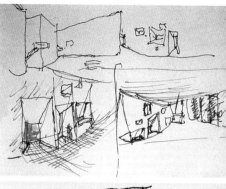

Buildings under construction have fascinated many architects. Le Corbusier's first manifesto of Modern architecture was the naked structure of the Maison Domino design prototype. Ludwig Mies van der Rohe photographed himself in front of the frame of his Farnsworth House (1946–50) while it was under construction. And the Eameses hopped on top of the frame of their house as soon as it was up. The structure as photo opportunity—as in those photographs of the Empire State Building showing workers hanging dangerously from the unfinished structure. But there are no photographs of the Gehry house under construction. For Gehry, this is not simply a stage of the project: the finished building is a construction site.

Le Corbusier continued to sketch his buildings again and again, even long after they were built. The process was more important than the final product. The sketch was the vehicle for the continuing life of the project. For Gehry, the house itself is a sketch. In fact, it is many sketches; the house, he says, is "a sketchbook for future projects."[39] Therefore it has to look unfinished, like a sketch: "I never think of the drawing as a finished product—they are a process to get to an idea."[40]

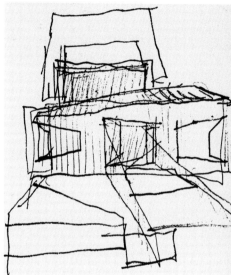

top: Le Corbusier, sketch for the chapel Notre-Dame-du-Haut (1950–53), Ronchamp, France. *bottom:* Sketch of Gehry Residence for 1977–78 renovation.

Sketching is combat mode, creative mode, Gehry fighting against his demons. When Gehry draws, he says, "it's almost like I'm grinding into the paper, trying to find the building."[41] But Gehry the fighter is also defensive Gehry. As long as the building is not finished, he is not accountable. The project cannot be criticized. The exposed inner structure is his armor.

Casual House

The perpetually unfinished condition of the house resonates with the unfinished condition of its materials. The chain-link fencing, the plywood, the corrugated steel, the asphalt—all are simply appropriated as found, none finished. The only finish is the house's cheap look. As Gehry tells *People* magazine, the house looks like "something that arrived in a packing crate that's been only partly torn away."[42] He presents himself as a "cheapscape" architect, offering various rationalizations for his use of cheap materials. Some critics pick up his arguments about the vernacular of California parking lots. Others hear his point about the

Living area, Gehry Residence, after 1977–78 renovation.

"jerry-built" structures of American do-it-yourself style. Then there are his references to the materials of children's playgrounds, the "throw-away and temporary" informality of the Los Angeles landscape, the poorness of his early clients and of himself, the social value of an affordable architecture, and so on.

But this cheap and casual look are carefully controlled: "My buildings look as if they are just thrown together. We work very hard to achieve this."[43] And it extends beyond the house to Gehry's own look. He wears chinos and open-collar shirts, the studied look of the "cheapscape" architect. But this look also protects him from attack. Modest, casual, informal, temporary, childlike, poor are hard to criticize. Informality is both weapon and defense.

Art House

From the beginning, the house has been presented as an artwork, a painting or a sculpture — as when Gehry complains that living in his house is "like living in your own painting,"[44] or when he says casually, "I had a funny notion that you could make architecture that you would bump into before you would realize it was architecture,"[45] a reference, in fact, to Barnett Newman's comment that sculpture is what you bump into when you back up to look at painting.

Repeatedly, Gehry drops the names of his artist friends, colleagues, collaborators, role models, and clients. The list has become enormous. Critics have added other names, so that now the whole history of avant-garde art — from Europe in the early twentieth century to southern California at the end of the century — has become involved.

Gordon Matta-Clark, *Splitting: Four Corners* (1974), Englewood, New Jersey.

For Gehry, artists are first of all role models because of the enviable control they have over their work. He traces specific qualities of his house to the influence of specific artists or movements: "If you look at the corner window you'll notice that one of the glass surfaces protrudes, unframed, beyond the corner. What I was trying to do there was to create a movement, almost like a Duchamp 'Nude Descending the Staircase.'"[46] "The wireglass in the skylights, which was not required by the building code, was intentionally used to portray a layer of lines that would relate to the diagonals of the chain-link so that it's almost like a Brice Marden layered drawing where a similar kind of depth is created with line work."[47]

"I guess I was interested in the unfinished — or the quality that you find in paintings by Jackson Pollock, for instance, or de Kooning, or Cézanne, that look like the paint was just applied."[48] With yet another list of artists, he points to their influence on the house without specifying exactly what influenced what.[49] But it is not just that artists affected the details of the house. The very idea that a utilitarian object could be transformed into an artwork was itself an idea that came from a particular set of artists: "I wanted to prove you could make an artwork out of anything. This is being done, of course, in sculpture, and I find myself influenced by artists such as Rauschenberg, Serra, Carl Andre, Donald Judd, Heizer."[50]

The critics of the house also have their lists of relevant artists and movements. The roll call includes Carl Andre, Chuck Arnoldi, Larry Bell, Billy Al Bengston, John Cage, Christo, Ron Davis, Louis Danziger, Giorgio de Chirico, Michael Heizer, Robert Irwin, Jasper Johns, Donald Judd, Ellsworth Kelly, René Magritte, Kazimir Malevich, Ed Moses, Bruce Nauman, Claes Oldenburg, Eric Orr, Kenneth Price, Robert Rauschenberg, Simon Rodia, Ed Ruscha, Kurt Schwitters, Richard Serra, David Smith, Frank Stella, Jacob van Ruisdael, Edouard Vuillard, Andy Warhol, Cubism, Dada, Constructivism, Expressionism, Futurism, Neoplasticism, Action Painting, Abstract Expressionism, Minimalism, Conceptual art, Process art, California environmental art, Pop, and so on.

Michael Graves, Benacerraf House (1969), Princeton, New Jersey.

Faced with such a pantheon of artists, one is left wondering, where is Gordon Matta-Clark, whose stripping, cutting, and exposure of the timber frame of an old house is perhaps the most obvious reference point in Gehry's house?[51] And before that, where does Michael Graves's Benacerraf House (1969) — a radically Modern addition to a traditional house in a traditional neighborhood in Princeton where the new elements slide out of the old — fit in all of this?[52]

Very rarely do Gehry or his critics refer to the influence of other architects. Indeed, artists seem to release him from the influence of architects. Gehry says, "Art gives you a sense of freedom. There were rigid rules in architecture and there don't need to be. Architects should be able to free associate."[53] Once again, the house is relieved of the usual scrutiny by architectural critics. It's off the hook.

Museum House

Many of the houses that Gehry has built have been for his artist friends, the domestic house becoming an art gallery and a reflection of its inhabitants' artistic philosophy. In this, Gehry's houses follow the tradition of Le Corbusier's domestic designs of the 1920s, where the house

was often also a studio and a gallery. Likewise, Gehry's own house is treated as an art gallery, a kind of museum of domestic life. Like Le Corbusier, Gehry describes it in terms of a promenade, a succession of events:

> *From the entrance gate onwards, entry is intended as a procession. As you walk up the stairs and enter the door you turn towards the cedar trees and in the evening the sun backlights them — a powerful image.... Once through the entrance door you are confronted by the entrance door of the old house — so that you really know that you are going in.... Throughout the house we left portions of cornices, moldings and frames: old windows became paintings on the wall in an exposed frame wall — all sculptural ideas for leaving parts of the old house as references.*[54]

The house is turned into a sequence of images, a trajectory encompassing paintings that might have been made by different artists. (The list of artists Gehry cites as inspiration starts to makes sense.) Gehry suggests that this became his way of thinking about architecture in general: "After I did my house I tried to see every event in a piece of architecture as a painting: the corner window, the front window, the kitchen window."[55]

The theme had already been studied by Le Corbusier. In his Villa Le Lac (1923–25), built for his parents on the shores of Lake Geneva, a "window" cut into a garden wall frames a view of the lake. The outside, the garden surrounded by a wall, is treated as an inside, and the landscape beyond becomes a painting on the wall, as though in a living room. For Le Corbusier, "the outside is always an inside."[56] For Gehry, on the other hand, the inside is always an outside. In his house, a twisted version of Le Corbusier's window is cut into the corrugated-metal fence, framing, from the street, a view of a huge cactus in the backyard. The window frames the cactus for the passerby, not the inhabitant. From the inside of Gehry's peek-a-boo house, multiple cuts frame fragments of the old house, foliage, the sky, the moon — but not the surrounding neighborhood. Inside, it is not possible to see the street from the above-eye-level windows.

If Le Corbusier's idea of the house as a place for a promenade was the idea of the house as a stage set for an imaginary film, Gehry's house is a stage set for an ongoing soap opera: the neighbors soap opera, the family soap opera, the architectural-world soap opera. As if to reinforce that sense, from the back of the house you see the theatrical props: the fencing wall held by diagonal bracing, the cactus propped up. From the street, these tricks are not visible. The cuts provide glimpses not only of the cactus and of architectural fragments, but of what is going on inside, the domestic life of the house's inhabitants, the ongoing soap opera.

The house as a sequential display of artworks becomes a gallery of Gehry and his life:

> It was to be like a sculptural gallery. I intended to walk around the house and each opening, each event, in the house would be something different and I would explore a different idea. What didn't work is that the ideas all look as though they came from the same person, from the same aesthetic. You can't do it unless you copy someone else's style.[57]

Gehry's house ends up being a museum of Gehry himself.

Drama House

> Sitting in the dining-room and looking toward the window of the old house is very surreal.... The feeling is of being outside the old house on the driveway—which is heightened by the asphalt paved floor. So there you are sitting on a driveway, having dinner, looking back at the old house...when somebody walks through the old house and you see them through the window from the dining room area or from the bay window in the kitchen, it's as if you're in a theatre, and there are people on stage.[58]

Philip Johnson said of Gehry's house that he liked the "sense of confusion in the dining room. I asked myself when I was there: 'Am I in the dining room or in the driveway?'"[59] Johnson was, in fact, replaying what Frank Lloyd Wright reportedly asked him on his visit to Johnson's Glass House (1949) when, according to Johnson, he "strode in and said, 'Philip, should I take off my hat or leave it on? Am I indoors or am I out?'"[60] It was a big compliment, then. It had the effect of positioning Gehry's house in a grand lineage of masters stretching back through Mies to Wright. In fact, Johnson even said on another occasion, "It is my house thirty years later."[61]

This lineage of architects struggling with the relationship between inside and outside goes back to Adolf Loos's experiments conducted in the early decades of the twentieth century in Vienna in which he examined the idea of the house as a theater of domestic life. If Loos was reacting to the emergent metropolis, Gehry was responding to the uniquely deterritorialized condition of Los Angeles. "The only important thing about my house is the neighborhood it's in,"[62] Gehry said early on. But, in fact, the house turns its back on that neighborhood. All of the house's windows, Gehry insists, are "above eye level" from the inside,

> [to] force your attention away from the street and give a sense of privacy from the street while maintaining a lot of openness to the trees and the sky. Inside it's very light and

airy and private, yet from the outside you can see into the house much more than into any of its neighboring houses. [63]

If Loos's houses turn their backs to the street to protect their intimacy and Mies's glass houses exhibit themselves to the public, Gehry's house simultaneously defends itself against the neighborhood and puts its intimacy on display. As Gehry notes, it is easier to look inside his house from the street than into any of the neighbors' houses. But at the same time, he blocks the view of the neighborhood from the inside of the house. From the windows of Gehry's double house, one can see fragments of the sky, or of trees, or of the interior of the other house (the interior of the interior). The house closes itself up to the street by doubling itself through a series of angled skins—or are they jabs?—and this opens up a distance, a protective gap, as if the house were defending itself from an attack while at the same time opening itself up to public view.

Gehry talks about how, when becoming "acquainted" with his future neighborhood, he became aware of the "body language of the neighbors' houses":

> *Window blinds are always closed to the street and for the most part, these pseudo-cute little structures which suggest humanity say "stay out; leave me alone."... I wanted to expose the beautiful specimen cactus in my garden to the public view. I wanted to present it like a public sculpture. I wanted to deal with the shut-out attitude of my neighbors, to demonstrate to them that one could have windows that offer views into the private realm of the house without compromising the privacy of the house.* [64]

Gehry Residence, after 1991–92 renovation.

And yet in photographs the windows in the front of Gehry's house always have their shades closed. Like his neighbors, Gehry is closed off. The dynamic confusion of inside and outside only really happens inside. Even if people cannot look in, they are portrayed as looking in—because Gehry talks that way. We do not even notice that the blinds are drawn.

And Gehry's house closes itself off more and more with time. In recent photographs trees and plants block the view of the house. The greenery is progressively cloaking the house in shadows as busloads of architectural tourists are driven past the front door. Not by chance, Gehry started to dream about a Miesian renovation of the house as early as 1983:

> *The house is complete although I continue to fantasize about it, like removing the interior and replacing it with a Miesian box, then tearing down the outside; or finishing it in conventional terms by painting it pink and covering it up with gypsum board. There's some bite in that for me.* [65]

In 1991–92, he carried out the renovation. A new door was opened in the front facade and the back of the house was completely transformed. The jumble of rough forms gave way to a series of smooth monolithic shapes. The pulverized concrete of the backyard became a sleek white terrace leading to a lap pool. Exposed stud walls disappeared. Exposed beams were covered with wood battens. The coarse plywood panels on the exterior were replaced with smooth metal surfaces. And inside, basic plywood surfaces were replaced with exotic hardwood. Suddenly, everything was a matter of finish and coherence. Gehry even complained that he did not have enough money to do a better job. Cheap, rough, informal, disjointed was no longer the name of the game. Once everybody had adjusted to the original provocation he did the only thing that could still provoke by embedding Miesian clarity and precision within the very symbol of California "cheapscape." Or perhaps this second renovation simply reflected new tendencies in Gehry's work.

Gehry Residence, after 1977–78 renovation.

The renovation was reported in the *New York Times*, but most critics act as if it never happened.[66] The original house lives on in everybody's imagination—where it lived from the very beginning.

Play House

Gehry's best friend when he was growing up, he says, was his maternal grandmother, who used to get down on the floor with him to build houses and cities out of wood scraps from his grandfather's hardware store: "That's what I remembered, years later, when I was struggling to find out what I wanted to do in life. It made me think about architecture. It also gave the idea that an adult could play."[67] Gehry describes his working method as child's play, more like the work of artists and scientists than the work of architects:

> When the artists and sculptors I know work, there's a sort of free play idea. You try things; you experiment. It is kind of naïve and childish, it's like kids in a playpen. Scientists work that way too.... It's kind of throwing things out and then following the ideas, rather than predicting where you're going to go.[68]

Not surprisingly, critics have also written about Gehry's house in terms related to play and children. The house is described either as an ideal place for children, "a timeless incarnation of all the houses that children have imagined in their dreaming and playing in attics,"[69] or as a place that appears as if it had been done by children: "It looks from the outside as though some energetic children had built it out of demolition-yard leftovers."[70]

The house seems to suggest a child's perspective. Within, a lot of the views involve looking up. Gehry's additions make parts of the old house seem to float higher. The main view from the kitchen is up at an angle. The bed is very low. The exposed structure of the ceiling becomes a major event, pulling the eyes toward it. The windows are above eye level. Which leads to another question: Are the occupants of the house, the visitors, and even the viewers of it in publications, like the critic and the architect, turned into permanent children?

And what kind of childhood would this be? In another continually repeated story, Gehry talks again about his adventures with his grandmother: "Every Thursday, we'd go to the Jewish market, we'd buy a live carp, we'd take it home … we'd put it in the bathtub and I would play with this … fish for a day … until she killed it and made gefilte fish."[71] The point is not, as Gehry suggests, that he ended up with a lifelong obsession with fish, an obsession that he would work into most of his projects. The point is that play and trauma are inseparable. The dismembering of the fish is inseparable from the intense pleasure of its shiny skin and endless movements. In the end, Gehry eats his playmate.

Couch House

He can put theory aside in order to raid his unconscious, like a refrigerator at night, for the hunches, whims and contradictions that make his best work inimitable.[72]

If most architects conceal their private life, Gehry flaunts it. The house is presented as his autobiography. From the very early coverage of the house, psychoanalysis enters the scene. Gehry repeatedly speaks about his personal problems, his separation from his first wife, Anita Snyder, his marriage to Berta, his two sons, his psychoanalyst, Milton Wexler, "a well-known shrink to the stars,"[73] whom he started seeing in the mid-1960s at the time of his separation from Anita. He even tells us what the psychoanalyst advised him in terms of his architecture: "Wexler hammered at me to be one thing or the other. … He'd say, 'Look, you're an artist. Just do jobs you can do. Don't try to be Skidmore, Owings & Merrill.'"[74] The shrink even makes comments to the press about Gehry (isn't this stuff supposed to be confidential?) and advances interpretations about his work, claiming that "the key to Gehry's work" is that "he has all the traits that a child has — loneliness, impulsiveness, playfulness, fighting the world"[75] — thus feeding one of the most insistent interpretations of Gehry.

The fact that Wexler is Jungian activates some of the critics, as when a skeptical journalist describes the house a "manifestation of nonlinear logic, visual symbolism and the Jungian collective unconscious. … They did this sort of thing some 65 years ago in Zurich and called it Dada."[76] A more sympathetic critic writes:

Through his preoccupation with the insides of a house, Gehry has discovered something about the inner mind, and in stripping away old shingles and plaster he also laid bare part of his soul, and part of ours as well.[77]

Even Gehry's sister, Doreen Nelson, joins in, interpreting the house in terms of family history:

Here's this flat sheet of metal outside and Frank saying: "I've parted it for you so you can come in." And what's inside is our grandparents' house in Toronto on Beverly Street, with the dark stairway leading up to the bedrooms. When Frank bought that pink house, he did a transformation not only on the house but on himself. He put all this stuff around it to present himself as a new person, but an old new person who's still connected to where he came from and who he was.[78]

The house is a form of therapy for Gehry, who treats himself as the patient. When an interviewer asks him how he managed to get free of the traditional constraints of architecture, he claims that it was the absence of an outside client and the enabling presence of his wife that allowed the process to go forward: "I didn't have a client to tell me no. I had my wife, who pushed me forward when I felt like chickening out."[79] He presents himself as simultaneously soft and tough: "In my life, I was always the quiet, nice guy, the pussycat, the 'Aw, shucks,' guy. The reality is I'm an angry s.o.b., pushy, ambitious like everyone else."[80] The house puts the anger on the outside and the pussycat inside. Gehry even explains his choice of materials in psychoanalytic terms. Of chain link, he says, "People used it in great quantities, and yet the denial syndrome was great.... Somehow there's the idea that if it is inevitable it's OK, but if it's a conscious or intentional use of the material, it's somehow threatening."[81]

Only much later, in 1997, did Gehry start thinking of himself as the shrink and the client as the patient. As he told Kurt Foster, "I am a good shrink. I listen."[82] In the same year, his design process was described in the *New Yorker* as "an intense sort of listening that involves paying attention not only to specific requests but to body language, facial expressions, unfinished thoughts, and other indicators. Having thus uncovered needs and desires that the client might not even have been aware of, Gehry starts making drawings."[83]

But what would it be to turn psychoanalysis toward the house itself? What would one make, for example, of the doubling of inside/outside? To look out through the windows of the old house only to see another inside is to delay the encounter with the outside. Perhaps the house is primarily a form of resistance. The house permanently under construction is another form of delay, delay of final critical response (another form of encounter with the outside).

Gehry is not finished and therefore cannot be criticized. He is protecting himself. The insistence that his architecture is developed without a critical apparatus can also be seen as an effort to keep critics at bay. Gehry offers us his biography instead of theory. But he is speaking for his building when he speaks for himself. The house built him. The house is him.

In Conclusion

These were ten of Gehry's stories, ten of his threads, but there are numerous others. So many lures for the critics.

Why does he spend so much time spinning these theories? Why is he so much the architect of critical reaction to the house? Why has his private space been made into the object of thirty years of public, even global, speculation? In controlling the reaction to his house, he is designing himself in architecture.

Before the house, Gehry was, as he is fond of saying, "in the service business,"[84] doing shopping malls for developers and other nondescript buildings for institutional clients, "straight stuff," as it has been called to differentiate it from his more experimental designs for private clients.[85] And then there was the house, the project that he built for himself and that in turn "built" him.

What the house really is, then, is the launching pad of a career. Like many of his contemporaries, and almost all of the twentieth century's most prominent architects, Gehry made it with a house. It is the house that builds the architect, not the other way around. It constructs the figure. Gehry is cannily aware of this: "The little jewel—a one family house—can be a powerful instrument for ideas, and [to] get attention."[86]

Notes

I am grateful to Jeannie Kim for her research assistance and suggestive insights.

1. Gehry, quoted in Carol Burns, "The Gehry Phenomenon," in Burns and K. Michael Hays, eds., *Thinking the Present: Recent American Architecture* (New York: Princeton Architectural Press, 1990), p. 76.
2. Gehry, commentary in *The Architecture of Frank Gehry*, exh. cat. (Minneapolis: Walker Art Center; New York: Rizzoli, 1986), p. 34.
3. John Dreyfuss, "Gehry: The Architect as Artist," *Los Angeles Times*, Nov. 7, 1979, part IV, p. 8.
4. Johnson, quoted in "Building of the Quarter: The Gehry House, Per Voco," *Archetype*, no. 2 (spring 1979), p. 23.
5. Riley, quoted in Calvin Tomkins, "The Maverick," *New Yorker*, July 7, 1997, p. 43.
6. Charles Jencks, "Frank Gehry—The Deconstructionist," *Art and Design* 4, no. 4 (May 1985), p. 14: "Just call me Daniel Boone, Frank Gehry said to me after I had called him that and everything else I thought appropriate: the Industrial Adhocist, the father of the Botched Joint, the son of Bruce Goff, the Noble Savage of Santa Monica, the Leonardo of Galvanised Sheet-Metal, the Malevich of Lighting and Rodchenko of the Non-Sequitur, . . . the Charlie Chaplin of Chain Link, the Over-

Psychoanalysed Jewish Master Builder, the Zen Priest of the Unfinished Finish, the Martin Escher of Reverse Perspective and Impossible Space, the first Deconstructionist Architect and so on.... The problem with Frank...is that many labels work. He is almost unclassifiable."

7. Tomkins, "The Maverick," p. 43.

8. Gehry, quoted in William Ted Georgis, "Interview: Frank Gehry," *Archetype*, no. 2 (spring 1979), p. 10.

9. Gehry, quoted in Rosemarie Haag Bletter, "Frank Gehry's Spatial Reconstructions," in *The Architecture of Frank Gehry*, p. 47.

10. Art Seidenbaum, "Opening Our Eyes to Buildings," *Los Angeles Times*, Dec. 28, 1977, pp. 1–2.

11. John Dreyfuss, "Gehry's Artful House Offends, Baffles, Angers His Neighbors," *Los Angeles Times*, July 23, 1978, part VIII, pp. 1, 24–25.

12. Gehry, quoted in Sarah Booth Conroy, "The Remodeled American Dream, East and West," *Washington Post*, May 25, 1980, p. D2.

13. See ibid.

14. See Barbaralee Diamonstein, "Frank O. Gehry" (interview), in Diamonstein, ed., *American Architecture Now* (New York: Rizzoli, 1980), p. 44; and Tomkins, "The Maverick," p. 42

15. See Thomas S. Hines, "Heavy Metal: The Education of F.O.G," in *The Architecture of Frank Gehry*, p. 13.

16. Tomkins, "The Maverick," p. 40.

17. See Charles Jencks, "Frank Gehry—The Deconstructionist," pp. 15–16, where Gehry is quoted: "So when Peter [Eisenman] came to LA for a visit I took him to an Italian restaurant where I know real mafioso—who owe me some favours. After dinner I arrange for Clarkie to sit down next to Peter and put in the knife: 'I hear you been messing around wit my friend Frangough. The boys don't like suckers who fink on their buddies, understand? I'm afraid you gotta lose more than one finger Mr. Egg-head.'"

18. Gehry, quoted in Tomkins, "The Maverick," p. 39.

19. Gehry, quoted in Michael Webb, "A Man Who Made Architecture an Art of the Unexpected," *Smithsonian* 8, no. 4 (April 1987), p. 54.

20. Frank Gehry, "Suburban Changes: Architect's House Santa Monica 1978," *International Architect* 1, no. 2 (1979), p. 34.

21. Gehry, quoted in Georgis, "Interview: Frank Gehry," p. 11.

22. Ibid., p. 10.

23. Tigerman, quoted in "Building of the Quarter," p. 24.

24. Gebhard, quoted in ibid., p. 25.

25. Vreeland, quoted in ibid.

26. Barbara Goldstein, "In California un Oggetto Architettonico," *Domus*, no. 599 (Oct. 1979), p. 9.

27. Sharon Lee Ryder, "Brutally Frank," *Residential Interiors*, Nov./Dec. 1979, p. 58.

28. Dreyfuss, "Gehry's Artful House Offends," p. 1.

29. Suzanne Stephens, "Out of the Rage for Order: Frank Gehry's House," *Progressive Architecture* 61, no. 3 (March 1980), p. 83.

30. Diamonstein, "Frank O. Gehry," p. 43.

31. Gehry, quoted in Conroy, "The Remodeled American Dream, East and West," p. D1.

32. Gehry, quoted in Bletter, "Frank Gehry's Spatial Reconstructions," p. 32.

33. Thomas Hine, "A Careless Design — Carefully Done," *Philadelphia Inquirer*, Jan. 13, 1980, p. 2K.

34. Gehry, quoted in Dreyfuss, "Gehry's Artful House Offends," p. 24.

35. Gehry, commentary in *The Architecture of Frank Gehry*, p. 56.

36. Wolf von Eckardt, "The Good, the Bad and the Tricky," *Los Angeles Times*, July 18, 1980, part V, p. 17.

37. Ross Miller, "The Master of Mud Pies" (conversation with Frank Gehry), *Interview* 20, no. 1 (Jan. 1990), p. 46.

38. Jane Holtz Kay, "Deconstructivist Architecture," *Nation*, Oct. 17, 1988, p. 360.

39. Gehry, quoted in Webb, "A Man Who Made Architecture an Art of the Unexpected," p. 54.

40. Gehry, quoted in "'No, I'm an Architect.' Frank Gehry and Peter Arnell: A Conversation," in Peter Arnell and Ted Bickford, eds., *Frank Gehry: Buildings and Projects* (New York: Rizzoli, 1985), p. xv.

41. Ibid.

42. Gehry, quoted in Sally Koris, "Renegade Frank Gehry Has Torn Up His House — and the Book of Architecture," *People*, March 5, 1979, p. 78.

43. Gehry, quoted in Hine, "A Careless Design — Carefully Done," p. 1K.

44. Gehry, quoted in Jayne Merkel, "It's Just a Colonial Turned Outside-In," *Cincinnati Inquirer*, Aug. 3, 1980, p. E8.

45. Gehry, quoted in Diamonstein, "Frank O. Gehry," p. 46.

46. Gehry, "Suburban Changes," p. 45.

47. Ibid., p. 42.

48. Gehry, quoted in Diamonstein, "Frank O. Gehry," p. 36.

49. For example, see Gehry, quoted in Kay Mills, "Prefab Aesthetics: Making Beauty Out of Junk Is Frank Gehry's Mission," *Los Angeles Times*, Jan. 18, 1981, part V, p. 2: "I think the real turning point in my work, my thoughts, is my interest in Southern California artists"; and Gehry, commentary in Friedman, *Gehry Talks*, p. 57: "The influences were from Joseph Cornell to Ed Moses to Bob Rauschenberg."

50. Gehry, "Suburban Changes," p. 34.

51. Only once, much later (in 1986), did Gehry mention Matta-Clark — not in relation to his Santa Monica house but to the unrealized renovation, Carriage House (1978), for Christophe de Menil in New York; see Gehry, commentary in *The Architecture of Frank Gehry*, p. 57: "Since I worked on it, the building [Carriage House] has been changed by Doug Wheeler and other artists; it was an interesting continuum. It fits my idea, which was to have the late Gordon Matta-Clark do the demolition and then work against it. I would have loved that."

52. Graves's project had an enormous impact on artists during the 1970s. Dan Graham, for example, says, "It influenced all of us. It influenced Matta-Clark and it influenced me and it may have influenced Frank Gehry." Graham, interview with the author, Feb. 2000.

53. Gehry, quoted in Mills, "Prefab Aesthetics," p. 2.

54. Gehry, "Suburban Changes," pp. 34 and 40.

55. Gehry, quoted in Miller, "The Master of Mud Pies," p. 48.

56. Le Corbusier, *Precisions* (Cambridge, Mass.: MIT Press, 1991), p. 64.

57. Gehry, quoted in Mills, "Prefab Aesthetics," p. 2.

58. Gehry, "Suburban Changes," p. 46.

59. Johnson, quoted in "Building of the Quarter," p. 23.

60. Philip Johnson, *Writings* (New York: Oxford University Press, 1979), p. 193.

61. Johnson, quoted in "Building of the Quarter," p. 24.

62. Gehry, "Suburban Changes," p. 34.

63. Ibid., p. 45.

64. Gehry, commentary in Friedman, *Gehry Talks*, pp. 38–39.

65. Gehry, quoted in Celant, "Reflections on Frank Gehry," in Arnell and Bickford, *Frank Gehry*, p. 10.

66. Herbert Muschamp, "The Gehry House: A Brash Landmark Grows Up," *New York Times*, Oct. 7, 1993, pp. C1 and C6.

67. Gehry, quoted in Tomkins, "The Maverick," p. 41.

68. Gehry, quoted in Diamonstein, "Frank O. Gehry," pp. 41–42.

69. Pastier, "Of Art, Self-Revelation and Iconoclasm," *AIA Journal* (May 1980), p. 172.

70. Conroy, "The Remodeled American Dream, East and West," p. D1.

71. Gehry, quoted in Hines, "Heavy Metal," p. 13.

72. Joseph Morgenstern, "The Gehry Style," *New York Times Magazine*, May 16, 1982, p. 48.

73. Gehry, quoted in Cathleen McGuigan, "A Maverick Master," *Newsweek*, June 17, 1991, p. 56.

74. Ibid.

75. Wexler, quoted in ibid.

76. Von Eckardt, "The Good, the Bad and the Tricky," p. 17.

77. Pastier, "Of Art, Self-Revelation and Iconoclasm," p. 172.

78. Nelson, quoted in Morgenstern, "The Gehry Style," p. 60.

79. Gehry, quoted in Miller, "The Master of Mud Pies," p. 48.

80. Gehry, quoted in McGuigan, "A Maverick Master," p. 56.

81. Gehry, commentary in *The Architecture of Frank Gehry*, p. 50.

82. Gehry, quoted in Cristina Bechtler, ed., *Frank O. Gehry/Kurt W. Forster* (Ostfildern-Ruit: Cantz, 1999), p. 83.

83. Tomkins, "The Maverick," p. 41.

84. Gehry, quoted in Georgis, "Interview: Frank Gehry," p. 10.

85. Stephens, "Out of the Rage for Order," p. 80.

86. Gehry, quoted in Webb, "A Man Who Made Architecture an Art of the Unexpected," p. 51.

Frankly Urban: Gehry from Billboards to Bilbao

Jean-Louis Cohen

Some wish to see Frank Gehry's great buildings as the expression of architecture as object, a contemptuous, at times violent response to the surrounding urban environment, essentially unconcerned about contextual coherence — perhaps even deliberately pitted against the city. And often this judgment is supported by the way in which the buildings are photographed and reproduced. Gehry notes, "When people photograph my buildings, they usually crop the context."[1]

The hypothesis proposed in these pages is precisely the opposite. The urban dimension has continually been part of the thought process behind Gehry's main projects since the end of the 1970s, although its role is quite often disguised. Almost none of his projects can be analyzed without considering their relationship to the urban space around them or reflecting on the question of cities in general. Like the often-noted rapport between Gehry's architecture and art, the reference to the urban is inherent to his designs. While it is particularly apparent in projects that incorporate several buildings, the reference is also obvious in many of his singular objects, in which formal decisions stem neither from purely internal concerns nor from an inattentiveness to the space surrounding them.

Learning from Los Angeles

Since the 1990s, Gehry has been considered an architect of international importance and has been asked to respond to the most varied situations, yet for a long time he was presented as an architect who was inextricably linked to the conditions of southern California. When Reyner Banham published Gehry's Danziger Studio and Residence (1964–65) in *Los Angeles: The Architecture of Four Ecologies* in 1971, the architect was inscribed within the tradition of radical Los Angeles Modernism. (Banham considered the project a critique of "commercial stuccoed cubes.")[2] In the interventions Gehry made to his own house in Santa Monica in 1977–78, he embodied *nolens volens*, a tenet of Postmodernism. The scale

Schnabel Residence (1986–89), Brentwood, California.

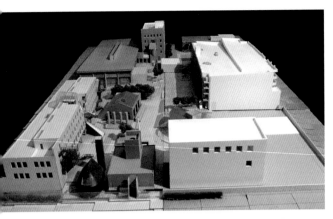

Site model, Loyola Law School (1978–), Los Angeles.

and textures of this project, and those of other houses and studios he designed in Venice, California, a few years later, shattered certain conventions cherished by Los Angeles domestic architecture.[3] His use of corrugated metal, chain-link fencing, and unfinished plywood in these projects exposed the prosaic materials with which the city is made—echoing, Gehry has often noted, the work of Joseph Cornell and Robert Rauschenberg.

The attention he paid in these projects not only to the materials, dimensions, and scale of the city he had lived in for thirty years, but also to his impalpable surroundings and emotions, was one of the first perceptible manifestations of his attempt to harness the resources of urban culture. Subsequent Los Angeles endeavors—which contain the seeds of projects developed in other cities—saw Gehry adopt three distinct strategies in pursuit of this goal.

The first of these strategies was to distort conventional or prosaic architectural types, which became subject to a process of decomposition. Gehry clearly applied this strategy in his house designs, which challenge common and comforting forms, juxtaposing them with prismatic, geometrically skewed volumes. In the Loyola Law School (1978–) in Los Angeles and in his unrealized design for the Screen Actors Guild (1981) in Studio City, Gehry tackled the low, horizontal building form known as the bar. In the case of the guild, elements were incised into the bar, which became a kind of frontal theater with large, dramatic windows opening onto the city. With the Loyola campus, on the other hand, extraneous elements were added to the predominant form. Gehry created a design that would protect against intrusion while providing a rich configuration of common space. His plan therefore offered more of "a visual opening to the outside" than a true openness to the urban environment.

Design process model, Screen Actors Guild (1981, unbuilt).

The second strategy concerned the placement of buildings and their dominant elements with regard to public space. It is clear from certain of Gehry's projects that he has internalized the principles of picturesque composition, but others, such as the Edgemar Development (1984–88) in Santa Monica or the Chiat Day Building (1985–91) in Venice, were based on another principle: the tangential—not frontal—view of buildings from the street. In these projects, the most important signs are placed in accordance with how they would be seen by someone driving past in a car. The sign Gehry designed for the parking lot of Santa Monica Place (1972–80), for example, shows him humorously adopting the scale and visual codes of the advertising billboard. The ironic presence of the buildings in which he assumes this strategy points to a subtle focus on urban rhythms. Each of the buildings creates its own context, with certain repeating or more subdued elements forming a background against which the figures that define the image of the program stand.

The third strategy Gehry pursued in his Los Angeles projects was an attempt to overturn the terms of the relationship between building and city. Here the architectural entity aimed to be a summary of the city, as if to echo Leon Battista Alberti's suggestion in *De re aedificatoria* (first published in 1485) that the house be a small town and the town a small house. Loyola represents the formulation of this principle in a public endeavor, but there are also domestic examples, specifically the houses in which rooms are isolated and stand in space

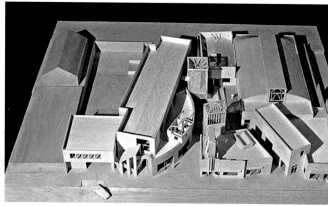

top: Final design model, Edgemar Development (1984–88), Santa Monica, California. Model courtesy Abby Sher.
bottom: Design process model, Tract House (1982, unbuilt).

like farms in a village. Explored in the House for a Film Maker (1981) in Santa Monica, the unrealized Tract House (1982), and again in the Winton Guest House (1983–87) in Wayzata, Minnesota, this principle was most fully realized in Los Angeles, at the Schnabel Residence in Brentwood (1986–89), a site that is both fragmented and centralized.

These three strategies are not embodied solely in Los Angeles projects, but they were deployed first in that metropolis, in which the very notion of the city is continually questioned and redefined. Gehry's thoughts on Los Angeles and on the form of the many cities in which he works are constantly shaped by his discovery and consideration of extremely contradictory scenes.

Gehry's Cities

Gehry is a pure product of the North American cities that have provided him with vivid personal experiences. He grew up in Toronto, which was and is similar to the largest North American metropolises that he subsequently discovered. But ever since he was young, Chicago has been especially significant to him. He assigned it "a special meaning," he says, "because I went there with my father," adding that he found it "fun to walk there." He states that "the body language of the city is more in the spirit of Paris" than in that of other American cities, and claims that what makes it "probably the best American city" is its successful relationship to Lake Michigan.[4] In the city's dense architectural landscape, Gehry is particularly interested in the buildings with unique features, like the Chicago Tribune Tower (1923–25) by Raymond Hood and John Mead Howells, the various buildings by Mies van der Rohe, and Bertrand Goldberg's Marina City (1959–64).

Bertrand Goldberg, Marina City
(1959–64), Chicago.

That other major North American metropolis, New York, has featured in Gehry's thoughts for more than twenty years, from his unrealized Carriage House (1978) renovation to his competition proposal, in collaboration with David Childs, for the New York Times Headquarters (2000). Gehry notes that what has made Manhattan such a remarkable urban setting is, most notably, its "zoning envelope relating to the steps"—the 1916 zoning laws that encouraged buildings to rise in ziggurat-like steps. He believes that "the setbacks have made an interesting city; they look good now." In this landscape whose "geometry is tight with towers and spires"—a "powerful context" described so well by the photographs of Berenice Abbott—the approach, he says, should be "keeping the discipline of the grid and disciplining it." The scale of the interventions is crucial: "Playing trivially with little interventions that don't count" is not the solution.

Design process model, New York Times Headquarters
(2000, unbuilt).

For Gehry, New York is as much a plastic system as it is a challenge of scale. Like his 1998 design for the Guggenheim Museum New York, which in some sense is implemented against the wall of buildings that would form a backdrop to the museum when viewed from across the East River, his New York Times project plays off the vertical landscape. The plastic distortions of the tower's curtain wall are the vehicle for this dialogue, both at street level, where the envelope covers the most public elements of the program, and at the top, where the facade unfurls like a fluttering flag, a fluid response to the crystalline geometry of the neighboring skyscrapers.[5]

Gehry's relationship to European cities is more complex. He discovered the urban landscape there at the beginning of the 1960s and became "enamored with Paris and the ends of the buildings with the chimney pots [that] reveal the different periods of history." This sedimentary scene inspired invention, precisely "because it was not perfect, you could integrate the interventions of Modernism." But Paris, because of its historicity and material density, is also a city that in some ways intimidates Gehry, as can be seen in the unusual attention he paid to evoking its urban fabric in his choice of light yellow stone and zinc for the exterior of his American Center (1988–94) there. Adopting typically Parisian textures, he used them in a way that broke from the quiet, if not dull, geometry of the city, successfully setting an essentially static material like stone into motion. Unfortunately, Parisian patrons have since had reservations about commissioning the architect, and so, while Gehry has been relatively reticent in Paris, Parisians have also remained amazingly reluctant to use him.

Berenice Abbott, *Wall Street Showing East River from Roof of Irving Trust Building*, 1938.

From Planning to Urban Design

The months Gehry spent in the city planning program at the Graduate School of Design at Harvard University in the 1950s played a decisive role in his education — not so much because of the program itself (which, under the direction of Reginald Isaacs, centered on government policy, whereas Gehry had enrolled in the program to attend Josep Lluís Sert's studios), but because of the range of issues he discovered there. Irritated by the exceedingly political aspects of the program in urban planning, Gehry was more interested in other classes, such as those offered by the Viennese historian Eduard Sekler. After Harvard, he saw Paris as more than an urban landscape; he also saw it as a place where architecture was practiced differently. While working as a designer with André Remondet in 1960 — Remondet had succeeded Auguste Perret as the head of one of the main studios at the École des Beaux-Arts in Paris — Gehry worked on the plan for Vélizy-Villacoublay, a new residential neighborhood to the southwest of Paris.

Paul Almsasy, view of Paris rooftops from the series *Les toits de Paris*, ca. 1950s.

Through Mark Biass, a Frenchman he met at Harvard, Gehry discovered the *Encyclopédie de l'Urbanisme* by Robert Auzelle and Ivan Jankovic and its methodical classification of historical and contemporary urban forms.[6] The book contains comparative plates, in the tradition of German treatises from the beginning of the twentieth century, and for Gehry, this collection of places, streets, and neighborhoods drawn to scale came to serve as a kind of mental catalogue of references essential to mastering the dimensions of elements in urban projects. Another important contact in Paris was Anatole Kopp, to whom Gehry was introduced by Herman Gutman, a fellow architect at Victor Gruen Associates in Los Angeles, where Gehry worked as an urban designer intermittently from 1954 to 1960. Having studied at the École Spéciale d'Architecture in Paris and then at the Massachusetts Institute of Technology (MIT), Kopp—a communist who supported the Algerian resistance—had devoted his pioneering research to Russian Constructivism, and he introduced Gehry to the social dimension of European urban planning.

While the training that Gehry received at Harvard and in Paris was, ultimately, disappointing, the experience he received at Victor Gruen Associates was rewarding. Gehry has stressed Gruen's diverse talents, and considers him "a businessman with design appreciation." Of the projects Gehry worked on at Gruen's office, he emphasizes the importance of Midtown Plaza in Rochester, New York, which opened in 1962, for its mixed-use program (a departure from the single-use developments encouraged by zoning laws in place at the time).[7] Despite the complexity of some of the firm's projects—which included, but were far from limited to, the first major shopping malls—Gehry has expressed, in hindsight, his "frustration of not being able to do city planning, except with Ed Loake from the Urban Development Corporation [a Gruen client], in the mould of Robert Moses." Yet his work at Gruen allowed him to better understand his own capabilities; Gehry asserts that he "found out what I did best, to make shapes, to understand how to use that in the service of function, uses without being trivialized." The Gruen firm was a kind of apprenticeship to reality, leading him to "accepting uses for uses," both on the community and city level.

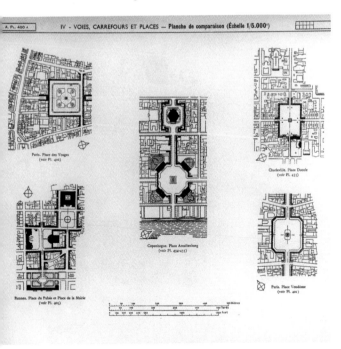

Comparative plans of urban squares from *Encyclopédie de l'Urbanisme*.

Establishing his own firm in 1962, Gehry took on numerous commercial projects over the next fifteen years, many of which were at a good-sized urban scale, including the Recreation Center (1972–73) in Cochiti Lake, New Mexico, and the projects he completed for the Rouse Company in various cities. With the decay of public-housing programs in Los Angeles (a rarity in the city in the first place), the work undertaken by the firm mostly involved office complexes and stores, which do not offer much scope for utopian thought.[8] Gehry found this professional situation dissatisfying, since his interests in urban planning continued to "derive from his political positions," which are fundamentally liberal. From the time that he began to consider "architecture as social responsibility," it was logical

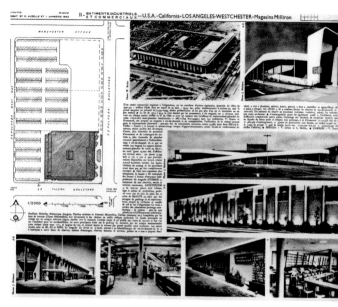

Victor Gruen Associates, Milliron Store, Westchester, Los Angeles, 1949.

that he "would rather be doing city planning and social housing" than large private residences or even cultural institutions. The absolute impossibility of bringing together an ideal, socially useful practice with the reality of his commissions drove Gehry to find a relationship with the city within the very conception of his projects.

Sitte Planning

Undoubtedly, the overinvestment of urban-planning strategies in Gehry's designs and discourse compensates for the absence of planning commissions in his practice. To use the concepts of Sigmund Freud, displacement and condensation are at play in certain of Gehry's designs, in which the relationship to the city is simultaneously concrete and imaginary. The major buildings that Gehry designed in the 1990s are not simply "urban pieces," fundamental to the revitalization of existing cities, but also configurations that interact with the most complex urban processes.

The process that led Gehry and Thomas Krens, Director of the Solomon R. Guggenheim Foundation to suggest the present site for the Guggenheim Museum Bilbao (1991–97) instead of the one originally proposed is telling. As soon as the project became the symbol of and the springboard for the renaissance of the Basque capital, it became essential to draw conclusions from its principal function: to lay a cornerstone for the transformation of the urban river valley. But implanting it in the expanded space of the valley involved considering the set of relationships between the building and the site. Gehry noted that everything happened as if "first [building] Notre-Dame and then Île de la Cité." In order to create this new

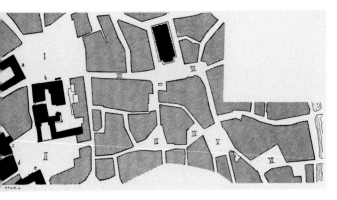

Camillo Sitte, plan of public squares in Bruges, Belgium.

island, an element of the new center, the Bilbao project developed on a different scale of building placement strategies, similar to those used for the much smaller Edgemar Development or for the Vitra International Manufacturing Facility and Design Museum (1987–89) in Weil am Rhein, Germany.

Edgemar and Vitra are, in fact, opposite versions of the same paradigm. In both cases, Gehry invested a site whose original components were fairly simple with new meaning: a lot in Santa Monica and a still-rural suburb of Basel. The strategy adopted for Edgemar was based on the play of empty space and the definition of outdoor pedestrian streets; Vitra was based on the play of solids and on covered hallways inside the Design Museum's galleries. The striking constructions of the two projects catch one's attention from a distance. The glass prisms and the fencing in Edgemar are vertical reference points, reminiscent of the urban landscapes of medieval Tuscan towns like San Gimignano and their play of tower and courtyard. Looking at Edgemar's superstructures from Santa Monica's Main Street, visitors are drawn into a maze of spaces that lead them to the heart of the complex. Vitra is distinguished by its collision of metal roofs and white walls, which form a spectacular contrast to the green of the surrounding fields. This dynamic—an echo of Rudolf Steiner's Goetheanum II (1924–28) in Dornach, Switzerland, and Le Corbusier's chapel Notre-Dame-du-Haut (1950–55) in Ronchamp, France, both of which are situated fairly close to Weil am Rhein—also bears the stamp of the Cubo-Futurist compositions created by Liubov Popova and Alexander Vesnin between 1915 and 1922, which were presented in *The Avant-Garde in Russia, 1910–1930: New Perspectives*, an exhibition of Russian Constructivism at the Los Angeles County Museum of Art in 1980 for which Gehry designed the installation.[9]

Above all, the play on pathways, the close and distant perspectives, and the contrast between singular elements and background in these projects directly and openly draw on Gehry's profound knowledge of Camillo Sitte's book *City Planning According to Artistic Principles*, a new edition of which was published in the United States in 1965.[10] Gehry does not, of course, agree with all the aesthetic positions taken by Sitte in this book, but he does share the Viennese architect's critical position concerning the monotony of many modern cities. In Edgemar's winding pathways and in the gallery system of Vitra, an often-abandoned urban sensuality takes shape.

In this way, Gehry was able to introduce at an urban level the attention he devotes to vision and the movement of the body at the building level. Relatively simpler designs by Gehry, such as the New York Times Headquarters, serve as monumental markers, as thresholds, or as urban centerpieces. The definition of singular points such as these, which allow us to comprehend depth or height and understand pathways, rests on anticipating the perception of inhabitants or visitors. This involves making the relationship between the components of the building, and moreover between the built space and its users, one that becomes increasingly complex and dense over time as building and people engage in a kind of process of shared growth. For Gehry, as Charles Darwin noted in relation to the natural world, "the way we grow is interaction."

Stata's Strata

Several sites raise the question of the relationship between the whole, calibrated to the scale of the city, and the part, shaped around smaller functional components. This relationship seems, in some cases, to be guided by the principle of unity in diversity, when an eruption of discrete volumes is lent a unifying external approach. In other cases, it involves more of a unified diversity, when a superior structure frames the play of individual elements. This hierarchical figure, which Gehry used for the first time in his unbuilt Screen Actors Guild, appears again in the Ray and Maria Stata Center (1998–) at MIT. Here the dominant structure is no longer a bar, but rather a bar with a vertical construction at either end, like a landscape framed by cliffs. Sheltered by this enveloping form, smaller volumes are fitted to the base of the building, which forms an open stage onto the campus.

Site model, Ray and Maria Stata Center (1998–), MIT, Cambridge, Massachusetts.

The Ray and Maria Stata Center also underscores a principle of differentiation, of vertical stratification through which Gehry redefined, in his own way, the familiar three-part division between base, middle, and top. The base of the building is part of the campus; on the inside, it allows technical circulation and the paths of researchers to be linked with MIT's resources, while on the outside it is accessible to students. Superficially, it could be understood as an arbitrary configuration, but in fact it urbanizes the center, allowing it to be rooted by its base to many of the institution's systems.

The echoes and tensions between the whole and its parts in Gehry's buildings stem from very varied tactics, involving either materials or empty space (as in the Edgemar and Vitra projects), or the very places where the parts are connected — that is, the junctures. It was the confidence that Gehry's firm gained in defining junctures between a building's framework and its facade that allowed them to go from the experimental sequences they conducted in the studio to construction. Without this control over the technological processes, the

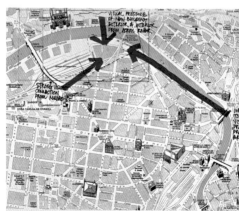

Map of Bilbao, with Gehry's handwritten notes, July 7, 1991.

flexibility and vigor of the models they produce as part of the design process would be lost at the construction site. The tactile jubilation with which Gehry takes interest in, say, the elasticity and compression ratio of corrugated cardboard when working on a model—or of strips of wood when working on furniture—is thus amplified in his buildings to an urban scale.

While the internal connections of Gehry's buildings are defined by their junctures, their links to exterior space rest on a different kind of elastic adjustment: the manipulation of empty space. Key to this adjustment is the definition of visual axes in the form of sight lines bordered by buildings, since Gehry's architecture inevitably restructures existing space by its presence. Asked to produce a new overall plan for MIT, he followed a city-planning approach that eventually created the context for the Stata Center.

Gehry applied different principles to attain unity in diversity in the three office buildings of Der Neue Zollhof (1994–99), constructed along the Rhine River in Düsseldorf. The buildings are clad in three different materials; unity is obtained here not through continuity of material, but through a continuity of plastic form (which distinguishes Gehry's structures from the orthogonal prisms of the surrounding buildings) and through the repetition of an identical window. The relationship between the city and the river is enhanced by the views framed by the buildings, which concentrate the relationship like an optical lens.[11]

Der Neue Zollhof (1994–99), Düsseldorf.

Elsewhere, Gehry has been able to bring together his overall vision of a site with the approach of other architects. The pleasure he takes in dialogue, in interaction with other architects, is illustrated by his suggestion that other architects contribute to the Vitra complex in Weil am Rhein, leading to projects being commissioned to Zaha Hadid and Alvaro Siza, among others. Gehry's well-known generosity is also evident in his collaborations with other architects, such as Rem Koolhaas and Jean Nouvel for various recent proposals.

The urban character that comes from the neighborly relationships his buildings have with their architectural context can be found in other, smaller European projects. Gehry readily adds that he "wouldn't have done those buildings in Los Angeles."[12]

Mimetic Games in Prague and Berlin

In a certain way, Gehry has captured the spirit of big cities in such projects as Vitra, which — while responding to specific situations — encapsulate themes that recur in his work. A common theme in his designs of the 1990s is the tower. Twisted and distorted, the tower — a fetish of modern urban planning — has undergone mutations in Gehry's hands. This nomadic element is key to the Guggenheim Museum Bilbao and it also appears in the Guggenheim New York on an entirely different scale.

The twisted tower is given a very different treatment at the Nationale-Nederlanden Building (1992–96) in Prague. Divided in two (this bipartite structure and the "swing" of its twist earned the building its nickname, "Fred and Ginger," in honor of Fred Astaire and Ginger Rogers), it acts as a juncture that links the nearby riverbank, bridge, and square. The playful lines of the facade overlooking the river — along which stand several of the best buildings from the Prague Secession — echo, in Gehry's words, "nineteenth-century texture and its finesse." Indeed, they recreate, in a single building, the undulation produced by

Nationale-Nederlanden Building (1992–96), Prague.

the staggered windows and roofs of the adjacent buildings. In this way, not only does the building encapsulate Secessionist or eclectic themes in specific parts such as its dome, but Czech Baroque shapes also emerge in its overall form.

Whereas in Prague the focus on local conditions includes an homage to plastic lyricism, in Gehry's DG Bank Building (1995–2001) at Pariser Platz in Berlin it involves the monotony of the urban landscape. Here "playing by the rules" implied accepting the principles of neighboring buildings — something that should not be confused with imitation. Gehry stresses the impression he received when he visited Erich Mendelsohn's Einstein Tower (1921) in Potsdam: the tower's "beautiful silhouette," he says, is part of a "beautiful sequence and there is context in that sequence, which you only can understand as in context." In discussing the DG Bank Building, Gehry states:

> I obey the golden rule. I think that the big issue is to be a good neighbor. That means that you respect what's around you and its context. It's again the Mendelsohn lesson, that you relate to it, that you bring something to it that wasn't there but is part of it. I have tried to do that here in relationship with the Brandenburg Gate, which is large, stony; it has a certain toughness and a certain character, and I made the facade on Pariser Platz of a character that would not detract or would not trivialize the Brandenburg Gate.[13]

This approach—which Gehry now says "applies to any place" and "might be conservative"—can be understood as a kind of self-criticism with regard to the iconoclastic character of the 1977–78 renovation of the Gehry House in Santa Monica house. It involves "somehow getting the sense of the place and respecting it, not being disrespectful"; a building should not "ignore the communal language that has been created." If we acknowledge, Gehry says, that "the city [has] a language invested by the inhabitants, as an Ausländer, a visitor, you have to understand it." With the Santa Monica house, he continues, "I knew they wouldn't like it, and I did it with a touch of anger, like many great artists." However, "when you're getting into a city, you play within the rules," and in Berlin, Gehry says, "I feel good that I have respected the rules and made a contribution they didn't expect." By accepting principles of height limitation and the supremacy of solids over empty space—restraints imposed on the new Berlin by the head of urban planning in the City Senate, Hans Stimmann—designing the DG Bank Building involved "making the new with urban features people like."

At the root of this urban courteousness, Gehry refers to the old adage "do unto others as you would have done unto you," also citing the children's rhyme "step on a crack, break your mother's back." More than humility in relation to context, this involves acknowledging a "Stadtgeist," a unique spirit that belongs to each city and that is made more of prosaic scenes than of monumental effects. For Gehry, "everything is a sculptural composition," and "in the city, with its chaos," he finds "banal scenes that are beautiful."

Back in Los Angeles for a "Repair Job"

An extraordinary accumulation of prosaic architecture, Los Angeles is a constant point of return for Gehry, a counterpoint to his endeavors in European cities. The similarity Gehry bears to many artists from southern California—like Ed Ruscha, an attentive observer of the textures and types of Los Angeles—is well known, and he has attempted on numerous occasions to manipulate references to the city's vernacular. One of his strangest designs is, without a doubt, Festival Disney (1988–93), a retail and entertainment center that is an extension of Disneyland Paris. Festival Disney does not imitate American urban space, as does Disneyland's Main Street; rather, it proposes a play on its materials and signs, the full effect of which can only be appreciated at night, when the scattered elements come together and are integrated by the illusion of an archway made of hundreds of little lights. In comparison to the contemporaneous American Center, in which Gehry embraced the conditions of Parisian space, Festival Disney acts as a European bridgehead of Los Angeles popular culture.[14]

As an advisor to the selection committee that chose Richard Meier to design the Getty Center for the J. Paul Getty Trust, Gehry proposed bringing the complex right down to the intersection of the San Diego Freeway and Sunset Boulevard, which is dominated by the cylinder of a Holiday Inn. In fact, he suggested creating a genuinely urban campus, based on a new combination of elements in the existing landscape. This proposition would not have resolved all the problems stemming from the choice of Brentwood as the center's site, but it would have enhanced its difficult link to the rest of the metropolis.

Gehry's relationship with Los Angeles has been crystallizing since 1987, when he first designed the Walt Disney Concert Hall.[16] The project was marked by a financial crisis when bids from contractors far exceeded the building's budget, but this eventually had a positive effect on the practice of Gehry's firm since it triggered the complete integration of the CATIA software system into the conception and construction of their buildings. The project went through complex changes, shaped by two intersecting factors: the first involved research relating to better acoustics for the hall, based on precedents like Hans Scharoun's Berlin Philharmonic Hall (1956–63), and the second was strictly urban in nature.

Site with competition model, Walt Disney Concert Hall (1987–), Los Angeles.

Situated on the edge of downtown Los Angeles, where the block system is interrupted by the Hollywood Freeway, the concert hall is adjacent to the existing Music Center. Gehry acknowledges that he should have attempted "to put together some of the disparate, horrible buildings" — that is, proceed with "a repair job." To integrate the various buildings in the center, Gehry suggested "a garden, which the city doesn't have, used for events." His proposal involved completely modifying the Music Center through a series of operations: "Cutting the [Dorothy] Chandler [Pavilion] and the [Mark] Taper [Forum] so that they are reproportioned, cutting the Ahmanson [Theatre]; integrating Disney Hall and MoCA [Museum of Contemporary Art]; extending Grand Avenue with a terrace, a gateway to the cultural district."

But disregarding the imposed limits was out of the question. It was therefore necessary for Gehry to play with the adjacent buildings, even if it meant restraining himself: "I took the curve of the Chandler and broke down the scale of Disney Hall so as not to disrupt the iconic preeminence of Chandler. I didn't want to because of a social commitment that goes back to the 1960s. I tried to make it better by what I did." This kind of process might be considered formal manipulation, but Gehry compares it to what he considers the "risk taking" of physicists who, for example, "still don't understand the forces of turbulence." For him, it's a similar adventure to introduce a new object in an urban space, at the risk of "looking stupid."

Without contempt and without subordinating himself to existing scales and textures, Gehry's relationship to cities goes more by way of experiment. It is based on the observation of what he calls the specific "body language" of each city. Only when it is grasped, sometimes intuitively, does the city's architecture find its place in Gehry's vision. As much as in their qualities of interiority, it is in the quasi-carnal vibration of the air separating his buildings from the cities enveloping them that his urban sensibility lies.

Translated from the French by Molly Stevens.

Notes

1. Frank Gehry, conversation with Kurt W. Forster, in *Frank Gehry, Kurt W. Forster: Art and Architecture in Discussion* (Ostfildern-Ruit: Cantz, 1999), p. 88.
2. Reyner Banham, *Los Angeles: The Architecture of Four Ecologies* (Harmondsworth: Penguin Books, 1971), p. 199.
3. In 1981, I emphasized the similarity between the Gehry Residence and the Eames House (1945–49) in Pacific Palisades, California, in terms of their relationship to the technologies of their respective eras. See Jean-Louis Cohen, "Charles Eames, Frank O. Gehry: La maison manifeste," *Architecture, mouvement, continuité*, no. 54–55 (June–Sept. 1981), pp. 77–85.
4. Frank Gehry, conversation with the author, Santa Monica, August 16 and 25, 2000. All following quotes, unless otherwise noted, are from this interview.
5. The design echoes certain elements of Gehry's 1991 project for the headquarters of the Los Angeles Rapid Transit District.
6. Robert Auzelle and Ivan Jankovic, *Encyclopédie de l'Urbanisme* (Paris: Vincent & Fréal, 1952–68).
7. See *Victor Gruen Associates: Architecture, Planning, Engineering* (Los Angeles: Victor Gruen Associates, 1966), unpaginated.
8. The best general survey of this early work can be found in the first comprehensive book on Gehry's work: Peter Arnell, Ted Bickford, and Germano Celant, *Frank Gehry: Buildings and Projects* (New York: Rizzoli, 1985).
9. San Gimignano, Steiner, and Le Corbusier are referred to in Mildred Friedman, ed., *Architecture + Process: Gehry Talks* (New York: Rizzoli, 1999), pp. 60; 97.
10. Camillo Sitte, *City Planning According to Artistic Principles*, trans. Christiane Crasemann Collins and George Collins (New York: Random House, 1965); reprinted in Christiane Crasemann Collins and George Collins, *Camillo Sitte: The Birth of Modern City Planning* (New York: Rizzoli, 1986). The first American translation was published in 1945, fifty-six years after the original German edition was published.
11. Thomas Rempen, *Frank O. Gehry: Der neue Zollhof* (Bottrop: Pomp, 1999).
12. Frank Gehry, in *Architecture + Process: Gehry Talks*, p. 207.
13. Frank Gehry, "Building at the Pariser Platz, Facets of a Challenge," lecture delivered at DG Bank Building, Berlin, May 31, 2000, typescript, p. 3.
14. See Jean-Louis Cohen, "Main Street Blues: Il Festival Disney di Frank O. Gehry," *Lotus*, no. 77 (June 1993), pp. 80–91.
15. See *Peter Eisenman and Frank Gehry*, exh. cat. (New York: Rizzoli, 1991).

Sites of Passage

J. Fiona Ragheb

Architecture has always represented the prototype of a work of art the reception of which is consummated by a collectivity in a state of distraction.

Walter Benjamin[1]

If every museum of our time is a child of Frank Lloyd Wright's Guggenheim,[2] then Frank Gehry's Guggenheim Museum Bilbao is a rebellious teenager. The unbridled energy of his design exhibits none of the reserve of Wright's landmark on Manhattan's Upper East Side, which acknowledges its setting by turning its back on Fifth Avenue, focusing its tightly wound spiral inward. Unruly and irrepressible, the Guggenheim Museum Bilbao (1991–97) by contrast makes the acquaintance of its neighbors in a spectacular fashion — sweeping along the riverfront, running under a bridge that crosses the Nervión River, and adapting itself as necessary to the nineteenth-century scale of its surroundings. Inextricably linked to its site, the building engages as well in a carefully choreographed dialogue with the paintings and sculptures for which it was intended — and in this lies the secret to Gehry's sensibility. For while Wright's interest in creating an "archeseum" overrode his concern for the art that would grace his building, Gehry's vocabulary is steeped in a lifelong engagement with the visual arts.

Despite Gehry's early interest in Wright's work, over the course of a nearly forty-year career he has developed an iconoclastic vocabulary as different from that of Wright as his early buildings, such as the Steeves Residence (1958–59) in the Los Angeles neighborhood of Bel Air, were similar. One of Gehry's very first commissions, the Steeves Residence — completed the same year Wright died and the year his Guggenheim was finally finished — reveals a debt to Wright in its low-slung profile, cruciform plan, and spatial relationships. By the next decade, however, Gehry had begun to experiment with not only the unusual materials that would become a hallmark of his aesthetic, but with the Modernist grid that he would eventually jettison completely — resonating with Wright's own longstanding ambition to destroy the architectural box in favor of a more organic and plastic expression. His interest in the work of Wright and in Japanese aesthetics and construction methods ceded to an aesthetic rooted in the vernacular and the expressive potential of unorthodox materials. The spare vocabulary and uniform scale of his earliest projects were gradually supplanted by a complex layering of

Guggenheim Museum Bilbao (1991–97).

Steeves Residence (1958–59), Bel Air.

forms and materials marked by a sense of the unfinished. Projects in California such as the O'Neill Hay Barn (1968) in San Juan Capistrano and the Davis Studio and Residence (1968–72) in Malibu reveal a nascent interest in investigating the conditions of perspective that underlie visual representation. Fittingly, the Davis Studio and Residence was designed for painter Ron Davis, whose own interest in perspective was explored in shaped canvases that distorted the convention of painting as a window on the world. Echoed in Gehry's design, this exploration was manifested in a gently skewed box that distorts visual conditions while at the same time acknowledging its site among the Santa Monica Mountains.

Gehry's perspective as an architect was informed by his early studies in the arts at the University of Southern California, which he eventually abandoned in favor of architecture, although he has continued to move readily between the two worlds. "Rather than be influenced only by dead artists, as many of my colleagues tend to be," Gehry has said, "I have always felt that living artists are working on the same issues I am."[3] Many of these artists could be counted among the architect's close friends; residing in southern California, Gehry befriended Chuck Arnoldi, Larry Bell, Robert Irwin, Ed Moses, and many other artists of his generation. His work with Davis would prove to be but one of the earliest of many projects designed for artists, in collaboration with artists, or for the presentation of the visual and performing arts. His earliest work in this vein was a studio and residence in 1964–65 for noted graphic designer Lou Danziger in Los Angeles, while his most recent projects include a performing-arts center for Bard College in Annandale-on-Hudson, New York, begun in 1997, and a 1998 proposal for a new Guggenheim facility to be located on the Lower Manhattan waterfront. In between, he has worked in an atmosphere steeped in the arts — collaborating with both visual and performing artists, creating exhibition installations, and designing or renovating numerous museums.

The design for the Davis Studio and Residence was significant in launching a move from an orthogonal language to a perspectival one. The spatial exploration of what is a perceptual condition resulted in a physical object that does not behave according to the laws of perspective. Instead, its built form emulates and thus exacerbates the conditions of forced perspective — the building doesn't merely seem to recede perceptually in space, it is actually constructed that way. By violating these laws, Gehry rejected a purely visual mode of perception. Confounding to the eye, the building cannot be understood with a quick glimpse, but requires instead that the observer navigate the whole of the building's perimeter. This physical experience became increasingly important as Gehry's projects evolved into more spatially complex buildings. That the body would become the field through which his architecture is understood was alluded to by the architect himself: "I had a funny notion that you could make architecture that you would bump into before you would realize it was architecture."[4]

Clad entirely in galvanized corrugated steel, the Davis Studio and Residence occupies the landscape like a sculptural object, its mass responding to the mass of the mountains that serve as its backdrop. Given his fascination with the compelling power of one-room buildings, Gehry would ultimately come to terms with a project's scale by articulating it as a series of individual masses, as in his House for a Film Maker (1980–81) in Santa Monica. "Think of the power of one-room buildings and the fact that historically, the best buildings ever built are one-room buildings.... I chose to break [the House for a Film Maker] into separate rooms, separate objects sitting together on the site, playing off one another and exploring different materials as a way of breaking down scale."[5] As he began to pull apart the elements of a project and disperse them across a site, the interstitial spaces that resulted took on increasing prominence. This play with the in-between was strategically employed in the renovation of Gehry's own home, despite the fact that the limitations of the narrow corner lot prevented him from creating multiple elements on the site. His renovation instead created two houses — one wrapped in the other — that occupy the same space, creating a tension that results in a continual oscillation between interiority and exteriority.

Davis Studio and Residence (1968–72), Malibu.

This materialized and physical experience of architecture was coincident with a rejection of a purely visual and transcendent experience of art among artists of Gehry's generation. In the late 1960s, critical debates surrounding the "new sculpture" focused on its relationship to its audience and its surroundings. Artist Robert Morris spoke of externalizing traditional notions of composition, in order to take "relationships out of the work and [make] them a function of space, light, and the viewer's field of vision...one's awareness of oneself existing in the same space as the work is stronger than in previous work."[6] This highly contextual and phenomenologically based approach that gives equal emphasis to "space, light, and the viewer's field of vision" was echoed in Gehry's comments on the Benson Residence (1979–84) in Calabasas, California, designed for a Loyola Law School professor. Given the tight budget constraints, Gehry chose to design a pair of boxes that would utilize short spans and thus prove less expensive to build than a single, larger structure. The strength of the project, according to Gehry, would derive in good measure from external conditions, as in Minimalist sculpture: "The richness in the project would be the differentiation of these pieces and the relationship of the different forms to each other and to the spaces they would create."[7]

These ideas are refined to their ultimate sculptural expression in the Winton Guest House (1983–87) in Wayzata, Minnesota, for while creating a mise-en-scène of diverse and varied forms is easily achieved in a project with an ambitious and long-term program like the Loyola Law School (1978–) in Los Angeles, realizing a similar feat within the limited program of a guest house — a paradigm of the one-room building — is a far more difficult undertaking. Yet here Gehry parsed the guest house into the smallest possible units in order to create a

Installation view, *The Tradition of the New: Postwar Masterpieces from the Guggenheim Collection,* Solomon R. Guggenheim Museum, 1994.

sculptural arrangement to play off the main house designed by Philip Johnson in 1952. "I started thinking, well, if I made a still life, if I made a Morandi, with three bottles and two pots, three big bottles and three little bottles, in order for each piece to retain its objecthood, the thing had to have the crack, it had to have the separation, it couldn't be a continuous structure."[8] To further emphasize the individually articulated components, each was sheathed in a different material.

"In order for each piece to retain its objecthood." Gehry's emphasis on the "objecthood" of the building's components resonates strikingly with the landmark debates that framed the critical discourse on Minimalism. In his now-famous invective against Minimal Art, Michael Fried railed against the increasingly temporal experience of an object—an experience that for Fried bordered on the "theatrical" and thus had no place in the hallowed realm of Modernism.[9] Picking up on Donald Judd's discussion of what he characterized as "specific objects," Fried argued that the defeat of "objecthood" was critical if the tenets of Modernist art were to be upheld. For the theatricality that was implicit to objecthood depended on a relationship to the viewer, who had been until then wholly absented from accounts of Modernism. The acknowledgment of the viewer introduced a contingency to the mechanics of reception, one that was predicated not solely on a visual relationship, but also on a corporeal one. It is in this context that we bump into Gehry's architecture, as we negotiate the changing spaces that give form to his designs.

The unusual materials that mark these projects share much with the industrial vocabulary of Minimalism. Atypical of residential applications, however, they do more than emphasize their objecthood. In the mid-1980s, Gehry's penchant for unusual materials blossomed into a profusion of shingles and colored tiles festooning the Wosk Residence (1981–84) in Beverly Hills, and the Norton Residence (1982–84) in Venice, California, alike. This bricolage is particularly pronounced in the Norton Residence, which is located on the beach. By this time, Gehry had recognized the importance of a project's surroundings to its design: "The way I perceive urban experience is in a fragmentary form which I try to express in the combination of more or less unrelated objects, which have a fundamental but not obvious relationship."[10] Taking delight in the vernacular materials and vocabulary of the urban landscape, Gehry's buildings reflect this in additive, free-form moves that suggest accretions over time, resulting in what have been called "objects that show a process of becoming."[11] The uniquely casual flavor of Venice Beach is thus captured in a residence most famously accented with a study in the form of a lifeguard shack overlooking the beach.

Yet whereas the artists who embraced a Minimalist vocabulary and created spare forms of industrial materials did so in part to remove the gestural touch of the artist, Gehry deployed these same materials to completely opposite effect—infusing his designs with a highly individual and handwrought sense of process and an idiosyncratic approach to form. The jarring juxtaposition of disparate materials is an effect the architect purposefully cultivates: "Even though I often put as much detail work into what I do as anyone, it always appears casual. That's the edge I'm after."[12] This edge lends his projects an air of the unfinished, and it is this air that breathes life into them. Rather than creating a machine for living, Gehry has chosen to humanize the machine and "de-deify" the details. By intentionally seeking out "awkward connections—like a jazz player just off the note,"[13] his buildings privilege rawness over beauty, laying bare the fissures and voids in order to reveal the cracks in the monolithic monument that is Modernist architecture.

The Guggenheim Museum by Frank Lloyd Wright is a unique and exemplary contribution to modern architecture.... It represents the manifestation of the search for an expression of liberty, an architectural ideal, where the lyric and poetic transcend space and form.

Santiago Calatrava[14]

If it is possible to speak of a spatial realm without figural contours yet possessing powerful bodily qualities, if ambulation can unlock the complexities of a building's order beyond the outlines of the plan, then the museum in Bilbao reawakens an architecture that has lain dormant for centuries.

Kurt Forster[15]

As the artist Richard Serra has noted of Gehry, "one of his greatest achievements is to collect the history of contemporary art and with an unabashed exuberance, wit, cunning and playfulness make it his own vocabulary."[16] That history is one which is inescapably clear in the evolution of Gehry's aesthetic, for just as an entire generation of artists began to reject the notion of a hermetic, self-referential work of art in favor of one that was inseparable from its surroundings, so too did the architect's work evolve into a highly contextual practice marked by spatial intricacies.

This paradigm shift is echoed in the iconic structures of the Guggenheim in New York and Bilbao. The truism that nominates the museum as the modern cathedral was all but explicit in the 1943 letter to Wright from Hilla Rebay, Solomon R. Guggenheim's art advisor, in which she implored him to design a museum for the burgeoning collection: "I need a fighter, a lover of space, an originator, a tester and a wise man.... I want a temple of spirit, a monument!"[17] Speaking more than half a century later, Gehry expressed a radically different ideal rooted in the more earth-bound realm of his new

Frank Lloyd Wright, Solomon R. Guggenheim Museum (1956–59), New York.

343

Guggenheim Museum Bilbao.

museum's site: "To be at the bend of a working river intersected by a large bridge and connecting the urban fabric of a fairly dense city to the river's edge with a place for modern art is my idea of heaven."[18]

By contrast, Wright was not concerned with context and site to the same degree, such that he began to design the Solomon R. Guggenheim Museum before a site was identified. Writing to Rebay in December 1943, he exhorted, "I hope we can get a plot before [late January] as I am so full of ideas for our museum that I am likely to blow up or commit suicide unless I can let them out on paper."[19] The profoundly muscular quality of the resulting design is a reaction against the relentless grid of Manhattan's streets. Despite the sensitivity to the landscape that marks Wright's work, and in particular his prairie houses, his design for the museum resulted in a building that turns its shoulder on Central Park and the surrounding residential neighborhood. This undoubtedly was the result of his averred dislike of the city and his conviction that the greatest luxury architecture could provide in a crowded city was a sense of light, air, and open space. Indeed, his Guggenheim Museum is "the rare one of his buildings not depending on context, surrounding landscape, or material conditions: the ideal model that could be planted everywhere."[20] So foreign was Wright's addition to the Fifth Avenue landscape, that upon its completion it was greeted with derision as a toaster or a spaceship that had landed in Central Park.

Like Wright's Guggenheim, Gehry's earliest designs did not acknowledge their surroundings. In designing the Danziger Studio and Residence, Gehry created a sculptural composition of rectilinear volumes partly dictated by the client's request for separate spaces for living and work. Sited on a heavily trafficked strip of Melrose Avenue, the building sits quietly in what is a highly commercial and visually congested area. The blank Melrose Avenue facade stands on guard against any intrusions from the outside. Looking back on the project, Gehry observes, "I realized that neglecting a potential interface with the city was a very limiting attitude. After this project I became much less moralistic about L.A. and more interested in developing a productive relationship between my architecture and the city."[21]

Danziger Studio and Residence (1964–65), Hollywood.

Wright's delocalized Guggenheim Museum stands in isolation as a monument not only to the architect, but also to Solomon R. Guggenheim himself, for whom the museum was renamed (from the Museum of Non-Objective Painting) after his death.[22] Privileging movement over monumentality, Gehry's Guggenheim Museum Bilbao, on the other hand, engages in a synergistic dialogue with the city. Says Gehry, "Making a building that has a sense of movement appeals to

344

me, because it knits into the larger fabric of movement in the city."[23] In contrast to the seamless, self-contained exterior of Wright's monolithic structure, Gehry's museum is rife with seams, evincing a gestural quality. Like the art of his contemporaries, Gehry's building looks to its physical site for its definition, twisting and bending in order to root itself more firmly into its surroundings.

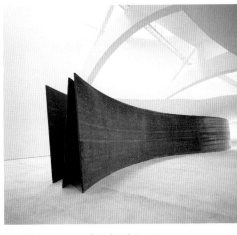

Installation view of Richard Serra's *Snake* (1994–97), Guggenheim Museum Bilbao.

The richness of Gehry's design comes from its dialogue between exteriority and interiority, solid and void, architecture and art. His rambunctious design engages in a flirtatious pas de deux with Jeff Koons's *Puppy* (1992/97), a monumental topiary sculpture positioned just outside its front door. Approaching the museum along the Calle de Iparraguirre, its cascading forms seem to slip their moorings and spill out across the site, embracing *Puppy*. All at once, the museum is transformed into a shimmering backdrop for the eager mutt, creating an oscillation between foreground and background that enriches the experience of the building in relation to the viewer and to its site. Gehry's sensitivity to the urban environment is translated to the interior, resulting in a building that successfully negotiates interior and exterior conditions simultaneously. With galleries that are variously configured as challenging spaces for the creation and presentation of contemporary art and as more conventional rectilinear volumes for easel painting, the interior is transformed into a profoundly complex and shifting terrain of ever-changing venues that require that the visitor explore them in order to fully understand their complexity. In this scheme, the atrium serves as a point of orientation from which museumgoers come and go, creating their own narratives as they travel through the building's galleries. In this, the museum recalls Gehry's vision for the renovation of his Santa Monica home some twenty years earlier: "I intended to walk around the house and each opening, each event, in the house would be something different and I would explore a different idea."[24] Founded upon an ambulatory and embodied observer, the museum echoes the city as a milieu of visual and spatial inquiry: "This was an opportunity to make something in the tradition of the great metaphorical cities. And that's what led to what's there, using the ramps and the stairs as a kind of metaphorical city — a metropolis."[25]

A fundamental symbol of the modern metropolis predominates Wright's interior of his Fifth Avenue landmark as well. If the episodic spaces of Gehry's museum are founded upon the corporeal experience of a mobile observer, which Serra has characterized as combining "a collision of unknown spaces with an overlay of anthropomorphism,"[26] Wright's interior is a constant, unchanging space that for Reyner Banham best exemplified the concept of route.[27] Indeed, the immediate precedent for Wright's design was his unrealized Gordon Strong Automobile Objective and Planetarium of 1924–25, which was wrapped by a massive spiral ramp along which cars could travel. Here the automobile and its driver

Interior, Guggenheim Museum Bilbao.

serves as a contemporary metaphor for the flaneur of Charles Baudelaire's nineteenth-century city, much like the detached observer who promenades along the ramps of Wright's later museum.

In striving to eliminate the "to and from, the back and forth,"[28] Wright was effectively erasing the body from the field of experience. As such, his museum replicates the structuring principles of Modern art, the prevailing history of which Rosalind Krauss has called "the modernist fetishization of sight."[29] The centripetal force of Wright's "temple of spirit" creates a monocular void, symbolized by the oculus that crowns the rotunda—the museum's defining and breathtaking central space that cannot be physically occupied. The extent to which the museum is bound to vision and experienced through sight alone is born out by the controversy surrounding Daniel Buren's contribution to the 1971 *Guggenheim International Exhibition*. The artist's *Inside (Center of Guggenheim)* sliced through the rotunda from the skylight nearly all the way to the floor and created an uproar among his fellow participants, who felt that it obstructed views of their own work. In creating a provocative installation that existed in an aggressive relationship to its environment—albeit briefly, since the piece was removed from the exhibition—Buren explicitly rejected the conventionally accepted notion that art is an autonomous entity, instead underscoring its dialectical relationship to historical conditions of artistic production and reception.

While some have argued that Wright's design compromises the aesthetic object, by extension it must then also compromise the object's transcendent authority. Significantly, then, it

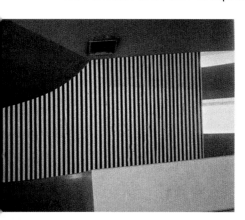

Installation view of Daniel Buren's *Inside (Center of Guggenheim)*, 1971, Solomon R. Guggenheim Museum, New York.

might be said to question the historically bounded character of the paintings for which it was originally intended.[30] Indeed, by the time the museum opened in 1959, Modernist painting had reached its apogee in the work of the Abstract Expressionists, and the direction of contemporary art was undergoing a sea change. Heralded by Wright's Guggenheim Museum, this paradigm shift reached its fullest expression in Gehry's Guggenheim, in which the experience of the architecture and the art contained therein results from an exchange between the object, the observer, and the environment. In the "expanded field" of art since the mid-twentieth century, the bold tectonics of Gehry's spaces provide an unparalleled opportunity for contemporary artists. While these landmark projects speak to the particularly mutable and resilient typology of museum architecture as it has evolved over the last several decades, they manifest profoundly different approaches that nonetheless both strike a resonating chord with the art of their time.

> *Let's frankly discard this queer antiquated little world and look with fully opened eyes at contemporary life as it rolls along, shifts, and brims over beside us.... Let's tackle the problem in all its scope. Let's organize the exterior spectacle. This is nothing more or less than creating "polychromed architecture" from scratch, taking in all the manifestations of current advertising.*
>
> Fernand Léger[31]

If the Guggenheim Museum Bilbao is a rebellious teenager, Gehry's recent Experience Music Project (EMP) (1995–2000) in Seattle is its extroverted cousin. In creating a sense of place, the museum in Bilbao drew worldwide attention to a city that had declined in tandem with the industries that had provided its economic base. But the EMP—dedicated to the history and celebration of popular music—attains spectacular new heights in this regard, unprompted by any need to be put on a map. Here, set among the remnants of the 1962 World's Fair, Gehry's building had a challenge of an altogether different sort. Competing for attention in the carnivalesque setting of Seattle Center and the Fun Forest (the amusement park just outside its entrance), the EMP had to fit in with its peers while simultaneously trying to stand out from the crowd.

A decade earlier, Gehry had designed an exhibition space devoted to the aerospace industry, which had at one time been an important part of the Los Angeles economy. His Aerospace Hall (1982–84) at the California Science Center is located in Exposition Park, which has existed in Los Angeles in some form or other for more than a hundred years and hosted

both the 1932 and 1984 Olympic Games. Built much like a stage set in front of the armory that previously housed aerospace exhibitions, Gehry's structure simultaneously masks and reveals its contents. The facade is marked by a Lockheed F-104 fighter jet seemingly caught in midflight—suggesting nothing so much as a billboard advertising a seller's wares. The exterior of the Aerospace Hall thus wears its heart on its sleeve—as if turned inside out, the building itself becomes part of the exhibition. Indeed, according to the architect, owing to a lack of financial resources, "It seemed possible that for two or three years the building itself would be the exhibit."[32]

Experience Music Project (EMP) (1995–2000), Seattle.

Aerospace Hall, California Science Center (1982–84), Los Angeles.

Like Aerospace Hall, the EMP reveals its inner secrets well before visitors walk through the front door. From the outside, its "swoopy" forms seem to hum with energy and excitement—a riot of stainless steel and painted aluminum shingles that cascade over the building's bulging and swelling forms. A monorail from the 1962 World's Fair adds to the energy level as it sweeps through the building, seeming to cause the exterior skin to flutter in its wake. Whereas a lone fighter jet accented the otherwise demur Aerospace Hall facade, the whole of the EMP's skin has been drawn into the action. Inspired by a shattered Fender Stratocaster guitar, its forms seem to have been completely absorbed and digested without any clearly identifiable trace, but for the brash coloration and the glass rooftop element that suggests the strings and frets of a guitar neck while playfully alluding to the adjacent amusement park's roller coaster. Here, the separately colored elements of the building seem to pulse and move individually to the rhythm of the music celebrated inside.

That the two projects are both sited in an exposition park or fairground is revealing. As such, they exist not primarily as structures, but as means of communication. As Umberto Eco notes, "In an exposition we show not the objects but the exposition itself. The basic ideology of an exposition is that the packaging is more important than the product."[33] With the EMP, rock and roll's subversive potential has been recuperated for consumption by the mainstream, neutralized for perpetuity in a museum, and repackaged in a building that has itself become the most arresting part of the show. What is so remarkable about the exuberance of Gehry's design is not simply that a built structure can be so utterly expressive of such abstract and personally felt content, but that in an age of instant communication the relatively slow and fixed medium of architecture can be deployed to such effect.

Flamboyant and flashy, the kaleidoscopic exterior is the ultimate expression of Gehry's ongoing interest in creating "a stronger sculptural statement of the shell"[34]—an interest that germinated in the Davis Studio and Residence of some thirty years earlier. According to Gehry, "The house I did for Ron Davis was that idea. I built the most beautiful shell I could do.... Then the user comes in and puts his junk in the shell in some way."[35] Indeed, on the inside, the EMP's exhibitionist impulses subside, revealing what is predominantly a raw, warehouselike space with exposed structural steel ready to be filled with exhibits of rock and roll memorabilia. Yet even here, the experience of the parts of the interior designed by Gehry —all contained within a public concourse that bisects the building and encompasses the ticket lobby, restaurant, museum shop, and other public amenities—is corporeally felt, for the brightly hued and highly polished metallic surfaces that animate the space prove as visually disorienting as the skewed form of the Davis Studio and Residence.

Having come around to developing a productive and synergistic relationship between his architecture and the city early in his career, by the time Gehry reached the EMP he had long since begun to reflect the cacophony of contemporary life in his sensibility. Finding the energy in his buildings' surroundings, his designs return it in undigested form, forging an inextricable relationship with the built environment and its inhabitants. That the EMP unwittingly heeds Léger's call to out-spectacle spectacle with a "'polychromed architecture'... taking in all the manifestations of current advertising" is thus no surprise in a contemporary society in which the explosion of information technology and the concomitant need for "content" has subjected entire areas of daily life to commercialization and mass consumption. What was previously unthinkable as prey for the workings of commodity culture and spectacle has now been commodified and can be voyeuristically experienced via the internet and "reality" television shows like "Survivor" and "Temptation Island."

Interior, Experience Music Project (EMP) (1995–2000), Seattle.

Few arenas have proved resistant to this dizzying spectacularization of the contemporary landscape, least of all the built environment and its mediatized representations. As much was clear from the outset of the Bilbao project, when Gehry was charged with taking his talents for place-making to new levels: "I was asked to make a building that has an international presence. Bilbao is not on the travel map for everybody, so this had to really stand out."[36] Articulating his critique of the society of spectacle in 1967, Guy Debord wrote of tourism and the elimination of geographical distance as by-products of commodity circulation and thus as symptoms of spectacle. With Bilbao, Gehry created not simply a *place*, as he had in his campus for Loyola Law School some twenty years earlier — giving an entirely new character to a one-block site in a gritty downtown neighborhood — but a *destination* in keeping with the tenor of a culture seemingly without national borders. In building exhibition and performance venues that have drawn people from all over the world at unprecedented levels, the impact of Gehry's exhibition spaces resonate with Georges Bataille's observations on the museum. Though writing in 1930 on the origins of the modern museum, his remarks are equally suited to contemporary culture. Bataille commented that museum visitors were themselves becoming the real spectacle therein, observing, "The museum is a colossal mirror in which man finally contemplates himself from all angles, finds himself literally admirable and abandons himself to the ecstasy expressed in all the art magazines."[37]

Notes

1. Walter Benjamin, "The Work of Art in the Age of Mechanical Reproduction," in *Illuminations*, Hannah Arendt, ed. (New York: Harcourt Brace Jovanovich, 1968), p. 239.

2. Paul Goldberger, "The Guggenheim Effect," *Guggenheim Magazine* 13 (fall 1999), p. 47.

3. Gehry, quoted in Coosje van Bruggen, "Leaps into the Unknown" in *The Architecture of Frank Gehry*, exh. cat. (Minneapolis: Walker Art Center, 1986), p. 124.

4. Gehry, quoted in Barbaralee Diamonstein, "Frank O. Gehry" (interview), in Diamonstein, ed., *American Architecture Now* (New York: Rizzoli, 1980), p. 46.

5. Gehry, quoted in *The Architecture of Frank Gehry*, p. 111.

6. Robert Morris, "Notes on Sculpture, Part II," *Artforum* 4, no. 2 (Oct. 1966), p. 21.

7. Gehry, quoted in *The Architecture of Frank Gehry*, p. 118.

8. "Conversation between Frank O. Gehry and Kurt W. Forster with Cristina Bechtler," in Cristina Bechtler, ed., *Frank O. Gehry/Kurt W. Forster: Art and Architecture in Discussion* (Ostfildern-Ruit: Cantz, 1999), p. 25. These thoughts are echoed in the architect's discussion of his own home, but here his interest in making something completely apart from architecture is more explicit: "I . . . changed it because it was looking too much like a village, and I really wanted the building not to look like buildings. I wanted to give them a different kind of objecthood." Gehry, quoted in Martin Filler, "Eccentric Space: Frank Gehry," *Art in America* 68, no. 6 (June 1980), p. 114.

9. Michael Fried, "Art and Objecthood," *Artforum* 5, no. 10 (June 1967), pp. 12–23.

10. Gehry, quoted in van Bruggen, "Leaps into the Unknown," p. 140

11. Joseph Giovannini, "Edges, Easy and Experimental," in *The Architecture of Frank Gehry*, p. 80.

12. Gehry, quoted in Carol Burns, "The Gehry Phenomenon," in Carol Burns and K. Michael Hays, eds., *Thinking the Present: Recent American Architecture* (New York: Princeton Architectural Press, 1990), p. 76.

13. Gehry, quoted in Mildred Friedman, "Fast Food," in *The Architecture of Frank Gehry*, p. 87.

14. Santiago Calatrava, quoted in "The Architecture World Pays Tribute to Frank Lloyd Wright's Guggenheim," *Guggenheim Magazine* 5 (spring/summer 1994), p. 5.

15. Kurt W. Forster, "Architectural Choreography," in Francesco Dal Co and Kurt W. Forster, *Frank O. Gehry: The Complete Works* (New York: Monacelli Press, 1998), p. 30 .

16. Richard Serra, quoted in Bechtler, *Frank O. Gehry/Kurt W. Forster*, p. 60.

17. Letter from Baroness Hilla Rebay to Frank Lloyd Wright, June 1, 1943, in Bruce Brooks Pfeiffer, ed., *Frank Lloyd Wright: The Guggenheim Correspondence* (Fresno, Calif.: Press at California State University, 1986), p. 4.

18. Gehry, quoted in Scott Gutterman, "Post-Industrial Heaven: Frank Gehry Designs the Guggenheim Museum Bilbao," Guggenheim Museum brochure, 1997, unpaginated.

19. Letter from Wright to Rebay, December 18, 1943, in Pfeiffer, *Frank Lloyd Wright: The Guggenheim Correspondence*, p. 22. A site was only identified by March 13 of the following year, at which time it did not include the full frontage along Fifth Avenue between Eighty-eighth and Eighty-ninth Streets.

20. Emilio Ambasz, quoted in "The Architecture World Pays Tribute to Frank Lloyd Wright's Guggenheim," *Guggenheim Magazine* 5 (spring/summer 1994), p. 6.

21. Gehry, quoted in Alejandro Zaero, "Conversations with Frank O. Gehry," *El Croquis* 74/75 (1995), pp. 10–11. A special issue on Frank Gehry projects, 1991–95.

22. The rootless character of Wright's monument resonates with Rosalind Krauss's discussion of the history of modern sculpture. The logic of sculpture is inseparable from what she calls the "logic of the monument," a logic triangulated by commemoration, representation, and symbolization, and one in which the object functions as a marker or chronicle on a symbolic level. Krauss argues that this logic ceased to operate in twentieth-century sculpture and pinpoints the turning of the tide in the work of Constantin Brancusi. Wholly abstract and self-referential in the acknowledgment of its process of construction and its mode of display, it thus evinces "an absolute loss of place" and reveals "meaning and function as essentially nomadic." See Rosalind Krauss, "Echelle/monumenalité, Modernism/postmodernisme: La ruse de Brancusi," in *Qu'est-ce que la sculpture moderne?* exh. cat. (Paris: Editions du Centre Pompidou, 1986), p. 246, and "Sculpture in the Expanded Field," in Krauss, *The Originality of the Avant-Garde and Other Modernist Myths* (Cambridge, Mass.: MIT Press, 1984), p. 279.

23. Coosje van Bruggen, *Frank O. Gehry: Guggenheim Museum Bilbao* (New York: Guggenheim Museum, 1997), p. 62.

24. Gehry, quoted in Kay Mills, "Prefab Aesthetics," *Los Angeles Times*, Jan. 18, 1981, part V, p. 3.

25. Gehry, quoted in Mildred Friedman, ed. *Gehry Talks: Architecture + Process* (New York: Rizzoli, 1999), p. 178.

26. Gehry, quoted in Bechtler, *Frank O. Gehry/Kurt W. Forster*, p. 23.

27. Reyner Banham, *Age of the Masters: A Personal View of Modern Architecture* (London: Architectural Press, 1975), p. 51.

28. Frank Lloyd Wright, in Pfeiffer, ed. *Frank Lloyd Wright: The Guggenheim Correspondence*, p. 111.

29. Rosalind Krauss, "Antivision," *October* 36 (spring 1986), p. 147. See also Norman Bryson, *Vision and Painting: The Logic of the Gaze* (New Haven: Yale University Press, 1983); Hal Foster, ed., *Vision and Visuality* (Seattle: Bay Press, 1988); and Rosalind Krauss, *The Optical Unconscious* (Cambridge, Mass.: The MIT Press, 1993).

30. Benjamin Buchloh, "Formalism and Historicity: Changing Concepts in American and European Art Since 1945," in *Europe in the Seventies: Aspects of Recent Art*, exh. cat. (Chicago: Art Institute of Chicago, 1977), p. 102.

31. Fernand Léger, *Functions of Painting* (New York: Viking, 1973), p. 46.

32. Gehry, quoted in Peter Arnell, "'No, I'm an Architect': Frank Gehry and Peter Arnell: A Conversation," in Arnell and Ted Bickford, eds., *Frank Gehry: Buildings and Projects* (New York: Rizzoli, 1985), p. XVI.

33. Umberto Eco, "How an Exposition Exposes Itself," in Neil Leach, ed., *Rethinking Architecture: A Reader in Cultural Theory* (London: Routledge, 1997), p. 204.

34. Gehry, quoted in van Bruggen, "Leaps into the Unknown," p. 128.

35. Gehry, quoted in Diamonstein, *American Architecture Now*, pp. 37; 40.

36. Gehry, quoted in Scott Gutterman, "Frankly Speaking," *Guggenheim Magazine* 11 (fall 1997), p. 26.

37. "Le musée est le miroir colossal dans lequel l'homme se contemple enfin sous toutes les faces, se trouve littéralement admirable et s'abandonne à l'extase exprimée dans toutes les revues de l'art." Georges Bataille, *Oeuvres complètes* (Paris: Gallimard, 1970), vol. 1, p. 240.

Construction view, Experience Music Project (EMP) (1995–2000), Seattle.

Roll Over Euclid: How Frank Gehry Designs and Builds

William J. Mitchell

Some architects are angry, really angry, with Frank Gehry. They see his late work as whimsical and capricious — a betrayal of the stern Modernist commitment to rational problem solving and economy of means. To them, he is a seducer of the public, promoter of frivolous fashions, and a corrupting influence on impressionable young designers.

Others are envious. They admire the spatial bravura of works like the Guggenheim Museum Bilbao (1991–97) and the Walt Disney Concert Hall (1987–) in Los Angeles, but dismiss them as singularities made possible by uniquely indulgent clients and generous budgets. Gehry seems somehow to have slipped the constraints that bind the average architectural Joe.

But both camps get it wrong. Gehry has, in fact, found a way of designing and building that is far more in tune with the realities of our digitalizing, globalizing age than are the stale dogmas of machine-age Modernism. He has created a powerful new architectural language of computer-constructed curved surfaces, nonrepeating parts, free-form composition, digital analysis, and globally distributed CAD/CAM (computer aided design/computer aided manufacturing) fabrication.

Euclid Rules

You cannot miss the curved surfaces. They challenge a deeply embedded tradition that goes all the way back to Euclid (ca. 300 B.C.). Euclid's Elements, as every schoolchild used to know, shows how to construct infinitely varied geometric compositions from points, straight lines, and arcs of circles. Parallels, perpendiculars, and congruencies figure prominently. And strictly speaking, the only instruments you need to explore this rigorously beautiful formal universe are a pencil, a straightedge, dividers, and compasses.

Traditional drafting instruments comprise these simple, ancient tools, plus some more-modern inventions that save the trouble of explicitly executing the commoner Euclidean constructions. T-squares and parallel bars allow the ready production of parallels. Triangles facilitate insertion of perpendiculars. Graph paper provides a modular framework of both parallels and

Paul Rudolph, Yale School of Art and Architecture (1959–63), New Haven, Connecticut.

perpendiculars. Graduated rulers and protractors simplify the subdivision of lines and angles. Tracing paper takes the tedious labor out of replicating shapes.

Many common fabrication and assembly techniques — craft-based and machine-based — are closely related. Saws most readily produce straight cuts and planar surfaces. Bricks and boards fit together plane-to-plane and at right angles. Brick walls have parallel sides and rise in parallel courses. Rolling and extrusion machinery generates straight lines, while lathes and other turning devices yield arcs and circles. Jigs and templates make it possible to repeat shapes exactly. The tools of the carpenter and the mason give the draftsman's graphic constructions material form at a larger scale — sometimes very literally, such as the corrugated concrete surfaces of Paul Rudolph's Art and Architecture Building (1959–63) at Yale University, from the parallel hatching of his drawings. Architects tend to draw what they can build, and build what they can draw.

Small wonder, then, that classical architectural treatises, from Vitruvius to the texts of the École des Beaux-Arts, are explicitly grounded in Euclid. Even before they introduce the classical orders, many of these texts provide geometry lessons cribbed from their great Greek predecessor. And John Dee's preface to the first English translation of Euclid (1570) addresses itself directly to architects; it has good claim, in fact, to be the first theoretical text on architecture in English.

Early applications of computer-aided design (CAD) technology in architecture simply (and rather unreflectively) reified this ancient tradition. CAD systems were mostly employed as accurate and efficient replacements for traditional drafting instruments in the production of construction documents. They provided points, straight lines, arcs, and circles as basic graphic primitives, and their operations for inserting these primitives into drawings were directly based on fundamental theorems of Euclid. Grids and snap operations were the electronic equivalent of graph paper; copy operations enabled rapid replication of existing shapes; and drawing "layers" explicitly harked back to the days of transparent tracing-paper sheets. By greatly enhancing the efficiency of traditional drafting practices, these systems further marginalized alternative practices.

The Countertradition Asserts Itself

There has, however, long been an extra-Euclidean countertradition. Despite its marginality, it has somehow managed to survive. It shows up briefly but significantly, for example, in the First Book (Chapter Thirteen) of Andrea Palladio's *Four Books of Architecture*. After remarking that Vitruvius gives no guidance on construction of the swelling profile of a column, Palladio sets forth his own method as follows:

> *The method I use in making the profile of the swelling is this; I divide the shaft of the column into three equal parts, and leave the lower part perpendicular; to the side of the extremity of which I apply the edge of a thin rule, of the same length, or a little longer than the column, and bend that part which reaches from the third part upwards, until the end touches the point of the diminution of the upper part of the column under the collarino. I then mark as that curve directs, which gives the column a kind of swelling in the middle, and makes it project very gracefully.*

In other words, Palladio resorted to bending a thin elastic spline to create the curve he wanted. This curve can be described by a precise formula—as later theoreticians of elastically deformed structures were to demonstrate—but Palladio did not delve into the mathematics. He simply employed what was, in effect, an efficient analog computation device to produce the required graphic output.

Antoní Gaudí made similar use of analog computation in designing the complex curved vaults of the Church of the Sagrada Familia (1883–1926) in Barcelona. In this case, the device was not a bent spline but a cable in tension. Hung with weights and supported at each end, the cable traced out a catenary curve. Inverted, the catenary specified an efficient and beautiful profile for a vault acting in compression.

Other architects, such as Félix Candela, Eduardo Catalano, and Eladio Dieste have worked with ruled surfaces. These are generated, in vast variety, by taking pairs of curves in space and connecting them at regular intervals by straight lines—a process most readily carried out by constructing wooden or wire models. The most familiar are the saddle-shaped hyperbolic paraboloid, as in Catalano's House (1954; destroyed 2001) in Raleigh, North Carolina, and the hyperboloid of revolution commonly seen in the cooling towers of power stations.

Yet other designers have been fascinated by minimal surfaces. One way to produce these, without becoming entangled in some fairly complex and tedious mathematics, is to dip a wire frame in soap solution; the resulting

Eduardo Catalano, Catalano House (1954), Raleigh, North Carolina.

355

soap films immediately give you what you want. With a bit more labor, you can get the same results with spandex. There is a conference room at the School of Architecture and Planning, Massachusetts Institute of Technology (MIT), with interior surfaces that were sculpted in this way by Frank Stella.

At the dawn of the computer graphics era, information technologists quickly realized that all these sorts of curves and surfaces, and many more, could now be generated by digital rather than analog means. The idea was to encode the mathematical formulas for various types of curves in software, let the user input parameters specifying particular instances of these curves, and then employ display routines to trace out these instances on screens or by means of printers or plotters. An active research community that focused on digital curved-surface modeling quickly sprang up in the 1960s and early 1970s, and developed a repertoire of highly specialized concepts and techniques with forbidding-sounding names: triangulated surfaces, parametric curves, bicubics, Coons patches, Bezier curves and patches, B-splines, and NURBS (non-uniform rational B-splines). Curved-surface CAD software based upon these concepts became an essential tool of automobile, aerospace, and ship design. In the entertainment industry, related software was put to work in production of three-dimensional computer animations. In these fields, with the aid of ever increasing computer power and ever more sophisticated display technology, free-form curved surfaces became as straightforward for designers to handle as straight lines, planes, circles, cylinders, and spheres were for architects.

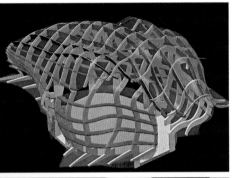

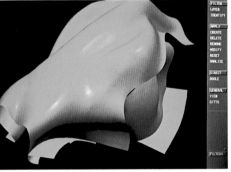

CATIA structural model and surface model, DG Bank Building (1995–2001), Berlin.

In the early 1990s, Gehry's partner James Glymph established the connection between the worlds of digitally designed airplanes, automobiles, and animated-cartoon dinosaurs and that of architecture. The breakthrough project was a monumental Fish Sculpture (1989–92) for the Vila Olimpica on the Barcelona waterfront. Its free-form curved surfaces were digitally modeled using CATIA, a CAD system primarily intended for use in aerospace. The digital model was used for design development, in structural analysis and design, and in place of traditional drawings as the primary repository of construction information. This opened the way to successful application of digital curved-surface modeling in far larger and more ambitious projects, such as the Guggenheim Museum Bilbao, the Walt Disney Concert Hall, Experience Music Project (EMP) (1995–2000) in Seattle, and the Ray and Maria Stata Center (1998–) at MIT. Gehry embarked on an exploration of a formal universe that was no less rigorously logical and mathematically elegant than that of ancient Greek geometry, but which — as a practical matter — had been inaccessible before computer-graphics technology unlocked it. If you were a Platonist, you could say that it had been lurking out there all the time, waiting for its cultural moment to arrive. It was curtains for the, well, hegemonic discourse of straightedge and compasses. Roll over Euclid. Tell Pythagoras the news.

The Role of Three-Dimensional Digitizing and Rapid Prototyping

It is technically possible to design directly at a curved-surface CAD workstation. Some younger architects have embraced this approach, and Gehry has flirted with it. The amazingly complex freestanding conference room—a horse-head shaped structure—at the heart of the DG Bank Building (1995–2001) in Berlin was done this way. But inserting curved-surface primitives and tweaking control points on the screen is not necessarily a very fluid or congenial way to explore design ideas. And it forces reliance on computer visualization as the primary means of understanding and evaluating forms and spaces, which turns out not to be entirely satisfactory.

The alternative is to sketch and sculpt forms using standard physical media as a first step, then to build a closely corresponding digital model by fitting mathematically defined curves and surfaces to the initial freehand shapes. This is the strategy mostly favored by automobile designers; curved surface modelers have not made them give up their felt-tip freehand sketches, their full-scale taped profiles, or their carefully crafted clay models. And it is also the strategy of Gehry, who greatly values the direct tactility of the physical model and the speed, freshness, and energy of the freehand gesture.

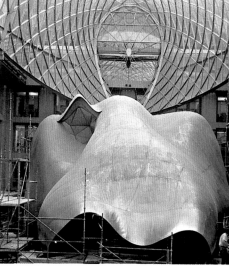

The trick in this process is to preserve the essential qualities of the initial two-dimensional or three-dimensional sketch. These qualities are easily lost, or subtly damaged, if unsuitable graphic primitives or inappropriate approximations are employed. When Jørn Utzon first sketched the saillike roof forms of the Sydney Opera House (1956–73), for example, he posed very difficult technical problems for the draftsmen who were to develop and precisely document the design, the engineers who were to analyze it, and the contractors who were to build it. Eventually these problems were solved by introducing a masterful simplification: the free-form surfaces were approx-

Construction views, DG Bank Building (1995–2001), Berlin.

imated by triangular patches from the surfaces of spheres, so that the composition became, in effect, an assembly of smaller versions of Eero Saarinen's Kresge Auditorium (1953–55) at MIT flipped on their sides and joined along their upper edges. It was a brilliant move, but it

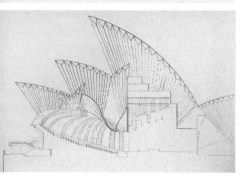

Jørn Utzon, sketch and longitudinal section, Sydney Opera House (1957–73).

carried a heavy penalty. The constructed building, while beautiful in its own way, is much stiffer and more classically geometric than the version that Utzon had originally imagined.

That was before computers and NURBS. Today, with the right equipment, painstaking care, and craftsmanship, it is usually possible to produce very close approximations that preserve the important nuances and subtleties of the original. In Gehry's office, the process begins with the use of a very accurate three-dimensional digitizer to capture vertex, edge, and surface coordinates from a large-scale physical model. Using CATIA, mathematical curves and surfaces are then fitted as closely as possible to these digitized points. Rapid-prototyping devices, such as computer-controlled three-dimensional deposition printers and multi-axis milling machines, are then used to "build back" physical models for visual inspection and comparison with the original. The process iterates, with adjustments as necessary to the digital model, until the design team is satisfied.

Computer Power Liberates Form

One of the important uses of the digital model is to provide input data for analysis software. And it is here that a crucial advantage becomes apparent.

In pre-CAD days, when design calculations were carried out by hand, increases in computational effort resulting from the introduction of complex shapes made an enormous practical difference. Anyone could quickly calculate the floor area of a rectangular room, for example. But it took greater mathematical knowledge, and considerably more work, to do the same for an irregularly polygonal room—and free-form curved rooms were a nightmare. An architect might be able to draw or physically model an arbitrarily shaped building, but would run into difficulty trying to calculate areas and volumes for costing and construction-management purposes, accurately visualize shading and shadows, and carry out structural, thermal, and acoustic analyses to evaluate performance. Producing accurate area and material takeoffs, and the necessary engineering analyses, might even turn out to be a technical impossibility.

Today, however, the availability of inexpensive computer power in huge quantities renders these differences in computational complexity almost entirely unimportant. Even monstrously complicated computations of area and volume are no problem for good geometric-modeling software running on a fast machine. And engineering-analysis procedures have been made far more flexible and powerful by eliminating the simplifying assumptions that had restricted their applicability. Thus, for example, the structural analysis formulas that I painfully learned in architecture school were restricted to rectangular beams, circular columns, semicircular arches and vaults, and the like, but today's finite-element software can efficiently and accurately analyze structures of pretty much any arbitrary shape. The same goes for ray-tracing and radiosity software that accurately simulates shades and shadows, for computational fluid-dynamics software that traces expected airflow in and around buildings, for dynamic-energy simulation software that predicts thermal performance, and for acoustic simulation systems.

Eero Saarinen, Kresge Auditorium (1954), MIT, Cambridge, Massachusetts.

From a technical viewpoint, simplicity and regularity hardly matter anymore. If designers want to emphasize these qualities, they must now do so on other grounds.

CAD/CAM Fabrication

One of these grounds, of course, has long been that simple, regular construction elements are easier and cheaper to fabricate than more complex ones. Furthermore, if designers can restrict themselves to using limited numbers of standardized, mass-produced parts, they can take advantage of industrial economies of scale. The formal implications of these principles were explored with exquisite poetry by Ludwig Mies van der Rohe, and rather less poetically by postwar exponents of industrialized component building in Europe. Throughout the twentieth century, the straightforward logic of industrial production seemed to provide an unassailable justification for the spare geometries of architectural Modernism.

But the implications of today's digitally controlled machinery differ radically from those of earlier industrial technology. This is vividly illustrated by the contrast between an old-fashioned printing press and a desktop laser printer. The printing press requires considerable time and effort to set up for a production run, but it then cranks out identical products in high volume and at low unit cost; it is a typical instrument of mass production. The laser printer has a higher unit cost, but it is much more flexible. It can rapidly and automatically be reset for every page, so it costs nothing extra for each one to differ from the last; this property makes it an instrument of computer-enabled mass customization. Even where small numbers of identical copies are required, the laser printer is more economical, since it eliminates the high, fixed preparation and setup costs of the printing press. It is only with large numbers of copies that unit costs begin to dominate and economies of scale effectively kick in.

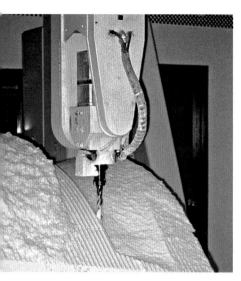

Computer milling of mold for glass panels for Condé Nast Cafeteria (1996–2000), New York.

Mass customization is particularly attractive in fabrication of construction components, since buildings are mostly one-off rather than mass-market products, and it is often difficult to get sufficiently long production runs to achieve major economies of scale. It is also well suited to just-in-time production and delivery, and similar up-to-date logistical strategies that take advantage of sophisticated, computerized management tools. And the very nature of buildings creates demands—which have too often been suppressed in modern buildings—for variation of components in response to their particular contexts. There are, after all, good, practical reasons to vary structural members according to their load conditions, windows according to their orientations, and so on.

CAD/CAM machinery now provides the means to mass-customize construction components. These devices are the architectural equivalents of laser printers. Just as a laser printer automatically translates a text file into tangible printed output, so a CAD/CAM fabrication machine automatically translates a three-dimensional CAD file into full-scale physical reality. It accomplishes this by performing the necessary physical operations, at high speed, under very precise digital control.

Application of CAD/CAM technology to structural steelwork fabrication has proven to be particularly effective. Numerically controlled machines can now shape, cut, and drill steel sections with great efficiency. This means that steel frames can economically be formed into complex shapes, and that the resulting complicated joints present little difficulty. Use of this technology has been crucial for Gehry in such projects as the Guggenheim Museum Bilbao, Walt Disney Concert Hall, EMP, and Ray and Maria Stata Center. In all of them, CAD renderings and construction photographs of the naked steel frames are jaw dropping.

For cutting flat sheet material into arbitrary shapes, CAD/CAM laser cutters, water-jet cutters, and routers have become commonplace. These are much like old-fashioned pen-plotters, with a powerful cutting device instead of the pen. Gehry has used them extensively to produce the irregular glass panels for the curtain wall of the Nationale-Nederlanden (1992–96) Building in Prague, and the sheet-metal cladding panels for the EMP.

Multi-axis milling machines extend the idea of computer-controlled cutting from two-dimensional sheets to three-dimensional solids. This technology is extensively used in the automobile industry for full-scale prototyping of metal parts. In architecture, it has the potential to reinvigorate the tradition of non-planar cut stonework, substituting high-speed, extremely precise mechanical action for the chisels of masons. It is now being utilized, to great effect, in the still-ongoing construction of Gaudí's Sagrada Familia. Gehry has employed it to shape the cut-limestone exterior of the American Center (1988–94) in Paris; and in full-scale prototyping of a curved stone wall for the Walt Disney Concert Hall, before that project was redesigned with a metal skin.

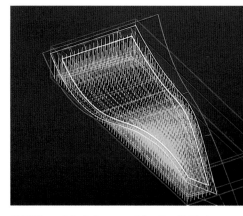

Three-dimensional milling, and other techniques such as three-dimensional deposition printing, can also be used to create concrete formwork, and molds for metal and glass. Thus, for example, the remarkable curved-glass shapes of the Condé Nast Cafeteria (1996–2000) in New York were produced by CAD/CAM fabrication of metal molds, then slumping heated glass sheets onto the mold surfaces.

CATIA model of glass panel for Condé Nast Cafeteria (1996–2000).

On-site assembly of complex, CAD/CAM fabricated elements can obviously present greater challenges than assembly of simpler, more standardized pieces. But here, too, the three-dimensional CAD model helps. It becomes the source of coordinates that can drive laser-positioning devices and other electronic construction aids. It can provide clear, detailed renderings of difficult assemblies. And it can even control construction robots that automatically carry out positioning and placement work.

The vigorous exploration of CAD/CAM fabrication technology by Gehry, his partners, and some highly skilled collaborators continues his long-standing interest in innovative uses of materials and construction techniques — an interest that earlier yielded his corrugated cardboard chairs, his use of chain-link fencing in provocatively unexpected contexts, and other such surprises. Like any such exploration, it requires embracing uncertainties and taking risks; and some innovations have proven more successful than others. But a growing body of successfully completed projects — with more in the pipeline — convincingly demonstrates that CAD/CAM fabrication works. Within schedule and budget frameworks that don't need to be extraordinary, it opens up an exciting new way of conceiving and making buildings.

Glass panel mock up for Condé Nast Cafeteria (1996–2000), New York.

Repeating and Non-Repeating Parts

In any building, there is a particular balance between repeating and unique elements, which gives the architecture much of its character. There is also some sort of balance between factory work and on-site handiwork. As Gehry has realized, CAD/CAM fabrication can shift these

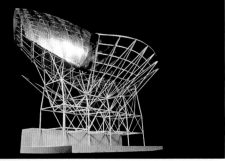

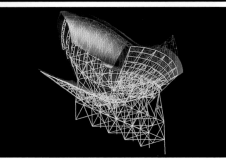

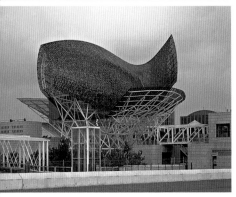

Model, CATIA model, and finished structure, Fish Sculpture (1989–92) at Vila Olimpica, Barcelona.

balances — so, one of the critical design issues is to figure out where they should be established for a particular project.

In the Barcelona fish sculpture, a simple conceptual division was created between structure and skin. The steel frame is all CAD/CAM, but the surface is made from copper strips that were hand-woven together in situ. At Bilbao, the external shapes and profiles were precisely specified by the CAD model, and there is no repetition or symmetry of the large-scale masses; but the titanium cladding panels are another matter. These were fabricated at a standard size and shape, and they were then bent and twisted into place on site. The result is an energetic and compelling interrelationship of mathematically smooth curves and surfaces at the macro scale; of discrete, repetitive panel rhythms at an intermediate scale; and of a micro-scale texture of wrinkles and kinks that resulted naturally from the panel fabrication and placement operations. The macro-scale curves visually connect to the river and the hills, the intermediate-scale panels to the fenestration patterns of nearby buildings, and the irregular reflective surface texture to the cloudy Basque sky.

The Der Neue Zollhof (1994–99) office buildings in Düsseldorf resolve the balances in quite another way. Here, the walls are fluid curves, but the windows are standardized, mass-produced rectangular elements. The difference between the two systems is resolved by an adjustable framing element, which allows each window to be fitted to its particular, nonstandard context.

At EMP, nothing on the exterior repeats. The major masses are free form, and if you look closely at their sheet-metal cladding panels you can see that these are all different. The surfaces were subdivided according to a logic that took account of local curvature and the technical properties of the material — particularly the limits on its capacity to bend. The CAD software performed the immense amount of intricate computation required to unfold each surface facet onto a plane. Then CAD/CAM cutting machinery accurately produced each unfolded shape from a flat sheet. These machine-cut sheets were efficiently transported to the site. Finally, they were bent back and fixed in place to produce exactly the right nonplanar polygonal facets.

Regular grids and repeating parts have been so fundamental to architectural composition for so long that most designers find it difficult to imagine life without them. But EMP begins to show how this is possible.

Reimagining Design and Construction

Three-dimensional digital models and CAD/CAM construction techniques not only have profound intellectual implications for designers; they also shake up the organization and everyday management of architectural practice. It can no longer be business as usual — the opportunities and demands fundamentally change.

Before computers, most architectural practices logged the bulk of their billable hours at the design development and construction documents phases of projects. This is where they really made their money. Then, when early CAD systems appeared, workstations took the place of drafting tables, and electronic computation replaced technical labor. The effect, pretty unexcitingly, was to automate the production of documents that had previously been prepared by hand. But more advanced CAD/CAM processes, as employed by Gehry, are far more revolutionary; they begin to eliminate, rather than automate, traditional construction documentation. CAD/CAM steel fabrication, for example, can now be a largely paperless process that relies on transfer of digital files rather than shop drawings.

Experience Music Project (EMP) (1995–2000) model being digitized and view of the completed building, Seattle.

In the now-fading industrial era, catalogues of manufactured components and materials have played an indispensable role in architectural practice. Architects spent a lot of their time searching, selecting, and procuring. In the context of CAD/CAM, though, the crucial thing is to know the capabilities and availability of the fabrication facilities offered by various vendors. Then, it becomes possible to design directly for those capabilities — a move that provides a great deal of creative freedom, and involves the architect far more directly in fabrication and construction processes.

It is easy to imagine that Gehry's high-flying, high-profile, international practice has few lessons to offer architects applying less advanced resources to more modest projects. But that would be to miss a vital point. Many of the digital-era strategies and techniques that he is pioneering now will be increasingly commonplace in the future, just as innovative uses of steel, concrete, and glass in early Modern buildings eventually became mainstream. His remarkable late projects will ultimately be remembered not only for the spatial qualities and cultural resonances that they have achieved, but also for the way in which they have suggested that everyday architectural practice can be liberated from its increasingly sclerotic conventions.

Biography

Born February 28, 1929, in Toronto, Frank Owen Gehry is one of the most inventive and pioneering architects working today. Based in Los Angeles—where he relocated with his family in 1947—he has developed a unique vocabulary that reflects both the urban vernacular and his long association with contemporary artists. In 1954, he received his undergraduate degree in architecture from the University of Southern California and in the years immediately following, worked in a number of firms including Victor Gruen Associates and Pereira and Luckman Associates.

After brief studies in urban planning at Harvard University's Graduate School of Design and a year in Paris working for André Rémondet, Gehry returned to California and opened a small office in Santa Monica in 1962. His earliest work evolved from a Modernist idiom suggesting the varied influences of such pioneers as Harwell Hamilton Harris, Richard Neutra, and Frank Lloyd Wright. His distinctive formal vocabulary developed in early residential commissions in which he explored the expressive potential of humble materials and infused the architectural envelope with a sense of movement. As his practice expanded, the scope of his commissions grew to include exhibition design, furniture, libraries, office buildings, restaurants, schools, and visual and performing arts venues. With each successive commission, Gehry breaks new ground in his ongoing negotiation of functional architecture and sculptural form.

This melding of unconventional materials and august forms continues in his highly acclaimed recent work. The award of the Pritzker Architecture Prize in 1989 brought increased recognition, and the years following have been among the most productive and rewarding of Gehry's career. The introduction of sophisticated computer software in the early 1990s, has facilitated the construction and engineering of complex building systems and successfully translated the gestural quality of his work from model to built form. In tandem with the increasing scope of their projects, Frank O. Gehry and Associates has grown to over 140 employees. Today, the geographic terrain covered by the firm's work includes the Czech Republic, France, Germany, Japan, Scotland, Spain, Switzerland, and the United States.

Selected Awards and Honors

In addition to the awards and honors listed below, Gehry has been recognized with more than one hundred awards from the American Institute of Architects.

1974	College of Fellows, American Institute of Architects
1977	Arnold W. Brunner Memorial Prize in Architecture, American Academy of Arts and Letters
1987	College of Fellows, American Academy of Arts and Letters
1987	Honorary Doctorate of Visual Arts, California Institute of the Arts
1987	Honorary Doctorate of Fine Arts, Rhode Island School of Design
1989	Pritzker Architecture Prize, Hyatt Foundation
1989	Trustee, American Academy in Rome
1989	Honorary Doctorate of Engineering, Technical University of Nova Scotia
1989	Honorary Doctorate of Fine Arts, Otis Art Institute
1991	College of Fellows, American Academy of Arts and Sciences
1992	Wolf Prize in Art, Wolf Foundation

1992	Praemium Imperiale Award, Japan Art Association
1993	Honorary Doctorate of Humanities, Occidental College
1994	Dorothy and Lillian Gish Prize, Dorothy and Lillian Gish Prize Trust
1994	Academician, National Academy of Design
1996	Honorary Master of Architecture, Southern California Institute of Architecture
1997	Honorary Consul of the City of Bilbao
1997	Honorary Doctorate of Architecture, Southern California Institute of Architecture
1998	Frederick Kiesler Prize, Frederick Kiesler Foundation
1998	Honorary Academician, Royal Academy of Arts
1998	Gold Medal, Royal Architectural Institute of Canada
1998	Chancellor of the City of Bilbao
1998	National Medal of Arts, National Endowment for the Arts
1998	Honorary Doctor of Laws, University of Toronto
1999	AIA Gold Medal, American Institute of Architects
1999	Lotos Medal of Merit, The Lotos Club
2000	Gold Medal, Royal Institute of British Architects
2000	Lifetime Achievement Award, Americans for the Arts
2000	Lifetime Achievement Award, National Academy of Design

Selected Solo Exhibitions

1984	Gagosian Gallery, Los Angeles, *Gehry: Unique Fish Lamps*
1984	Ballenford Architectural Books, Toronto, *Frank Gehry Recent Drawings*
1984	Metro Pictures, New York, *Frank Gehry: Fish and Snake Lamps*
1985	Gallery MA, Tokyo, *Frank O. Gehry: Recent Projects*
1986	Castello di Rivoli, Turin, *Frank O. Gehry*
1986	Walker Art Center, Minneapolis, *The Architecture of Frank Gehry*; traveled to Contemporary Art Museum, Houston; Art Gallery at Harbourfront, Toronto; High Museum of Art, Atlanta; Museum of Contemporary Art, Los Angeles; Whitney Museum of American Art, New York
1988	Hoffman/Borman Gallery, Los Angeles, *Frank O. Gehry: New Cardboard Furniture*
1989	Galerie für Architektur und Raum, Berlin, *The Work of Frank Gehry*
1989	Architekturmuseum, Basel, *Frank O. Gehry*; traveled to Museum of Finnish Architecture, Helsinki; Center of Contemporary Art, Warsaw; de Singel Kunstcentrum, Antwerp; Arkitekturmuseet, Stockholm; Danish Architectural Center-Gammel Dok, Copenhagen
1989	Art Store Gallery, Los Angeles, *Frank O. Gehry. Sketches of Recent Projects*
1990	b. d. Madrid Gallery, Barcelona, *Frank O. Gehry. Muebles y dibujos*
1991	Centre Georges Pompidou, Paris, *Frank O. Gehry, Projects en Europe*
1991	Dansk Arkitekturcenter, Copenhagen, *Frank O. Gehry*
1991	Fundació Joan Miró, Barcelona, *Frank O. Gehry*
1992	Montreal Museum of Decorative Arts, *Frank Gehry: New Bentwood Furniture Designs*; traveled to American Craft Museum, New York; Saint Louis Art Museum

1994	Vitra Design Museum, Weil am Rhein, Germany, *Frank O. Gehry*
1994	*Frank O. Gehry*, Charlottesville, University of Virginia, in conjunction with Thomas Jefferson Medal of Architecture
1994	Aedes Gallerie und Architekturforum, Berlin, *Frank O. Gehry. Europäische Projekte*
1994	Wetsman Gallery of Twentieth-Century Decorative Art, Birmingham, Michigan, *Frank O. Gehry: Innovation in Furniture Design, 1969 to the Present*
1996	Vitra Design Museum, Weil am Rhein, Germany (organized in cooperation with the Center of Contemporary Art, Warsaw), *Frank O. Gehry. Design i Architektura*; traveled to Panstwowa Galeria Sztuki, Sopot, Poland
1998	Louisiana Museum of Modern Art, Humlebæk, Denmark, *Frank O. Gehry. The Architect's Studio*; traveled to Soanes Museum, London; Dundee Contemporary Arts Centre, Scotland; Architectuuinstituut, Rotterdam; Les Fonds Régionaux d'Art Contemporain, Bordeaux; Henry Art Gallery, Seattle
1999	Gagosian Gallery, Los Angeles, *Frank O. Gehry: A Study*

Selected Exhibition Designs

1965	Los Angeles County Museum of Art, Los Angeles, *Art Treasures of Japan*
1966	Los Angeles County Museum of Art, Los Angeles, *Assyrian Reliefs*
1968	Los Angeles County Museum of Art, Los Angeles, Norton Simon Sculpture Courtyard installation
1968	Los Angeles County Museum of Art, Los Angeles, *Billy Al Bengston*
1978	Los Angeles County Museum of Art, Los Angeles, *Treasures of Tutankhamen*
1980	Los Angeles County Museum of Art, Los Angeles, *The Avant-Garde in Russia 1910–1930: New Perspectives*
1980	Corderie dell'Arsenale, *La presenza del passato: Strada Novissima*, First Architecture Biennale, Venice
1981	Los Angeles County Museum of Art, Los Angeles, *Seventeen Artists in the Sixties*
1983	Los Angeles County Museum of Art, Los Angeles, *German Expressionist Sculpture*
1983	Museum of Contemporary Art, Los Angeles, *Available Light*
1986	San Francisco Museum of Modern Art, Los Angeles, *Lawrence Halprin: Changing Places*
1986	Walker Art Center, Minneapolis, *The Architecture of Frank Gehry*
1992	Los Angeles County Museum of Art, Los Angeles, *Degenerate Art: The Fate of the Avant-garde in Nazi Germany*
1997	Los Angeles County Museum of Art, Los Angeles, *Exiles + Emigrés*
1998	Solomon R. Guggenheim Museum, New York, *The Art of the Motorcycle*; redesigned for travel to Guggenheim Museum Bilbao; Guggenheim Las Vegas

Teaching Positions

1979	The William Bishop Chair, Yale University
1982	Charlotte Davenport Professorship in Architecture, Yale University
1984	Eliot Noyes Chair, Harvard University
1985–89	Charlotte Davenport Professorship in Architecture, Yale University
1996	Visiting Scholar, Federal Institute of Technology, Zurich
1998	Visiting Professor, University of California at Los Angeles
1999	Charlotte Davenport Professorship in Architecture, Yale University

Project Information

Davis Studio and Residence

Malibu, California 1968–72

Client: Ron Davis

Program: Two-bedroom residence and painter's studio

Area (sq. ft.): 4,000

Materials: Wood frame, galvanized corrugated steel, plywood

Project team: Frank O. Gehry, C. Gregory Walsh, Jr., Stephen Dane

Easy Edges Cardboard Furniture

1969–73

Program: Low-cost furniture

Materials: Glued and laminated corrugated cardboard with Masonite edge banding

Project team: Frank O. Gehry, C. Gregory Walsh, Jr., Jack Brogan, Stephen Dane

Collaborating Artist: Robert Irwin

Gehry Residence

Santa Monica, California 1977–78; 1991–92

Client: Frank and Berta Gehry

Program: Residential remodel

Area (sq. ft.): 3,400

Materials: Wood frame, galvanized corrugated steel, chain link, plywood

Project team: Frank O. Gehry, Paul Lubowicki, Jon Drezner

Wagner Residence (unbuilt)

Malibu, California 1978

Client: Georgie Fink Wagner

Program: Single-family residence and office space

Area (sq. ft.): 3,200

Materials: Wood frame, galvanized-corrugated-metal roofing and siding, plywood; carport: concrete block, stucco; chain link

Project team: Frank O. Gehry, C. Gregory Walsh, Jr., John Clagett

Familian Residence (unbuilt)

Santa Monica, California 1978

Client: Gary and Elizabeth Familian

Program: Single-family residence

Area (sq. ft.): 3,600

Materials: Wood frame, stucco

Project team: Frank O. Gehry, C. Gregory Walsh, Jr., John Clagett

Loyola Law School

Los Angeles 1978–

Client: Loyola Marymount University

Phase I: Fritz B. Burns Student Center, 1978–82

Program: Master plan and four-story student center with student and faculty offices, meeting rooms, seminar rooms, cafeteria, bookstore

Area (sq. ft.): 42,250

Materials: Steel frame, concrete, stucco

Phase II: Merrifield Hall, Donovan Hall, Hall of the 70s, and Chapel of the Advocate, 1978–84

Program: Three 80–120 seat classroom buildings and a non-denominational chapel

Area (sq. ft.): 8,800

Materials: Merrifield: wood frame, brick, sheet metal; Donovan: wood frame, stucco; Hall of the 70s: wood frame, stucco; Chapel: wood frame, Finnish plywood (later, copper sheet metal)

Phase III: William M. Rains Library Renovation, 1983–85

Program: Renovation of existing building, including law library, moot court, and classrooms

Area (sq. ft.): 55,000

Materials: Wood frame, plaster

Phase IV: Rev. Charles S. Casassa Building and Hall of the 80s, 1989–91

Program: Library annex, classrooms, and student and administrative offices

Area (sq. ft.): 34,600

Materials: Steel frame, stucco

Phase V: Parking Garage, 1992–94
Program: Seven-level, 850-automobile parking garage;
acoustical renovation of Merrifield Hall
Area (sq. ft.): 325,000
Materials: Concrete, stainless-steel sheet metal

Phase VI: Girardi Trial Advocacy Center, 1999–
Program: Three-story building to house an ethical lawyering
center, trial court, and classrooms
Area (sq. ft.): 15,000
Materials: Wood frame, stucco

Project team: Frank O. Gehry, James M. Glymph, Randy
Jefferson, Robert G. Hale, Craig Webb, Jon Drezner, Edwin
Chan, Josh Schweitzer, C. Gregory Walsh, Jr., Hak Sik Son,
Tomaso Bradshaw, Brad Winkeljohn, Carroll Stockard, Rene
Illustre, Bob Cloud, Ana Henton, David Kellen, Dane
Twichell, Mok Wai Wan, Adam Wheeler, Sharon Williams,
Ed Woll, Bryant Yeh

Indiana Avenue Studios
Venice, California 1979–81
Client: Charles Arnoldi, Laddie Dill, Guy Dill, Bill Norton
Program: Artists' lofts
Area (sq. ft.): 4,500
Materials: Wood frame, concrete, asphalt shingles,
unpainted plywood, stucco
Project team: Frank O. Gehry, C. Gregory Walsh, Jr., Rene
Illustre, Adolph Ortega, Ed Woll

Experimental Edges Cardboard Furniture
1979–82
Program: Low-cost furniture
Materials: Glued and laminated corrugated cardboard
Project team: Frank O. Gehry, Paul Lubowicki

Aerospace Hall, California Science Center
Los Angeles 1982–84
Client: California Office of the State Architect, Museum of
Science and Industry
Program: Exhibition galleries, 430-seat theater, terraces, and
gardens

Area (sq. ft.): 28,000
Materials: Steel frame, concrete, asphalt shingles, stucco,
sheet metal
Project team: Frank O. Gehry, Rene Illustre, John Clagett,
Ron Johnson, Patricia Owen, C. Gregory Walsh, Jr., Yuk
Chan, Dean Perton
Structural engineer: Kurily & Szymanmski
Mechanical/electrical engineer: Store, Matakovich &
Wolfberg

Norton Residence
Venice, California 1982–84
Client: Lynn and William Norton
Program: Single-family residence and studio/office space
Area (sq. ft.): 2,500
Materials: Wood frame, stucco, concrete block, glazed tile,
wood logs
Project team: Frank O. Gehry, John Clagett, David Kellen,
Rene Illustre

Winton Guest House
Wayzata, Minnesota 1983–87
Client: Penny and David M. Winton
Program: Guest house
Area (sq. ft.): 2,500
Materials: Wood frame, sheet metal, brick, Finnish plywood
Project team: Frank O. Gehry, Robert G. Hale, John Clagett,
C. Gregory Walsh, Jr., Adolph Ortega, Mitch Lawrence,
Carroll Stockard
Associate architect: Meyer, Scherer, Rockcastle

Fish and Snake lamps
1983–86
Client: Formica Corporation and New City Editions
Program: Light-fixture prototype designs
Materials: Wire frame, Formica chips
Project team: Frank O. Gehry, Tomas Osinski, Fred
Hoffman, Joel Stearns, Daniel Sachs

Sirmai-Peterson Residence
Thousand Oaks, California 1983–88
Client: Mark Peterson and Barbara Sirmai

Program: Single-family residence
Area (sq. ft.): 3,000
Materials: Wood frame, stucco, galvanized metal, concrete block, unpainted plywood
Project team: Frank O. Gehry, C. Gregory Walsh, Jr., Patricia Owen, Sergio Zeballos, Rene Illustre

Edgemar Development

Santa Monica, California 1984–88
Client: Sher Development
Program: Mixed-use development including exhibition space, restaurant, retail shops, office space, parking
Area (sq. ft.): 34,500
Materials: Steel, concrete, wood, ceramic tile, stucco, chain link
Project team: Frank O. Gehry, David Denton, Sergio Zeballos, C. Gregory Walsh, Jr., Rene Illustre, David Pakshong, Roberta Weiser
Structural engineer: Kurily & Szymanski
General contractor: Tyler & Cobleigh

Chiat Day Building

Venice, California 1985–91
Client: Chiat/Day Advertising, Inc.
Program: Regional corporate headquarters, including office space and parking
Area (sq. ft.): 75,000
Materials: Precast concrete, steel, stucco, copper sheet metal
Project team: Frank O. Gehry, David Denton, C. Gregory Walsh, Jr., Craig Webb, Alan Au, Gerhard Auernhammer, Perry Blake, Thomas Duley, Anne Greenwald, Robert G. Hale, Victoria Jenkins, Alex Meconi, Clive Wilkinson
Associate architect: Leidenfrost/Horowitz & Associates
Collaborating artists: Claes Oldenburg and Coosje van Bruggen

Schnabel Residence

Brentwood, California 1986–89
Client: Marna and Rockwell Schnabel
Program: Single-family residence
Area (sq. ft.): 5,700

Materials: Wood frame, stucco, lead-coated copper panels
Project team: Frank O. Gehry, David Denton, C. Gregory Walsh, Jr., Tom Buresh, Kevin Daly, Rene Illustre, Adolph Ortega, Carroll Stockard, Sergio Zeballos
Mechanical engineer: Kurily & Szymanski; Storms & Lowe
Electrical engineer: Athans Enterprises
Landscape architect: Nancy Goslee Power & Associates
General contractor: Blackoak Development

Vitra International Manufacturing Facility and Design Museum

Weil am Rhein, Germany 1987–89
Client: Vitra International, Ltd., represented by Rolf Fehlbaum
Program: Furniture assembly plant with adjacent office, mezzanine, and distribution areas; small furniture museum with library and offices; master plan including new entrance road and gate house, future expansion of the factory, museum parking, and ancillary facilities
Area (sq. ft.): 98,000
Materials: Concrete frame, stucco, plaster over masonry, titanium-zinc panels
Project team: Frank O. Gehry, Robert G. Hale, C. Gregory Walsh, Jr., Berthold Penkhues, Liza Hansen, Joseph Bonura, Edwin Chan
Associate architect: Gunter Pfeifer Associates
Collaborating artists: Claes Oldenburg and Coosje van Bruggen

Team Disneyland Administration Building

Anaheim, California 1987–96
Client: Disney Development Company
Program: Office building with cafeteria, exercise facility, 200-seat auditorium, and parking garage
Area (sq. ft.): 333,000
Materials: Steel frame, stucco, galvanized-stainless-steel sheet metal
Project team: Frank O. Gehry, Randy Jefferson, Bruce Biesman-Simons, Edwin Chan, Kevin Daly, Jonathan Davis, Jim Dayton, David Gastrau, Robert G. Hale, Patricia McCaul, Michael Resnic, Todd Spiegel, Randall Stout, Lisa Towning, C. Gregory Walsh, Jr., Tim Williams

Associate architect: Langdon Wilson Associates, Jim House, Douglas Gardner, Behrooz Kooklan, Nial Kelly

Structural engineer: Martin & Associates

Mechanical engineer: Rosenberg & Associates

Electrical engineer: Kocher & Schirra

Lighting consultant: LAM Partners, Inc.

Preconstruction services: Dinwiddie Construction Company

Vitra International Headquarters

Birsfelden, Switzerland

1988–94

Client: Vitra International Ltd., represented by Rolf Fehlbaum

Program: Corporate headquarters, including flexible work spaces, conference and meeting rooms, cafeteria, switchboard, and mailroom

Area (sq. m.): 6,200

Materials: Steel frame, concrete, masonry, stucco, zinc panels

Project team: Frank O. Gehry, Robert G. Hale, Vincent Snyder, James M. Glymph, Liza Hansen, Peter Locke, Eva Sobesky, David Stein, Randall Stout, Laurence Tighe, Dane Twichell, Brian Yoo

Associate architect: Gunter Pfeifer Associates

Bent Wood Furniture Collection

1989–92 (manufactured 1992–)

Client: The Knoll Group

Program: Lightweight wooden chairs and tables

Materials: Maple veneer laminated strips, glass, glue

Project team: Frank O. Gehry, Daniel Sachs, Tom MacMichael

Frederick R. Weisman Art Museum at the University of Minnesota

Minneapolis 1990–93

Client: Frederick R. Weisman Art Museum at the University of Minnesota

Program: Exhibition galleries, auditorium, sales shop, rental gallery, print study room, administrative offices, frame shop, carpentry shop, storage, and parking

Area (sq. ft.): 47,300 (museum); 42,426 (parking)

Materials: Concrete, steel frame, brick, painted and mill-finish stainless-steel panels

Project team: Frank O. Gehry, Robert G. Hale, Edwin Chan, Victoria Jenkins, Matt Fineout, David Gastrau, Richard Rosa

Associate architect: Meyer, Scherer & Rockcastle

Mechanical and electrical engineer: Ericksen, Ellison & Associates

Structural engineer: Meyer, Borgman & Johnson, Inc.

Civil engineer: Progressive Consulting Engineers

Lighting consultant: Pha Lighting Design Inc.

Transportation/parking engineer: Damon Farber & Associates, Inc.

Cost consultant: Ted Jage and Associates

Specification consultant: Jack Lindeman

Fish Sculpture at Vila Olimpica

Barcelona 1989–92

Client: Travelstead Group

Program: Waterfront retail and commercial complex

Area (sq. ft.): 150,000

Materials: Stone, steel, glass

Project team: Frank O. Gehry, David Denton, James M. Glymph, Michael Maltzan, C. Gregory Walsh, Jr., Douglas Hanson, David Reddy, Rick Black, Karl Blette, Christopher Joseph Bonura, Kevin Daly, Peter Locke, Michael Sant, Dane Twichell

Hotel development architects: Bruce Graham and Skidmore, Owings & Merrill

Contractor: Permasteelisa

EMR Communication and Technology Center

Bad Oeynhausen, Germany 1991–95

Client: Elektrizitatswerk Minden-Ravensburg GmbH

Program: Center for regional power distribution, including offices, technical facilities, exhibition hall, dining area, and conference center

Area (sq. m.): 4,300

Materials: Steel, glass, sheet metal, plaster

Project team: Frank O. Gehry, James M. Glymph, Randall Stout, Vince Snyder, Michael Maltzan, Tomaso Bradshaw, Jonathan Davis, Matthias Seufert, Todd Spiegel, Hiroshi Tokumaru, Laurence Tighe, Tim Williams

Associate architect: AKNW, Hartwig Rullkötter

Structural engineer: John A. Martin Jr.

Mechanical engineer: Dipl. Ing. Albert Grage; Herford

Electrical engineer: Rodinghausen-Bruchmülen,

Lighting consultant: LAM Partners, Inc.

Landscape design: Nancy Powersis & Associates

Lewis Residence (unbuilt)

Lyndhurst, Ohio 1989–95

Client: Peter B. Lewis

Program: Single-family residence, two guest houses

Area (sq. ft.): 22,000

Project team: Frank O. Gehry, James M. Glymph, Craig Webb, Susan Desko, Vincent L. Snyder, Terry Bell, George Metzger, Laurence Tighe, Rich Barrett, Karl Blette, Naomi Ehrenpreis, John Goldsmith, Michael Jobes, Michael Mantzoris, Jay Park, David Reddy, Philip Rowe, Rick Smith, Eva Sobesky, Kevin Southerland, Tensho Takemori, Robert Thibodeau, Lisa Towning, Dane Twichell, Scott Uriu, Jeff Wauer, Kristin Woehl, Nora Wolin, Brian Yoo

Associate architect: Van Dijk, Pace, Westlake, & Partners

Collaborating architect: Philip Johnson

Structural engineer: DeSimone, Chaplin and Dobryn Consulting Engineers, P.C.

Mechanical/electrical engineer: Cosentini Associates

Collaborating artists: Larry Bell, Maggie Cheswick Jencks, Frank Stella, Claes Oldenburg and Coosje van Bruggen, Richard Serra

Landscape architect: Hanna/Olin, Ltd.

Interior programming consultants: Lewis Wallack & Associates, Inc.

Guggenheim Museum Bilbao

Bilbao, Spain 1991–97

Client: Solomon R. Guggenheim Foundation/ Consorcio Del Proyecto Guggenheim Bilbao

Program: Art museum, including permanent collection and temporary exhibition spaces, administrative offices, 300-seat auditorium, restaurant, retail, public plaza and water gardens

Area (sq. ft.): 297,000

Materials: Concrete, steel, Spanish limestone, titanium, glass

Project team: Frank O. Gehry, Randy Jefferson, Vano Haritunians, Douglas Hanson, Edwin Chan, Rich Barrett, Karl Blette, Tomaso Bradshaw, Matt Fineout, Robert G. Hale, Dave Hardie, Michael Hootman, Grzegorz Kosmal, Naomi Langer, Mehran Mashayekh, Patricia McCaul, Chris Mercier, George Metzger, Brent Miller, David Reddy, Marc Salette, Bruce Shepard, Rick Smith, Eva Sobesky, Derek Soltes, Todd Spiegel, Jeff Wauer, Kristin Woehl, Nora Wolin

Associate architect and engineer: IDOM, Bilbao, Jose Asumendi, Luis Rodriguez, Cesar Caicoya, Anton Amann, Fernando Perez, and Armando Bilbao

Structural engineer: Skidmore, Owings & Merrill, Chicago, Hal Iyengar, John Zils, Bob Sinn

Mechanical engineer: Cosentini Associates, New York, Marvin Mass and Igor Bienstock

Titanium contractor: Permasteelisa

Lighting consultant: LAM Partners, Inc., Boston, Paul Zaferiou

Acoustical consultant: McKay, Conant, Brook, David Conant, Ron McKay, Tim Hart

Curtain wall consultant: Peter M. Muller

Mechanical and electrical engineer: Consentini Associates consulting engineers, Marvin Mass, Igor Bienstock, Tony Cirillo, Ed Martinez

Graphics consultant: Vignelli Associates, Massimo Vignelli, J. Graham Hanson

Nationale-Nederlanden Building

Prague 1992–96

Client: Nationale-Nederlanden/International Netherlands Group, Yan Scheere and Paul Koch

Program: Office building with conference rooms, café-bar, and restaurant

Area (sq. ft.): 58,000

Materials: Steel, glass, precast concrete with plaster finish

Project team: Frank O. Gehry, James M. Glymph, Marc Salette, Edwin Chan, Douglas Giesey, Masis Mesropian, Eva Sobesky, Thomas Stallman, Lisa Towning, Philip Rowe, Kristen Woehl, Nora Wolin

Executive architect: Kappa, S.R.O.

Engineering: Atipa, S.R.O.

Collaborating architect: Studio Vlado Milunic

Curtain wall contractor: Permasteelisa

General contractor: Les Entreprises SBBM, Sic
Construction SA

Services contractor: Croon

Goldstein Süd Housing

Frankfurt 1991–96

Client: Nassauische Heimstatte

Program: 162-unit public housing

Area (sq. m.): 11,000

Materials: Masonry, zinc panels, colored plaster

Project team: Frank O. Gehry, James M. Glymph, Randall
Stout, Michael Maltzan, Tomaso Bradshaw, Jonathan Davis,
David Denton, Mara Dworsky, Robert G. Hale, Michael
Resnic, Matthias Seufert, Eva Sobesky, Hiroshi Tokumaru,
Tim Williams

Associate architect: Nassauische Heimstatte, Andreas Varnai

Landscape design: Hanna/Olin

Executive landscape architect: Corinna Endress, BWN&P

Vontz Center for Molecular Studies, University of Cincinnati

Cincinnati 1993–99

Client: University of Cincinnati

Program: Research laboratories, offices, and academic
spaces

Area (sq. ft.): 128,000

Materials: Steel frame, brick, glass

Project team: Frank O. Gehry, James M. Glymph, Randall
Stout, Michael Maltzan, Hiroshi Tokumaru, Terry Bell,
Richard Claridge, Matt Fineout, Michael Gale, John
Goldsmith, Stefan Hellwig, Wai Wan Mok, Gaston Nogues,
Jay Park, Todd Spiegel, Tensho Takemori, Nora Wolin

Executive architect: Baxter Hodell Donnelly Preston, Inc.

Structural engineer: THP limited

Mechanical/electrical engineer: H.A. Williams Associates

Laboratory consultant: Earl Walls Associates

Lighting consultant: LAM Partners, Inc.

Walt Disney Concert Hall

Los Angeles 1987–

Client: Walt Disney Concert Hall Committee

Program: 2,300-seat concert hall, 250-seat multi-use theater,
a pre-concert performance space, retail shop, café, outdoor
amphitheater, garden plaza, and 2,500-car parking garage

Area (sq. ft.): 200,000

Materials: Steel frame, stainless steel panels, glass, stone,
Douglas fir

Project team: Frank O. Gehry, James M. Glymph, Craig
Webb, Michael Maltzan, Craig Webb, Vano Haritunians,
Terry Bell, Andrew Alper, Suren Ambartsumyan, Larik Ararat,
Kamran Ardalan, Herwig Baumgartner, Pejman Berjis, Rick
Black, Kirk Blaschke, Tomaso Bradshaw, Earle Briggs, John
Carter, Padraic Cassidy, William Childers, Rebeca Cotera,
Jonathan Davis, Jim Dayton, Denise Disney, Jon Drezner,
Nick Easton, Jeff Guga, David Hardie, James Jackson,
Victoria Jenkins, Michael Jobes, Michael Kempf, Gregory
Kromhout, Naomi Langer, Jacquine Lorange, Gary Lundberg,
Gerhard Mayer, Alex Meconi, Emilio Melgazo, George
Metzger, Brent Miller, Julianna Morais, Rosemary Morris,
Mathias Mortenson, Gaston Nogues, David Pakshong,
Michael Resnic, David Rodriguez, Christopher Samuelian,
Michael J. Sant, Robert Seelenbacher, Michael Sedlacek,
Matthias Seufert, Bruce Shepard, Tadao Shimizu, Rick
Smith, Eva Sobesky, Randall Stout, Thomas Swanson, John
Sziachta, Tensho Takemori, Laurence Tighe, Hiroshi
Tokumaru, Jose Catriel Tulian, Dane Twichell, William
Ullman, Monica Valtierra-Day, Tim Williams, Kristin Woehl,
Brian Yoo, Brian Zamora

Structural engineer: John A. Martin and Associates, Trailer
Martin, George Norton, Barry Schindler, Vernon Gong

Mechanical engineer: Levine Seegel Associates, Anil Shenoy,
Anil Shinde, Gary Dunn; Consentini Associates Consulting
Engineers, Marvin Mass, Igor Bienstock

Electrical engineer: Frederick Russell Brown & Associates,
Frederick Brown, Simon Younan

Acoustical consultant: Nagata Acoustics, Minoru Nagata,
Yasuhisa Toyota; Charles M. Salter Associates, David
Schwind, Tom Schindler

Theater consultant: Theatre Projects Consultants, Richard Pilbrow, Victor Gotesmant, Jeremy Godden, Mark Stroomer, George Ellerington
Civil engineer: Psomas and Associates, Don Gordon, Fred Muller, Steven Gregorson
Exterior wall consultant: Gordon H. Smith Corporation, Gordon Smith
Landscape designer: Melinda Taylor
Organ builders: Rosales Organ Builders & Glader Gotz
Graphics consultant: Bruce Mau Design
Lighting consultant: L'Observatoire International, Herve Descottes
General contractor: Mortenson

Der Neue Zollhof
Düsseldorf 1994–99
Client: Kunst-und Medienzentrum Rheinhafen GmbH, Thomas Rempen, Werner Scholz, Norbert Gams, and Holzmann BauProjekt
Program: Commercial office space, public plaza, and below-grade parking.
Area (sq. m.): 28,000
Materials: Concrete, steel, glass, plaster, stainless steel panels
Project team: Frank O. Gehry, Randy Jefferson, Craig Webb, Terry Bell, Tomaso Bradshaw, Brent Miller, Lisa Towning, Kristin Woehl, Jim Dayton, John Goldsmith, Jeff Guga, Michael Jobes, Naomi Langer, Jorg Ruegemer, Charles Sanchez, Bruce Shepard, Rick Smith, Eva Sobesky, Todd Spiegel, Tensho Takemori, Laurence Tighe, Scott Uriu, Flora Vara, Jeff Wauer, Nora Wolin
Executive architect: Beucker, Maschlanka & Partners, Thomas Beucker, Christoph Haselhoff, Holger Amft, Wieland Freudiger, Silke Frischbutter, Michel Laudert, Klaus Peek, Martin Strauch, Scott Williams
General contractor: Philipp Holzmann AG, Alexander Jonas

DG Bank Building
Berlin 1995–2001
Client: DG Immobilien Management GmbH and Hines Grundstucksentwicklung GmbH

Program: Ten-story office building with conference center and residential component
Area (sq. m.): 20,000
Materials: Steel, limestone, glass, alabaster, sheet metal
Project team: Frank O. Gehry, Randy Jefferson, Craig Webb, Marc Salette, Tensho Takemori, Kirk Blashke, Nida Chesonis, Tom Cody, Jim Dayton, John Goldsmith, Jeff Guga, Leigh Jerrard, Michael Jobes, George Metzger, Jorg Ruegemer, Bruce Shepard, Tadao Shimizu, Rick Smith, Eva Sobesky, Laurence Tighe, Scott Uriu, Nora Wolin
Executive architect: Planungs AG - Neufert Mittmann Graf, Michael Heggemann, Achim Hauser, Johannes Wilberz, Masoud Afchar
Structural engineer: Ingenieur Büro Müller Marl GmbH, Thomas Frankenstein, N.C.P. Nagaraj, Schlaich Bergermann und Partner, Dr. Jörg Schlaich, Dr. Hans Schober, Thorsten Helbig, Dorothea Krebs, Andrea Kratz
Mechanical/electrical engineer: Brandi Ingenieure GmbH, Burkhard Feimann, Niels Wehlau, Peter Johanni
Facade consultant: Planungsbüro für Ingenieurleistungen, Klaus Glass, Karl Spanier
Lighting consultant: A.G. Licht, Wilfried Kramb
Elevator consultant: Jappsen & Stangier Berlin GmbH, Hans Jappsen, Matthias Kramer
Acoustician: Audio Consulting Munich, Michel Schreiber
Audio visual consultant: R.R. Ingenieurbüro Für Gebaudetechnik, Ralph Ammelung
Kitchen consultant: Ingenieurbüro Schaller, Ernst Schaller
Fire safety consultant: Technische Prüfgesellschaft Lehmann, Klaus Kieke
Glass contractor: Josef Gartner GmbH & Co.

Experience Music Project (EMP)
Seattle 1995–2000
Client: Experience Music Project
Program: Museum of contemporary music, including exhibition galleries, electronic library, sound laboratories, performance hall, screening room, administration, archival storage, store, café, and bar
Area (sq. ft.): 140,000
Materials: Steel frame, concrete shell, interference colored stainless steel panels, painted aluminum panels, and glass

Project team: Frank O. Gehry, James M. Glymph, Craig Webb, Terry Bell, George Metzger, Laurence Tighe, Jeffrey Wauer, Kenneth Ahn, Kamran Ardalan, Rich Barrett, Herwig Baumgartner, Elizabeth Beasley, Anna Helena Berge, Kirk Blaschke, Karl Blette, Rebeca Cotera, Jon Drezner, Douglas Glenn, Jeff Guga, David Hardie, Gary Lundberg, Yannina Manjarres-Weeks, Kevin Marrero, George Metzger, Brent Miller, Gaston Nogues, David Pakshong, Douglas Pierson, Steven Pliam, Daniel Pohrte, Paolo Sant'Ambrogio, Christopher Seals, Dennis Sheldon, Bruce Shepard, Tadao Shimizu, Rick Smith, Eva Sobesky, Randall Stout, Tensho Takemori, Hiroshi Tokumaru, Lisa Towning, Scott Uriu, Adam Wheeler, Nora Wolin

Associate architect/exhibition architect: LMN Architects, Seattle

Engineer: Young + Dring

Structural & civil engineer: Skilling Ward Magnusson Barkshire (SWMR)

Mechanical engineer: Notkin Engineering (NEI)

Metal skin fabricator: A. Zahner Company

Structural steel fabricator: Columbia Wire and Iron

Roof sculpture: Permasteelisa

Electrical engineer: Sparling

Acoustical engineer: Jaffe Holden Scarbrough Acoustics; Cerami Associates

Consultants for sound lab: VanSickle and Rolleri Quatrefoil

Sky Church designers: The Floating Company

Sky Church lighting designer: Willie Williams

Sky Church video production: eMotion Studios

Artist's Journey technical production: Lester Creative, Inc.

Artist's Journey architects: Cuningham Group

Blue Lounge architects: Boora Architects

ADA accessibility: Mcguire and Associates

Code consultant: Robert Pielow and Associates

Show audio/video/lighting: Soundelux Showorks/Candela

Signage/graphic design: Skidmore, Owings & Merrill

Theater projection equipment design: Harrah's Theatre Equipment

Geotechnical: Shannon and Wilson

Surveyors: Bush, Roed and Hitchings

Roofing consultant: Wetherholt and Associates

Testing and inspectors: Mayes Testing Engineers

Video vendor: Sony Electronics, Inc.

Security consultant: Schiff and Associates, Inc.

Kitchen designer: CMA Restaurant Supply and Design, Inc.

General contractor: Hoffman Construction

Electrical contractor: Holmes Electric, Evergreen Electric

Mechanical contractor: Mckinstry Inc.

Exhibit fabrication/installation: Maltbie Associates

Fireproofing, paint and acoustics: Clayton Coatings

Glazing: Benson, Herzog

Carpentry/casework: J.S. Perrott/Nicolai

Signage/graphics fabrication/installation: TubeArt Sign and Sports

Millennium Park Music Pavilion and Great Lawn

Chicago 1999–

Client: Millennium Park

Program: Open-air music pavilion with fixed seating for 4,000 and additional lawn seating for 6,000

Materials: Stainless steel panels, glass, and Douglas fir

Project team: Frank O. Gehry, Randy Jefferson, Craig Webb, Lynn Pilon, Reza Bagherzadeh, Chris Banks, Tom Besai, Manucher Eslami, James Jackson, Kurt Komraus, Jason Luk, David May, Chris Mazzier, Frank Medrano, Sy Melgazo, Chris Mercier, Julianna Morais, Diego Petrate, Birgit Schneider, Tensho Takemori, Karen Tom, Scott Uriu, Adam Wheeler, Nora Wolin

Structural and civil engineer: Skidmore, Owings & Merrill, Chicago, John Zils, Robert Sinn, Brian Schirmer

Electrical engineer: OWP & P Engineers, Kevin Christensen

Lighting consultant: Schuler & Shook

Landscape architects: Terry Guen Design Associates and Gustafson Partners

Condé Nast Cafeteria

New York 1996–2000

Client: The Condé Nast Publications, Inc.

Program: Employee cafeteria with private dining areas for meetings and presentations

Area (sq. ft.): 10,800

Materials: Titanium panels, curved glass panels, and ash flooring

Project team: Frank O. Gehry, Randy Jefferson, Edwin Chan,

Chris Mercier, Michelle Kaufmann, Leigh Jerrard, Kamran Ardalan, Douglas Glenn, Julian Mayes, David Nam, Bruce Shepard, Rick Smith, Kristin Woehl, Nora Wolin
Executive architect (interiors): Mancini-Duffy, Anthony Schirripa, Joyce Afuso, Tony Schirripa, and Peter Black
Titanium contractor and cafeteria contractor: Permasteelisa
Glass panel fabricator: C-TEK, Erik Adickes, Fred Adickes, and Javier Valdivieso
Glass panel connector fabricator: Tripyramid, Tim Eliassen, Michael Mulhern, and Michael Samra
Acoustical engineer: Cerami & Associates and Paul S. Veneklasen & Associates
Food service consultants: Beer Associates
General contractors (interiors): Tishman Interiors
Glass consultant: Donald Vild
Glass load engineer: DeSimone Consulting Engineers

Performing Arts Center at Bard College

Annandale-on-Hudson, New York 1997–
Client: Bard College
Program: Performing arts center with two multi-purpose theaters, rehearsal rooms, conference rooms, and administrative offices.
Area (sq. ft.): 105,000
Materials: Stainless steel panels, concrete, glass, and wood
Project team: Frank O. Gehry, Randy Jefferson, Craig Webb, John Bowers, Suren Ambartsumyan, Guillermo Angarita, David Blackburn, Kirk Blaschke, Earle Briggs, Nida Chesonis, Matt Fineout, Sean Gale, Craig Gilbert, Jeff Guga, James Jackson, Julian Mayes, Chris Mazzier, Frank Medrano, John Murphey, David Pakshong, Yanan Par, Lynn Pilon, David Rodriguez, Tadao Shimizu, Karen Tom, Jose Catriel Tulian, Mok Wai Wan, Yannina Manjarres-Weeks, Adam Wheeler, Brad Winkeljohn, Nora Wolin, Brian Zamora
Structural egineer: DeSimone Consulting Engineers, Vincent DeSimone, Christopher Cerino
Consulting engineer: Cosentini Associates, Marvin Mass, Igor Bienstock
Theater consultant: Theatre Projects Consultants, Richard Pilbrow, John Tissot
Acoustical consultant: Nagata Acoustics, Yasuhisa Toyota

Lighting consultant: L'Observatoire International, Herve Descottes, Maria Machado
Landscape consultant: Olin Partnership, Laurie Olin, Cindy Sanders, Lundy Clark, Maty Porteous, Brian Suchy
Geotechnical engineer: Maxim Technologies
Civil engineer: Morris Associates
Curtain wall consultant: Peter M. Muller

Peter B. Lewis Building, Weatherhead School of Management, Case Western Reserve University

Cleveland 1997–
Client: Case Western Reserve University, Al Weatherhead School of Business
Program: Five-story center for the business school containing classrooms, offices, and study space
Area (sq. ft.): 143,000
Materials: Brick, stainless steel panels, concrete, glass
Project team: Frank O. Gehry, James M. Glymph, Edwin Chan, Douglas Hanson, Gerhard Mayer, Rachel Allen, Thomas Balaban, Steven Brabson, Henry Brawner, Heather Duncan, Matt Fineout, Bryan Flores, Jason Luk, Christopher Mazzier, Julian Mayes, Frank Medrano, Robyn Morgenstern, John Murphey, Brian Papke, Yanan Par, Jonathon Rothstein, Marc Salette, Frank Sheng, Rick Smith, Derek Soltes, Friedrich Tuczek, Frank Weeks, Brad Winkeljohn, Nora Wolin
Structural engineer: DeSimone Consulting Engineers, Vincent DeSimone, Steve DeSimone, Derrick Roorda, Mark Tobin, Nathan Ingraffea
MEP engineer: Bard, Rao + Athanas, Theodore Athanas, Mike Fahey, Grant Anderson, Jim Wilson, Ronald Parsley
Construction manager/general contractor: Huber, Hunt & Nichols, William Mullen, Bruce Wylam, Ronald Graham, Dan Seib
Code consultant: Rolf Jensen & Associates, Daniel Gemeny, Nathan Wittasek
Acoustical and audiovisual consultant: McKay, Conant, Brook, David Conant, Thomas McGraw, Timothy Hart
Elevator consultant: Hesselberg, Kessee & Associates
Civil engineer: Euthenics

Hotel at Marques de Riscal

Elciego, Spain 1998–

Client: Vinos de los Herederos del Marques de Riscal

Program: Hotel containing 11 guest bedrooms, a conference facility, restaurant, wine tasting room, and exhibition facility. Additional work to include additional guest bedrooms and parking

Area (sq. m.): 3,300

Materials: Stone, and titanium panels in silver, gold, and dusty rose

Project team: Frank Gehry, Randy Jefferson, Edwin Chan, Richard Barrett, Guillermo Angarita, Kamran Ardalan, Anand Devarajan, Chad Dyner, Matt Gagnon, Albert Lee, Steffen Leisner, Andrew Liu, Colby Mayes, Joejohn McVey, Jonathon Rothstein, Zohar Schwartz, Nora Wolin

Executive architect: IDOM, Cesar Caicoya, Fernando Perez, Karl Blette, Amando Castroviejo, Javier Arostegui, Jorge Berezo, Alvaro Gutierrez, Julio Aretxaga

Guggenheim Museum New York

New York 1998–

Client: The Solomon R. Guggenheim Foundation

Program: Art museum, including permanent collection and temporary exhibition spaces, performing arts space, multi-media production facilities, administrative offices, auditorium, restaurant, retail, public plaza and water gardens

Project team: Frank O. Gehry, Randy Jefferson, Edwin Chan, Michelle Kaufmann, Kamran Ardalan, Tom Balaban, Christoph Deckwitz, Chad Dyner, Matt Gagnon, Sean Gale, Albert Lee, Andrew Liu, Frank Mendelez, Ross Miller, David Nam, Gaston Nogues, Catriel Tulian, Adam Wheeler, Nora Wolin, Brian Zamora

Ray and Maria Stata Center, Massachusetts Institute of Technology

Cambridge, Massachusetts 1998–

Client: The Massachusetts Institute of Technology

Program: Office, laboratory, and conference space for the Laboratory for Computer Science, Artificial Intelligence Laboratory, Laboratory for Information and Decision Systems, and the Department of Linguistics and Philosophy

Area (sq. ft.): 424,000

Materials: Brick, stainless steel panels, painted aluminum panels, titanium panels, and glass

Project team: Frank O. Gehry, James M. Glymph, Craig Webb, Marc Salette, Laurence Tighe, Rachel Allen, Helena Berge, Henry Brawner, Vartan Chalikian, Christine Clements, Edward Duffy, Yono Hong, James Jackson, Thomas Kim, Jason Luk, Yannina Manjarres-Weeks, Emiliano Melgazo, Yanan Par, Doug Pierson, David Plotkin, David Rodriguez, Derek Sola, Karen Tom, Steve Traeger, Monica Valtierra-Day, Yuwen Wang, Jeff Wauer, Chris Banks, Christopher Barbee, Herwig Baumgartner, Tom Bessai, Tomaso Bradshaw, Tina Chee, Susannah Dickinson, Brian Flores, Raymond Gaetan, Craig Gilbert, Jeff Guga, Dari Iron, Michael Kempf, Kurt Komraus, Frank Medrano, Frank Melendez, Clifford Minnick, Robyn Morgenstern, Ngaire Nelson, Janine Nesseth, Robert Seelenbacher, Dennis Shelden, Bruce Shepard, Suren Sumian, Birgit Schneider, Gavin Wall, Nora Wolin, Bryant Yeh, Bryan Zamora

Associate architect: Cannon Design, John D. Cannon, Mark Mendell, Bob Peterson, Debi Lacey McDonald, Frank McGuire, Dave Ordorica, Tom Tostengard, Ed Duffy, Christine Clements, Julie McCullough, George Trandel, James Spencer, Nancy Chan, Steve Palasciano, Paul Ditto, Scott Morris

Structural engineer: John A. Martin and Associates, Trailer Martin, Ron Lee, Marcello Sgambelluri, Martha Gonzalez, Marvin Mittelstaedt, Mark Day

Construction manager/general contractor: Beacon Skanska Construction Company, Jim Becker, Tony Esteves, Paul Hewins, Blane Petterson, Paul Hewins, Claude LeBlanc

Exterior wall consultant: Martin/Martin, Steve Judd

Local associates: CBI Consulting, Craig Barnes

MEP and telecom engineer: RG Vanderweil Engineers, Gary Vanderweil, Joe Manfredi, John Daly, Dave Courtemanche, Robert Chaves, Edita Brooks, Chris Schaffner, James Kasteff, Chris Brooks, Demetri Tsatsarones, Amy Hughes, John Rattenbury, Seth Johnson, James Scales, Elise Russo, Krysten Bettano, Murray Shafiroff, Shawn Niles

Acoustical and audiovisual consultant: McKay, Conant, Brook, Dave Conant, Tom McGraw, Tim Hart, Brad Beattie

Landscape Architect: Olin Partnership, Laurie Olin, Keith McPeters, Yue Li, Chris Canning

Lighting consultant: a.g. Licht, Wilfried Kramb, Hans-Jurgen Schmitz

Code, life-safety, and accessibility consultant: Rolf Jensen and Associates, Ray Grill, Dan Gemeny, Nate Wittasek, Rockwood Edwards

Elevator consultant: Lerch Bates North America, Mike Farris

Childcare consultant: Gail Sullivan Associates, Gail Sullivan, Lisa Hiserodt

Playground consultant: Johansson Design Collaborative, Sonja Johansson, Holly Ben-Joseph, Willow Cheeley

Graphics consultant: Bruce Mau Design

Maggie's Centre Dundee

Dundee, Scotland 1999–

Client: Maggie's Centre Cancer Caring Foundation

Program: Hospice with sitting areas, physical therapy room, library, kitchen

Area (sq. m.): 250

Materials: Stainless steel panels, plaster, wood, glass

Project team: Frank Gehry, James M. Glymph, Craig Webb, Tomaso Bradshaw, Michael Cranfill, Saffet Bekiroglu, Meaghan Lloyd, Colby Mayes, Joejohn McVey, Wai Wan Mok, Jose Catriel Tulian, Nora Wolin, Bryant Yeh

Executive architect: James F. Stephen Architects, James Fred Stephen, Douglas Reid

New York Times Headquarters (unbuilt)

New York 2000

Client: The New York Times Company, and Forest City Ratner

Program: Forty-story office building with offices for the New York Times and speculative office space

Area (sq. ft.): 1,300,000

Materials: Glass and curved glass panels

Project team: Frank O. Gehry, Randy Jefferson, James M. Glymph, Edwin Chan, George Metzger, David Nam, Sean Gallivan, Matthew Gagnon, Ana Henton, Steffen Leisner, Christopher Deckwitz, Anand Devarajan, Jose Catriel Tulian, Michelle Kaufmann, Kamran Ardalan, Cara Cragan, Chad Dyner, Sean Gale, Eric Jones, Meaghan Lloyd, Diego Petrate, Birgit Schneider, Zohar Schwartz, Nora Wolin, Brian Zamora

Associate architect: Skidmore, Owings & Merrill, New York, David Childs, Marilyn Taylor, Ross Wimer, TJ Gottesdiener, Scott Duncan, Ursula Schneider, Donald Holt, Michael Fei, Tran Vinh, Samer Bitar, Simone Pfeiffer, Dale Greenwald, Shashi Caan, Peter Buendgen, Kaz Morihata

Structural engineer: Skidmore, Owings & Merrill, Chicago, William Baker, Hal Iyengar

Selected Bibliography

Interviews and Statements by the Architect

Balaban, Tom, Greg Dunn, Terrance Galvin. "Frank O. Gehry." *The Fifth Column. The Canadian Student Journal of Architecture* (Montreal) 8, no. 4 (1994), pp. 30–38.

Campbell, Clayton; Helena Kontova and Giancarlo Politi. "Frank Gehry: The Artist Is the Pig, the Architect Is the Chicken." *Flash Art* (New York) 31, no. 198 (January–February 1998), pp. 76–81.

Diamonstein, Barbaralee, ed. "Frank O. Gehry." *American Architecture Now*. New York: Rizzoli, 1980, pp. 35–46.

Esterow, Milton. "How Do You Top This?" *Art News* (New York) 97, no. 7 (summer 1998), pp. 74–80.

Fillip, Janice. "The Illusion of Chaos: An Interview with Frank O. Gehry, FAIA." *Architecture California* (Sacramento) 9, no. 5 (September–October 1987), pp. 18–25.

Garfield, Donald. "The Next Thing Now: Designing the Twentieth Century Museum." *Museum News* (Washington) 95, no. 1 (January–February 1996), pp. 39–42.

Gehry, Frank. "Frank O. Gehry & Associates, Inc." *Designers West* (Los Angeles) (May 1969), p. 31.

———. "Suburban Changes: Architect's House, Santa Monica 1978." *International Architect* (London) 1, no. 2 (1979), pp. 33–46.

———. "Beyond Function." *Design Quarterly* (Minneapolis) 138 (winter 1987), pp. 2–11.

———. "Frank O. Gehry Talks on his Works." *A+U: Architecture and Urbanism* (Tokyo), 184 (January 1986), p. 61.

———. "Walt Disney Concert Hall." *L'Architecture d'Aujourd'hui* (Boulogne sur Seine) 261 (February 1989), pp. 36–37. In French and English.

———. "Up Everest in a Volkswagen." *Design Quarterly* (Minneapolis) 155 (spring 1992), pp. 17–19.

Gehry, Frank O., and Richard Serra, "Connections." *Collaborations: The Artists and Architects*. New York: Watson-Guptill Publications, 1981, pp. 156–59.

Georgis, William Ted. "Interview: Frank Gehry." *Archetype* (San Francisco) 1, no. 2 (summer 1979), pp. 10–11.

Ivy, Robert. "Frank Gehry: Plain Talk with a Master." *Architectural Record* (New York) 187, no. 5 (May 1999), pp. 184–92, 356, 359–60.

Lace, Bill, and Susan de Menil, eds. "Interview." *Angels and Franciscans: Innovative Architecture from Los Angeles and San Francisco*. New York: Rizzoli, 1992, pp. 8–16.

Leclerc, David. "La Vie comme elle vient, conversation avec Frank Gehry." *L'Architecture d'Aujourd'hui* (Boulogne sur Seine) 286 (April 1993), pp. 86–91. In French and English.

Selected Books and Exhibition Catalogues

The Architecture of Frank Gehry. Exh. cat., The Walker Art Center, Minneapolis. New York: Rizzoli, 1986. Essays by Rosemarie Haag Bletter, Coosje van Bruggen, Mildred Friedman, Joseph Giovannini, Thomas S. Hines, Pilar Viladas; commentary by Gehry.

Arnell, Peter, and Ted Bickford, eds. *Frank Gehry: Buildings and Projects*. New York: Rizzoli International Publications, Inc., 1985. Includes interview with Gehry.

Bechtler, Christina, ed. *Frank O. Gehry/Kurt W. Forster. From Art and Architecture in Discussion*. Berlin: Cantz, 1999. Includes interview with Gehry.

Dal Co, Francesco, and Kurt W. Forster. *Frank O. Gehry: The Complete Works.* New York: Monacelli Press, 1998.

Frank O. Gehry. Exh. cat., Castello di Rivoli, Torino, 1986. Text by Germano Celant. In Italian.

Frank O. Gehry: Design Museum Vitra. Exh. cat., Aedes Galerie für Architektur, Berlin, 1989. Entries by Kristin Feireiss, Kurt W. Forster, and Ulrike Jehle-Schulte Strathaus. In German and English.

Frank O. Gehry: Projets en Europe. Exh. cat., Centre de Création Industrielle. Paris: Editions du Centre Pompidou, 1991. Includes interview with Gehry and texts by Olivier Boissière, Odile Fillion, Kurt W. Forster, Alain Guiheux, and Werner Oechslin. In French.

Frank Gehry: New Bentwood Furniture Designs. Exh. cat., The Montréal Museum of Decorative Arts, Montreal, 1992. Includes texts by Andrew Cogan, Martin Filler, Daniel Sachs, commentary by Gehry.

"Frank O. Gehry: America come contesto." From the series *Quarderni di Lotus.* Electa: Milan, 1994. Includes texts by Kurt W. Forster and Mirko Zardini. In Italian and English.

Frank O. Gehry: Arkitekturens værksteder/The Architect's Studio. Exh. cat., Louisiana Museum of Modern Art: Humlebaek, Denmark, 1998. Includes texts by Nicolai Ouroussoff and Steen Estvad Petersen. In Danish and English.

Friedman, Mildred, ed. *Gehry Talks: Architecture + Process.* New York: Rizzoli, 1999. Includes texts by Gehry and Michael Sorkin.

Jencks, Charles, ed. *Frank O. Gehry: Individual Imagination and Cultural Conservatism.* London: Academy Editions, 1995.

Knapp, Gottfried. *Frank O. Gehry, Energie—Forum—Innovation.* Stuttgart: Axel Menges, 2000.

Ragati, Manfred, and Uta Kreikenbohm. *Frank O. Gehry: The Energie-Forum-Innovation in Bad Oeynhausen.* Bielefeld: Kerber, 1996. Includes interview and speech by Gehry.

Rempen, Thomas, ed. *Frank O. Gehry: Der Neue Zollhof Düsseldorf.* Bottrop: Peter Pomp, 1999. In German.

Saggio, Antonino. *Frank Owen Gehry: Architetture Residuali.* Turin: Testo & Immagine, 1997. In Italian.

Steele, James. *Schnabel House: Frank Gehry.* London: Phaidon Press, 1993.

———. *California Aerospace Museum: Frank Gehry.* London: Phaidon Press, 1994.

Van Bruggen, Coosje. *Frank O. Gehry: Guggenheim Museum Bilbao.* New York: Guggenheim Museum, 1997.

The Vitra Design Museum: Frank Gehry Architect. New York: Rizzoli, 1990. Includes texts by Oliver Boissière, Martin Filler, and Gehry.

Selected Articles and Essays

Adams, Brooks. "Frank Gehry's Merzbau." *Art in America* (New York) 76, no. 11 (November 1988), pp. 139–145, 205.

Ambasz, Emilio. "Stickhandling." *I.D.* (New York) 39, no. 2 (March–April 1992), pp. 74–83.

Anderton, Frances. "Frank Words on LA." *Architectural Review* (London) 182, no. 1090 (December 1987), pp. 67–68.

Bierman, Lindsay. "Metallic Muse." *Architecture* (New York) 83, no. 6 (June 1994), pp. 84–93.

Bode, Peter. "Frank O. Gehry: Der Gigant von Bilbao." *Art: Das Kunstmagazin* (Hamburg) 6 (June 1997), pp. 58–68. In German.

Boissière, Olivier. "Frank O. Gehry: Les Tribulations de FOG." *L'Architecture d'Aujourd'hui* (Boulogne sur Seine) 261 (February 1989), pp. 2–35. In French and English.

————. "Frank O. Gehry: Chroniques Gehriennes." *L'Architecture d'Aujourd'hui* (Boulogne sur Seine) 271 (October 1990), pp. 146–52. In French and English.

Brandolini, Sebastiano. "La Progettazione della casualità." *Casabella* (Milan) 49, no. 514 (June 1995), pp. 56–63. In Italian and English.

"Building of the Quarter: The Gehry House, Per Voco." *Archetype* (San Francisco) 1, no. 2 (summer 1979), pp. 23–28.

Celant, Germano. "Il Terremoto dell'architettura." *Casabella* (Milan) 49, no. 514 (June 1995), pp. 52–55. In Italian and English.

Cohen, Jean-Louis. "Exception." *L'Architecture d'Aujourd'hui* (Boulogne sur Seine) 261 (February 1989), pp. 38–41. In French and English.

Davidsen, Judith. "Birth of a Chair." *Architectural Record* (New York) 180, no. 2 (February 1992), pp. 74–78.

Davies, Colin. "Energetic Assemblage." *Architecture* (New York) 85, no. 3 (March 1996), pp. 100–09.

Drohojowska, Hunter. "Frank Gehry's Grand Illusions." *Art News* (New York) 87, no. 8 (October 1998), pp. 116–21.

Emmons, Paul F. "Whole Amidst Part: Perceiving the Architecture of Frank Gehry." *Midgard* (Minneapolis) 1, no. 1 (1987), pp. 91–103.

Filler, Martin. "Eccentric Space: Frank Gehry." *Art in America* (New York) 68, no. 6 (summer 1980), pp. 111–19.

————. "Sticks and Stains." *Design Quarterly* (Minneapolis) 155 (spring 1992), pp. 13–16.

————. "Breaking the Rules and Getting Away with It." *House and Garden* (New York) 152, no. 9 (September 1980), pp. 148–53, 200.

————. "Maverick Master." *House and Garden* (New York) 158, no. 11 (November 1986), pp. 208–17, 252–54.

————. "The Well-Furnished Museum." *House and Garden* (New York) 162, no. 5 (May 1990), pp. 193–96.

Forster, Kurt W. "Volumini in libertà: Frank Gehrys architektonische Improvisationen." *Archithese* (Niederteufen) 18, no. 2 (March–April 1988), pp. 53–58. In German.

————. "Visions of Urban Transparency. On Frank Gehry's Concert Hall Project for Los Angeles." *Daidalos* (Berlin) 31–34 (September 1989), pp. 26–35. In German and English.

————. "Il Pesce e il Serpente al Vertice." *Zodiac* (Milan) 2 (1989), pp. 182–195. In Italian.

Fraker, Harrisson. "Spatial and Material Conventions: Frank Gehry's Artistic References." *Midgard* (Minneapolis) 1, no. 1 (1987), pp. 105–15.

"Frank O. Gehry: Davis Studio/Residence." *GA Houses* (Tokyo) 2 (April 1977), pp. 54–59.

"Frank O. Gehry & Associates: Gehry Residence, Santa Monica, California." *GA Document: Special Issue 1970–1980* (Tokyo) 12 (summer 1980), pp. 300–01.

"Frank O. Gehry: Indiana Project." *GA Houses* (Tokyo) 11 (May 1982), pp. 26–33.

"Frank O. Gehry & Associates." *GA Document* (Tokyo) 5 (1982), pp. 72–91.

"Frank O. Gehry & Associates." *GA Document* (Tokyo) 12 (January 1985), pp. 4–21.

Frank O. Gehry & Associates. Special issue of *Progressive Architecture* (New York) 67, no. 10 (October 1986). Includes texts by Adele Freedman, Joseph Giovannini, Paul Goldberger, Esther McCoy, Pilar Viladas, and Leon Whiteson.

"Frank O. Gehry: FOG Exhibition/Recent Works." *GA Document* (Tokyo) 17 (April 1987), pp. 8–39.

"Frank O. Gehry & Associates: Vitra International Furniture Manufacturing Facility & Design Museum, Weil am Rhein, West Germany." *GA Document* (Tokyo) 27 (September 1990), pp. 66–85.

Frank Gehry: 1985–1990. Special issue of *A & V* (Madrid) 25 (September–October 1990). Includes texts by Luis Fernández-Galiano, Kurt Forster, Justo Isasi, Sylvia Lavin, and Rafael Moneo. In Spanish with English summary.

Frank O. Gehry: Work 1987–1990. Special issue of *El Croquis* (Madrid) 45 (November 1990). Includes texts by David Cohn, Josep María Montaner, and Alejandro Zaera. In Spanish and English.

Frank Gehry. Special issue of *Archithese* (Niederteufen) 21, no. 1 (January–February 1991). Includes texts by Jean-Louis Cohen (in French), Kurt Forster (in German and French), Sylvia Lavin (in German), Carol McMichael Reese (in German).

"Frank O. Gehry & Associates." *GA Document* (Tokyo) 32 (March 1992), pp. 8–31.

"Frank O. Gehry." *GA Document* (Tokyo) 38 (February 1994), pp. 8–37.

"Frank O. Gehry." *GA Document* (Tokyo) 40 (July 1994), pp. 62–83.

Frank O. Gehry: 1991–1995. Special issue of *El Croquis* (Madrid) 74/75 (January 1995). Includes interviews by Alejandro Zaera with Gehry, James Glymph, and Randy Jefferson. In Spanish and English.

"Frank O. Gehry: EMR Communication and Technology Center, Bad Oeynhausen, Germany." *GA Document* (Tokyo) 45 (December 1995), pp. 30–47.

"Frank O. Gehry." *GA Document* (Tokyo) 51 (April 1997), unpaginated.

"Frank O. Gehry: Guggenheim Bilbao Museoa." *GA Document* (Tokyo) 54 (January 1998), pp. 1–93. In Japanese and English.

"Frank O. Gehry." *GA Document* (Tokyo) 63 (November 2000), pp. 10–37. In Japanese and English.

Friedman, Mildred. "Frederick R. Weisman Art Museum." *A+U: Architecture and Urbanism* (Tokyo) 285 (June 1994), pp. 8–140. Includes statement by Gehry.

Gandee, Charles. "The Right Stuff." *Architectural Record* (New York) 173, no. 1 (January 1985), pp. 114–123.

———. "Norton House, Venice, California." *Architectural Record* (New York) 173, no. 5 (mid-April 1985), pp. 86–93.

Garcia-Marquez, Francesca. "Frank O. Gehry & Associates/Claes Oldenburg & Coosje van Bruggen: Office Building, Venice/California." *Domus* (Milan) 735 (February 1992), pp. 29–37; XXII.

Giovannini, Joseph. "Will Success Spoil Frank Gehry?" *Metropolitan Home* (New York) 21, no. 8 (August 1989), pp. 61–63, 138, 150.

———. "Back Lot Bravado." *Architecture* (New York) 85, no. 7 (July 1996), pp. 62–69.

———. "Fred and Ginger Dance in Prague." *Architecture* (New York) 86, no. 2 (February 1997), pp. 52–63.

———. "Gehry's Reign in Spain." *Architecture* (New York) 86, no. 12 (December 1997), pp. 64–77.

———. "Experience Music Project." *Architecture* (New York) 89, no. 8 (August 2000), p. 91.

Goldberger, Paul. "Three Works of Frank O. Gehry." *A+U: Architecture and Urbanism* (Tokyo) 184 (January 1986), pp. 55–66. In Japanese and English.

———. "Architect of Dreams." *Vanity Fair* (New York) 478 (June 2000), pp. 184–191; 206–208.

Goldstein, Barbara. "Frank O. Gehry & Associates." *Progressive Architecture* (New York) 61, no. 5 (May 1980), pp. 69–75.

———. "Frank Gehry." *Architectural Review* (London) 168, no. 1001 (July 1980), pp. 26–32.

Gough, Piers. "The Building as Jujitsu." *Modern Painters* (London) 9, no. 4 (January 1997), pp. 50–55.

Jencks, Charles. "Frank Gehry: The Deconstructionist." *Art & Design* (London) 4, no. 4 (May 1985), pp. 14–19.

Ketcham, Diana. "Frank Gehry in Vogue." *The New Criterion* (New York) 6, no. 7 (March 1988), pp. 50–57.

Knobel, Lance. "Frank Gehry: Los Angeles: Links in a Context of Fragmentation." *The Architect's Journal* (London) 176, no. 51/52 (December 22 & 29, 1982), pp. 28–31.

Kugel, Claudia. "Modern Baroque Ensemble." *Architectural Review* (London) 199, no. 1190 (April 1996), pp. 28–33.

———. "Frankfurt Collage." *Architectural Review* (London) 201, no. 1204 (June 1997), pp. 62–65.

Lace, Bill. "Penn Station/Madison Square Garden Redevelopment." *Angels & Franciscans. Innovative Architecture from Los Angeles and San Francisco.* New York: Rizzoli, 1992, pp. 18–25.

Lavin, Sylvia. "A proposito di Gehry." *Zodiac* (Milan) 15 (March/August 1996), pp. 52–87. In Italian and English.

Leclerc, David., "Un moment de vérité." *L'Architecture d'Aujourd'hui* (Boulogne sur Seine) 286 (April 1993), pp. 78–91. In French and English.

———. "Le Walt Disney Concert Hall: Un projet et sa méthode." *L'Architecture d'Aujourd'hui* (Boulogne sur Seine) 293 (December 1993), pp. 78–90. In French and English.

LeCuyer, Annette. "Building Bilbao." *The Architectural Review* (London) 202, no. 1210 (December 1997), pp. 43–45.

Linn, Charles. "Creating Sleek Metal Skins for Buildings." *Architectural Record* (New York) 188, no. 10 (October 2000), pp. 173–78.

Macrae-Gibson, Gavin. "The Representation of Perception: Gehry House, Frank O. Gehry and Associates." *The Secret Life of Buildings: An American Mythology for Modern Architecture.* Cambridge, Mass.: MIT Press, 1985, pp. 2–29.

Marder, Tod A. "Gehry House, Santa Monica, California." *The Critical Edge: Controversy in Recent American Architecture.* Cambridge, Mass.: MIT Press, 1985, pp. 101–11.

Marshall, Alex. "How to Make a Frank Gehry Buidling." *The New York Times Magazine*, April 8, 2001, pp. 64–66.

"Meet the Architect: Stanley Tigerman vs. Frank O. Gehry." *GA Houses* (Tokyo) 6 (1979), pp. 18–171.

Miklosko, Helga. "Dancing House." *Architectural Record* (London) 201, no. 1202 (April 1997), pp. 38–44.

Munson, Andrew. "Fog una sedia come un'architettura/Fog, a Chair as Architecture." *Domus* (Milan) 820 (November 1999), pp. 56–59. In Italian and English.

Murphy, Jim. "A Venice Collaboration." *Progressive Architecture* (New York) 73, no. 3 (March 1992), pp. 66–73.

Muschamp, Herbert. "In the Public Interest." *The New York Times Magazine*, July 21, 1996, pp. 38–41.

———. "The Miracle in Bilbao." *The New York Times Magazine*, September 7, 1997, pp. 54–59, 72, 82.

Newman, Morris. "Rancho Delux." *Architectural Review* (London) 181, no. 1147 (September 1992), pp. 22–24.

Novitski, B.J. "Gehry Forges New Computer Links." *Architecture* (New York) 81, no. 8 (August 1992), pp. 105–10.

Osborne, Lawrence. "Kiss the Sky." *Metropolis* (New York) 19, no. 8 (May 2000), pp. 90–95; 107; 109; 111.

Pastier, John. "Of Art, Self-Revelation and Iconoclasm: A House Remade by Frank Gehry in Santa Monica, California." *AIA Journal* (Washington) 69, no. 6 (mid-May 1980), pp. 168–73.

———. "Distillation of a Paradoxical City." *Architecture* (New York) 74, no. 5 (May 1985), pp. 202–07.

———. "Recent Works of Frank Gehry." *GA Document* (Tokyo) 17 (April 1987), pp. 6–7.

———. "Part of Both Show and Audience." *Architecture* (New York) 76, no. 5 (May 1987), pp. 134–37.

Pehnt, Wolfgang. "Il nuovo Zollhof di Düsseldorf/The Neue Zollhof in Düsseldorf." *Domus* (Milan) 819 (October 1999), pp. 8–17. In Italian and English.

Rabeneck. Andrew. "Positive Space: The California Space Museum." *Arts and Architecture* (Los Angeles) 3, no. 4 (February 1985), pp. 75–79.

Russell, James S. "Experience Music Project, Seattle." *Architectural Record* (New York) 188, no. 8 (August 2000), pp. 126–37.

Shapiro, Lindsay Stamm. "A Minimalist Architecture of Allusion: Current Projects of Frank Gehry." *Architectural Record* (New York) 171, no. 6 (June 1983), pp. 114–25.

Shirvani, H. A. "Gehry and Deconstructivism: A Matter of Difference in Text," *Avant-Garde* (Denver) 1 (winter 1989), pp. 63–77.

Slessor, Catherine. "Atlantic Star." *Architectural Review* (London) 202, no. 1210 (December 1997), pp. 30–42.

———. "Digitizing Düsseldorf." *Architecture* (New York) 89, no. 9 (September 2000), pp. 118–25.

Slessor, Catherine. "Are You Experienced?" *Architectural Review* (London) 208, no. 1244 (October 2000), pp. 72–77.

Steele, James "Frank Gehry: Los Angeles and Its Discontents." *Los Angeles Architecture: The Contemporary Condition*. London: Phaidon, 1993, pp. 73–103.

———. "Schnabel House. Brentwood, California 1990." *Contemporary California Houses*. London: Phaidon, 1999, unpaginated.

———. "The Myth of L.A. and the Reinvention of the City." *Architectural Design* (London) 62, no 7/8 (July/August 1992), pp. 66–67.

Stein, Karen D. "Project Diary: Guggenheim Museum Bilbao, Bilbao, Spain." *Architectural Record* (London) 185, no. 10 (October 1997), pp. 74–87.

Stephens, Suzanne. "Out of the Rage for Order. Frank Gehry House." *Progressive Architecture* (New York) 61, no. 3 (March 1980), pp. 81–85.

———. "The Bilbao Effect." *Architectural Record* (New York) 187, no. 5 (May 1999), pp. 168–73.

———. "Vontz Center, University of Cincinnati." *Architectural Record* (New York) 188, no. 2 (February 2000), pp. 80–87.

———. "Condé Nast Cafeteria, New York City." *Architectural Record* (New York) 188, no. 6 (June 2000), pp. 116–23.

Sudjic, Deyan. "Gehry's Blockbuster." *Blueprint* (London) 106 (April 1994), pp. 38–40.

Thea, Carolee. "The Guggenheim Museum in Bilbao." *Sculpture* (New York) 17, no. 2 (February 1998), pp. 71–73.

Tomkins, Calvin. "The Maverick." *The New Yorker* (New York) 73, no. 18 (July 7, 1997), pp. 38–45.

Van Bruggen, Coosje. "Waiting for Dr. Coltello: A Project by Coosje van Bruggen, Frank O. Gehry, and Claes Oldenburg." *Artforum* (New York) 23, no. 1 (September 1984), pp. 88–95.

Vidler, Anthony. "Opere recenti di Frank O. Gehry." *Casabella* (Milan) 53, no. 555 (March 1989), pp. 4–21; 59–60. In Italian and English.

Viladas, Pilar. "Form Follows Ferment." *Progressive Architecture* (New York) 66, no. 2 (February 1985), pp. 67–77.

———. "Outdoor Sculpture." *Progressive Architecture* (New York) 68, no. 13 (December 1987), pp. 60–67.

———. "House(s) on the Lakeside." *Progressive Architecture* (New York) 70, no. 13 (December 1989), pp. 74–81.

———. "Cranked, Curled, and Cantilevered." *Progressive Architecture* (New York) 71, no. 5 (May 1990), pp. 94–99.

———. "Pavilions on the Edge." *House and Garden* (New York) 162, no. 7 (July 1990), pp. 60–69, 136.

Webb, Michael. "The Trouble With Frank." *Metropolis* (New York) 15, no. 7 (March 1996), pp. 50–53, 74–75.

Wigley, Mark. "Frank O. Gehry." *Deconstructivist Architecture*. Exh. cat., The Museum of Modern Art, New York; Boston: Little Brown, 1988, pp. 22–33.

"Works and Projects: Frank O. Gehry, Guggenheim Museum Bilbao, Bilbao, Spain, 1991–97." *El Croquis* (Madrid) 88/89 (January 1998). n.p.

Zardini, Mirko. "Los Angeles as Context: Frank O. Gehry's Edgemar Development." ss (Milan) 74 (August 1992), pp. 98–108.

———. "Frank Gehry Reinvents the Chair." *Blueprint* (London) 90 (September 1992), pp. 27–34.

Lenders to the Exhibition

Germano Celant and Argento Celant

Jay Chiat Collection

Frank O. Gehry & Associates

Frank and Berta Gehry

Library, Getty Research Institute, Los Angeles

Fred and Winter Hoffman, Santa Monica, California

Jasper Johns

MAK-Austrian Museum of Applied Arts, Vienna

The Montreal Museum of Fine Arts

The Museum of Modern Art, New York

Doreen Nelson

Claes Oldenburg and Coosje van Bruggen

Joan and Jack Quinn, Beverly Hills, California

Thomas Rempen

San Francisco Museum of Modern Art

Susan I. Spivak

William and Ruth True, Seattle, Washington

Frederick R. Weisman Art Museum, University of
  Minnesota, Minneapolis

Private collectors who wish to remain anonymous

Photographic Credits and Copyright Notices